X Thinking
Building Better Brands in the Age of eXperience

Jason Huang
Michael T Lai

X Thinking Institute
Shanghai   Columbus, Ohio

+86-21-60746536
info@x-thinking.com
www.x-thinking.com

Isbns
Hardback 978-1-7376952-0-2
Paperback 978-1-7376952-1-9
E-ISBN 978-1-7376952-2-6

Copyright © 2022 Jason Huang, Michael T Lai and X Thinking Institute
All rights reserved. No part of this book may be reproduced or transmitted in any form or by any means, electronic or mechanical, including photocopy, recording or any information storage and retrieval system, without permission in writing from the copyright owners.

Every reasonable attempt has been made to identify owners of copyright. Any errors or omissions brought to the publisher's attention will be corrected in subsequent editions.

LIBRARY OF CONGRESS CATALOGING-IN-PUBLICATION DATA
Names: Lai, Michael, 1979- author. | Huang, Jason, 1980- author. |
  Pine, B. Joseph, writer of foreword.
Title: X thinking : building better brands in the age of experience /
  Jason Huang [and] Michael T. Lai ; [foreword by] B. Joseph Pine II.
Description: Shanghai : X Thinking Institute, 2022. | Series: X thinking, bk. 1.
Identifiers: LCCN 2022901598 (print) | ISBN 978-1-7376952-0-2 (hardcover) |
  ISBN 978-1-7376952-1-9 (paperback) | ISBN 978-1-7376952-2-6 (ebook)
Subjects: LCSH: Branding (Marketing) | Corporate image. | Marketing--China. |
  Business planning. | Communication in marketing. | BISAC: BUSINESS & ECONOMICS / Marketing / General. | BUSINESS & ECONOMICS / Strategic Planning.
Classification: LCC HF5415.1255 H83 2022 (print) | LCC HF5415.1255 (ebook) |
  DDC 658.8/27--dc23.

Foreword for X Thinking
BUILDING BETTER BRANDS IN THE AGE OF EXPERIENCE

B. Joseph Pine II

Today, we live in the Experience Economy.

Goods and services are no longer enough; what consumers want are experiences — memorable events that engage each individual in an inherently personal way. In industry after industry, goods and services have become commodities, with little or no differentiation purchased primarily on price. In order to create differentiation companies must innovate in experiences, reaching inside of people and engaging them emotionally, physically, intellectually, or even spiritually.

Experience innovation is of course the focus of X Thinking: Building Better Brands in the Age of Experience. Jason Huang and Michael Lai show how brands can better engage with their customers — engagement again being core to the very definition of economic experiences — and thereby create value within customers, and economic value for the company. For in today's Experience Economy, as the authors write in Chapter 1, "Value is created as brands engage and interact with consumers, building a mutual relationship through meaningful experience."

The need for experience innovation hit home for me a number of years ago when I was in Milan, Italy, giving a boardroom presentation with a number of different companies. One of the participants was a vice-president of Maxwell House, and he said something that floored me, "There's been no innovation in the coffee industry in 15 years." I responded, "Have you never heard of Starbucks?" As a coffee manufacturer, this executive had totally missed the innovation in the coffee-drinking experience that Howard Schultz created. The irony? It was the coffee culture of Milan that inspired Schultz to create places where people could spend their time drinking the cup of coffee made just for them. Such places enable Starbucks to turn a commodity, worth $.02-.04 USD a cup, into a premium offering worth $3-5 USD (or more) per cup.

I first discovered the Experience Economy in the mid-1990s and wrote about it with my partner Jim Gilmore in such places as Strategy & Leadership, The Wall Street Journal, and the Harvard Business Review, and then in 1999 we published our book The Experience Economy: Work Is Theatre & Every Business a Stage. We used to have to argue with people that this economic shift was happening, marshalling economic data, case studies, and logical arguments to make the case. Today I just have to state it, and everyone gets it. Experiences are now in the air that we breathe.

That's why in our 2011 Updated Edition we stopped using phrases like the "forthcoming", the "nascent", the "emerging" Experience Economy. It was here. But it wasn't sitting still; the Experience Economy continued to grow, to spread, to generate innovation after innovation in arenas even we had never imagined. And our understanding of it continued to grow as well, yielding new insights, new principles, and new frameworks that first described the phenomenon and then prescribed what companies should do as a result.

One key insight that we focused on in our 2020 re-release was right there in the new subtitle Competing for Customer Time, Attention, and Money. That is what every company in the world does — compete against every other company in the world for the time, attention, and money of individual customers. That is why you must design experiences that get customers to spend time with you, give you their attention, and then buy your offering as a result — whether that offering is a good, a service, or even the experience itself.

Focusing on time — for it is the currency of the Experience Economy — recognizes that experience thinking means designing the time customers spend with you. What people seek from experiences is time well spent. What they value is that time, and you must design it to flow through a series of events that rise up to a climax and come back down again. Places that forego this come off as flat, with little or no dramatic structure, and do not rise to the level of an experience but remain at the service level. With services, customers seek time well saved – nice, easy, convenient, frictionless interactions that get some functional job done. So important is the time of individual human beings — it is, after all, the most precious resource on the planet – that customers want both goods and services to be commoditized so they can spend their hard-earned money and their harder-earned time on the experiences they value.

Of course, COVID-19 changed the value equation tremendously, especially for experience stagers. Physical experiences were devastated by the pandemic, because anywhere people gathered was a place no one wanted to be. But people did not give up their experiences! No, they just switched them from physical to digital, from out there to in here, from social and communal to individual and familial. And even as people everywhere bought more online with home and/or contactless delivery, still they recognized that the stuff we buy does not define who we are. It is the experiences we share with our loved ones, our friends, our colleagues that give life meaning. In that sense I believe the pandemic actually created an acceleration in the Experience Economy.

The rise of digital technology that burst forth to new levels during the pandemic was perhaps the biggest change in the world since I first discovered the Experience Economy. This has four wide-ranging effects. First, digital technology is the greatest force of commoditization ever invented, for the frictionless digital marketplace means customers can instantly compare prices across all vendors, which tends to push prices down to the lowest possible point. Second, anything you can digitize you can customize, so it has enabled companies in almost every industry to mass customize their offerings. As I've long said, customizing goods turn them into services and customizing services turns them into experiences. (Understanding this is in fact how I discovered the Experience Economy.) Third, digital technology enables us to fuse the real and the virtual, resulting in new and wondrous experiences that have never been envisioned, engendered, or encountered before. And finally, digitization facilitates new ways of interacting with customers across the spectrum of life, most notably in retail.

It is in this last effect of digital technology where it is clear that Chinese consumers are leading the way. Their daily use of smartphones is perhaps the highest in the world, but its their innovative and sophisticated ways of using them that should cause everyone to stand up and take notice. This is particularly apparent in the rise of "SuperApps" that combine search, shopping, social media, financial transactions, and similar functions in a manner that is always on and so very often used – and mass customized to the needs of each user in the moment. One related innovation I first saw in China is the use of digital channels in physical stores, with sales associates broadcasting to a store's followers, producing their own media show as they turn the store into a product showcase. Jason, Mike, and their colleagues at TANG have helped lead this innovation in a number of Chinese companies — innovations that predict where other consumers around the world are headed. As they state quite succinctly, "New Retail = E-commerce + Offline Commerce". Do not miss their discussion of this, nor the case studies throughout the book that demonstrate X Thinking principles and really make the concepts come alive — including how they helped Starbucks understand and incorporate Chinese characteristics.

You may have noticed that I referred to "discovering" the Experience Economy a number of times. I didn't invent it; rather, I discovered what companies were naturally doing to create more economic value, and simultaneously how much more consumers were valuing their time and craving experiences.

Similarly, Jason and Mike didn't invent the methods companies use to create experiences, but they have honed their insights into more science than art, more understandable than opaque, more hit than miss. And with this book you can take advantage of the lessons they have learned, the tools they have devised, and the techniques they have developed for creating great experiences – or eXperiences, as they define them.

In fact, I'm not sure anyone has done more to inspire experience innovation in China than Jason Huang and Mike Lai. As they bring X Thinking to the US and western countries, it's important to pay attention, because it is not just an approach to experience design, it's a philosophy, one that embraces the Experience Economy and will help you prosper in going beyond mere goods and services to creating experiences for your individual customers.

— B. Joseph Pine II
Strategic Horizons LLP
Stillwater, MN USA

Preface
X THINKING: SUSTAINABLE GROWTH IS HUMAN-CENTERED

When X Thinking was originally published in China in 2020, it introduced a new business philosophy built around experience. It identified common challenges brands faced connecting with consumers in China, and the unforeseen factors companies that were new to China discovered as they adapted their products and services to a new culture.

But in many ways, China offers a glimpse of the future beyond its borders. Its consumers are sophisticated and savvy. Technologies that are still struggling to achieve widespread adoption elsewhere are already well-established in China. Customer expectations are high and social media influence is pervasive. Brands that understand these trends and embrace these lessons will likewise discover advantages over their competitors who are slow to adapt to business environments evolving at an unprecedented pace.

Even the English translation and adaptation of X Thinking proved prophetic. The 12-hour time zone difference between the authors and editors illustrated the metaphor profoundly. It's already tomorrow in China.

Whether you're a thought leader, decision maker, or brand manager, X Thinking offers insights into the future of consumer behavior — from the value of relationships and identifying the right customers to strategic planning and digital transformation. Designers and developers, engineers and entrepreneurs, in fact anyone intrigued by innovation and the processes behind it will find more than just a new point of view. X Thinking reveals the cultural context for changes in China that will define consumer experience for the next decade, and those to come, throughout the world.

Despite China's accelerated industrialization and impressive expansion of urban development, high-speed rail, and economic upward mobility, the cultural underpinnings that made this rapid transformation possible remain a mystery for many. We'll pull back the curtain and share the history and opportunity the emergence of the internet, integration of physical and digital retail, and the ubiquity of smartphones have created for Chinese consumers. Eager to reach new markets, global brands soon learned they couldn't simply "lift and shift" their existing business models, and even established Chinese brands struggled to adapt to new social and generational alignment among once predictable patrons.

Unlike the agricultural, industrial, and service economies that preceded, experience aggregates elements of each in exciting new ways. Consumers with a world of options soon moved beyond the predictable measures of value to something more meaningful, yet less tangible. Experience has become the new standard for every brand interaction.

When we discuss experience in the context of X Thinking, we use the term "eXperience". But that distinction doesn't apply to every customer encounter. That's because eXperiences are branded, intentional, and superlative — concepts we'll define and refine in the chapters ahead. However, X Thinking also represents an element of the unknown, often elusive, because not all consumers share the same understanding of people, value, and sustainability — core principles we'll also discuss in detail as fundamental to the success of every business. X Thinking helps turn uncertainty into clarity, answering the questions brands may not even know to ask.

Customer eXperience is a journey, and so is our exploration of X Thinking. The organization of this book mirrors that journey, leading readers from philosophical understanding to tactical and strategic objectives for businesses to apply and embrace. There are also several case studies along the way highlighting the implementation of specific insights from the preceding chapters.

Included are discussions of Chinese brands that will be unfamiliar to many readers, as well as those from global companies who reinvented themselves to appeal to the needs, wants, and desires of Chinese consumers. We've also added lessons from brands beyond China that are perhaps more familiar, but with backstories and lessons that are likely new even to readers who recognize their names.

Translations are rarely literal, and this book is no exception. For example, the four Chinese characters for Peking University literally translate to "North Capital Big School". Though no knowledge of Chinese is necessary to read and appreciate X Thinking, we've included select names and ideas in English as well as Chinese, particularly those for which a perfect translation proves challenging, to remain faithful to the original text.

The convention for individual names may also be new for some readers. In Chinese, family names appear first, followed by given names, so when you see someone referenced, you'll notice the order appears reversed for English readers. But when adding our perspectives, we use our "English names", Jason and Mike, which are interchangeable in our professional and personal lives interacting with those who may only speak English. Both formats are accurate and intentional.

Though Jason was born in China, and Mike in the United States, our influences are far more global, educated across three continents and with a balance of industry and academic experience serving clients through TANG Consulting, and pioneering and championing the concepts contained in this book through the X Thinking Institute.

Iteration is at the heart of innovation. But many companies view this process from the inside out, instead of the point of view of their customers. Our book distills this complex process into a practical approach for any organization to solve today's business challenges, as well as those over the not so distant horizon.

| Foreword | I |
| Preface | XI |

Chapter 1: The Need for a New Business Philosophy — 5

    Section 1: Understanding Changes in China — 9
    Section 2: Preparing for the Future — 27
    Section 3: Introducing X Thinking — 41

Chapter 2: The Relationship Between People and Brands — 59

    Section 1: Understanding Connections — 63
    Section 2: Applying the X Thinking Relationship Model — 79
    Case Study: Amway — 95

Chapter 3: The Value of eXperiences — 109

    Section 1: Understanding eXperiences — 113
    Section 2: Defining Ideal and Holistic eXperiences — 125
    Section 3: Measuring Return on eXperience (ROX) — 137
    Case Study: Xiao Guan Tea — 151

Chapter 4: The Source of All Change — 163

    Section 1: Understanding Consumers — 167
    Section 2: Identifying Meaningful Opportunities — 179
    Section 3: Prioritizing the Seven Types of Consumers — 197
    Case Study: China Merchants Bank — 209

Chapter 5: The Challenge of Execution — 223

    Section 1: Understanding Brand Value Proposition — 227
    Section 2: Delivering, Planning, and Managing eXperiences — 239
    Section 3: Creating an X Strategy — 249
    Case Study: WM Motor (Weltmeister) — 271

Chapter 6: The Evolution of Engagement — 279

    Section 1: Understanding Connectivity — 283
    Section 2: Driving Digital Transformation — 293
    Case Study: Starbucks — 303

Chapter 7: The Integration of X Thinking — 313

    Section 1: Understanding People, Value, and Sustainability — 317
    Section 2: Initiating Organizational Change: Chief eXperience Officer (CXO) and the X Maturity Model — 325
    Section 3: Incorporating Insights from the Future — 335

Acknowledgments — 355

Endnotes — 359

About the Authors — 365

"It is the framework which changes with each new technology and not just the picture within the frame."

— *Marshall McLuhan*

CHAPTER 1

The Need for a New Business Philosophy

Understanding Changes in China

Preparing for the Future

Introducing X Thinking

INTRODUCTION

We live in unprecedented times. New innovations, new businesses, new opportunities. There has never been a period in history when humanity has advanced so quickly. Yet inherent to innovation and change is uncertainty, which may still prove daunting for even the most seasoned and experienced leaders and innovators.

Innovation occurs where opportunities exist, and businesses rise to support these advances. China is an entirely unique business environment with distinct characteristics and consumers who are digital and demanding, smart and savvy. It's increasingly become a test market for introducing and refining products and services around the world. In Understanding Changes in China, we'll examine development in recent years, discuss three major trends in business, and how consumers are the catalyst of that change.

In the world of business innovation, we face a constantly shifting landscape and unknown future. When we face challenges, as businesses and individuals, we rely on experience to evaluate and understand our situation, then plot a course forward. In Preparing for the Future, we'll examine common business challenges and how to address them. Some of these strategies are from the West, some have originated in China.

From this complex and evolving environment, something new has emerged, a business philosophy that applies the lessons of the past and the advances of the present to understand what comes next. In Introducing X Thinking, we'll share our way, a new way, to address these and future unforeseen challenges.

Section 1
UNDERSTANDING CHANGES IN CHINA

Something remarkable is happening in China, and we are fortunate to witness it firsthand. Everywhere you look, China is in the midst of transformation.

China's rise wasn't instantaneous. It's been a long time coming. A major milestone was in 2010 when China passed Japan becoming the world's second largest economy. At its current trajectory, experts project that China's economy will surpass the United States to become the biggest economy in the world as early as 2028. [1]

New highrises are changing familiar city skylines. In 2016, China built 84 of the world's 128 skyscrapers in a single year. In 2018, ten of the world's 20 tallest buildings were built in China in a single decade. As of 2020, 11 of the 20 tallest buildings in the world are in China. By comparison, only two buildings in the United States break into the top 20 tallest buildings, One World Trade Center and Central Park Tower.

China's cities are connected by a high-speed railway system that spans the entire country with trains running at speeds up to 400 km/h (248 mph). Even though China's first high-speed train line launched in 2008, the fastest commercial train in the world is the Shanghai Maglev, and the second fastest is the Fuxing. Less than a decade later, there were more than 4,000 bullet trains in China, carrying 4 million passengers every day, covering more than 37,900 km (23,500 miles). More than two-thirds of the world's high-speed train tracks are in China. By comparison, the United States doesn't have a single high-speed rail line reaching the international standard of more than 250 km/h (160 mph), and only has 2.6 million air passengers on an average day. [2,3,4,5]

Chinese cities are often described in a hierarchy of tiers (中国城市等级制). Though this is not an official government designation, the terminology is used by industry and academia as a common point of reference for denoting relative size, income, education, sophistication, and opportunity. Beijing, Shanghai, Guangzhou, Shenzhen and a growing set of emerging cities are Tier 1 — similar to New York, Los Angeles, Chicago, and Washington DC. Tier 2 cities are slightly smaller, but growing quickly, while Tier 3 cities are more regional in their influence.

All of this change isn't just about initiatives and infrastructure championed by China in recent years. These advances have created substantial changes and improvements for consumers. Chinese net worth doubled in the past decade. With their new found wealth, Chinese consumers are spending. In 2020, China accounted for 20 percent of the personal luxury goods market, nearly double the previous year. They're also traveling abroad and seeing the world. The number of annual overseas visits has increased 255 percent to 170 million from 2009 to 2019. In 2019, Chinese citizens spent the most money on international tourism at $255 billion USD. That's almost a fifth of all global tourism spending and nearly equivalent to the next three countries (United States, Germany, and United Kingdom) combined. [6,7]

Daily life in China has also changed dramatically, and in some ways has surpassed certain aspects of life in leading developed countries. It's arguably a glimpse of what life might be like for the rest of the world in the near future. A big part of that is the introduction of mobile payments through Ant Financial's AliPay Wallet mobile app and Tencent's WeChat Pay in 2013. Since then, China has moved from a primarily cash-based society to a cashless society, with millions of consumers skipping credit cards completely. Mobile payments are accepted almost everywhere, from high-end restaurants and luxury fashion boutiques down to street vendors and taxis, even street musicians and panhandlers. For many people, it has become the preferred way to pay just about everything. [8]

But it's not just payments that are being conducted from smartphones, virtually every interaction can be achieved right from the palm of one's hand. Ordering a cab or black car on DiDi. Watching short videos on Douyin on the commute to work. Ordering takeout and having it delivered via Ele.me for lunch. Communicating via text, voice, and video communications for work or personal lives on WeChat. Ordering and paying for dinner at a restaurant by scanning a QR code, without talking to the server. Playing PlayerUnknown's Battlegrounds on the phone while waiting for dinner. Shopping on Taobao and Tmall, also operated by Alibaba. Ordering groceries and having them delivered to your home within 30 minutes from Freshippo. Rather than going out to consume goods and services, now anything and everything can be ordered from your smartphone and delivered right to your door.

Though some of these companies may have started by replicating western concepts, they've since adapted, evolving into more original and refined platforms built for the needs of Chinese consumers. WeChat has become so intertwined with everyday life, global brands have created WeChat Official Accounts, also called "Gong Zhong Hao" (公众号), much like official Twitter and Facebook accounts, but more robust. Such trends are no longer just a copy of earlier concepts, but made for China.

CHANGING BUSINESS ENVIRONMENT

With China changing so quickly, brands need to understand the latest trends in order to remain competitive or risk disruption. Three of the most important business trends facing brands in China are new retail, the service economy, and digital transformation.

New Retail

All around the world, there is talk about how retail is quickly becoming replaced by e-commerce. But is that truly the case? Is the evolution from traditional to online sales just another retail option or an entirely different experience? New Retail is the collective term for the next evolution of e-commerce.

E-commerce VS Offline Commerce

China knows more than most about e-commerce. In 2020, online sales in China exceeded those of the US and Europe combined, and accounted for 44.8 percent of total retail sales in China, an increase of 27.5 percent over the previous year. [9] [10]

There are several significant advantages to e-commerce over traditional retail stores. For businesses, online stores aren't limited to a specific geographic location like brick and mortar stores. They have a lower financial cost compared to creating and maintaining a physical retail presence. They can gain access to customer data and analyze customer behavior and purchases that are difficult to track in the offline world.

For customers, they can access goods and services from all over the country, or around the world. They can easily compare prices and find opinions about products, either through reviews or soliciting advice on social networks. Because online stores are open 24/7, customers may shop whenever and wherever they prefer. And lastly, orders are delivered right to their doorsteps.

But for all the advantages of shopping online, there are some aspects of shopping offline that e-commerce just can't deliver. Specifically, customers can't try before they buy. Some products and services need to be experienced in person. Clothing and footwear need to be tried on to experience how they feel to wear and use. Perfumes, particularly cosmetics, rely on senses and application an online store can't offer.

Many older brands that primarily relied on brick and mortar sales have adapted to the new reality of online shopping by supporting both traditional and internet sales channels, reaching customers wherever they are more comfortable. However, new channels can create competition among the existing channels that may lead to confusion and frustration for customers — like when retail and online stores have different prices on the same item.

New Retail = E-commerce + Offline Commerce

Addressing these challenges between e-commerce and offline commerce, Jack Ma, co-founder and executive chairman of Alibaba (China's leading e-commerce company with Taobao as China's largest C2C platform and Tmall as China's largest third-party B2C retail platform) proposed the concept of "New Retail" as the next evolution of e-commerce.

> *'E-commerce' is rapidly evolving into 'New Retail.' The boundary between offline and online commerce disappears as we focus on fulfilling the personalized needs of each customer.*
>
> *– Jack Ma, Co-founder and Executive Chairm*

According to Ma, the New Retail concept is "the online, offline, logistics, and customer data across a sing

What this means is that customers don't need to choose between shopping at an online store or an offline store, because they are the same store. Consumers choose how they shop based on their unique situations and needs, not based on the location of the channels. [12]

By integrating logistics, brands can always ensure products are available to their customers as quickly as possible. Products are always available at the offline store if customers choose to buy offline. If customers choose to buy online, the brand ensures products reach customers when they want it. In addition, data on purchasing patterns ensures that there is enough merchandise to meet customer demand, but not too much, which may exceed inventory space or goes to waste due to spoilage (for products that have a limited shelf life).

Regardless of where and how consumers interact with brands, whether it is browsing online, buying offline, sharing on social media, customer data is captured and analyzed to create a comprehensive profile. By leveraging big data and AI, businesses gain a more detailed understanding about their customers, to generate new opportunities by improving products, the supply chain, marketing, and distribution.

New Retail Example: Freshippo (Formerly Hema Xiansheng)

One of the classic examples of New Retail is Alibaba's Freshippo supermarket. Products can be purchased online via smartphone app or in-person at the traditional supermarket. Once an order is placed on the app, store staff receive it on their mobile devices then gather the order items and place them in designated bags. Once all the items are collected, the bag is put on a conveyor belt to a waiting army of electric scooters that deliver orders to the doors of their customers. Those who live within three kilometers, or a little less than two miles, of the store can have their order delivered for free within half an hour.

Offline, the supermarket shopping eXperience is augmented through the same app customers use to place online orders. Inside ᐁ store, free WiFi is available for customers and the app adapts to support additional services only available inside the store. Customers can use the app to scan the price tag for any item for more information, such as the origin and recipes using the ingredient. After filling their shopping cart and confirming their shopping list, checkout is completed through an automated kiosk with payment made within the app, connected to Alibaba's Alipay. If customers find any items along the way they prefer to have delivered instead, they can add those to the app's online cart as well.

In addition to groceries, there is also an on-site food court. One of the store's key differentiators is their selection of fresh seafood flown in from all over the world. Customers can select fresh, live seafood from the tank, have it cooked by the staff in a variety of styles, and enjoy the dish in Freshippo's in-store food court.

Chinese consumers value being able to see the seafood alive all the way to being cooked. Instead of farm-to-table, think "alive-to-table". In American markets and restaurants, you rarely see a tank of live fish. But in Chinese groceries and restaurants they are the norm, not the exception. In fact, the Chinese meaning of the word "fresh" literally translates to "alive and fresh" making the terms effectively synonymous, explaining the cultural connection to the expectation.

Another benefit of including the food court within the supermarket is the reduction of food waste by preparing produce from store shelves and including them as ingredients in the dishes before they expire.

Eighteen months after the launch of the New Retail supermarket concept, Alibaba revealed at their investor conference that daily sales of Freshippo were about ¥800,000 RMB ($118,000 USD) per day. More than 60 percent of sales were from customers shopping online. [13]

Since Jack Ma coined the term in 2016, "New Retail" has become one of the hottest business buzzwords in China. That trend has no signs of slowing down with competitors Tencent and JD forming similar strategies termed "Smart+Retail" and "Unbounded Retail" respectively.

The New Retail revolution has also been gaining momentum outside of China with international media coverage from the likes of Forbes, Fortune, and Bloomberg.

Even US-based Starbucks is getting in on the "New Retail" action with the opening of the Starbucks Roastery in Shanghai. The world's largest and most extravagant Starbucks is powered by Alibaba technology to enable a seamlessly integrated online and in-store eXperience by leveraging Alibaba's Taobao mobile app and augmented reality (AR) technology. [14]

Service Economy

How brands deliver value to consumers has been shifting from manufacturing and selling products to delivering services. This realignment is likewise evident in China as services slowly outpace the economic impact of agricultural and industrial products.

Manufacturing and Selling Products

Traditionally, the moment of transfer of value between brand and consumer is when a product is exchanged for money from their customer. Prior to that moment, the brand needs to invest large amounts of money to design, develop, and manufacture or acquire the product to sell. They generate their revenue at the time of sale. If the customer dislikes the product, or stops using the product, the brand still profits at the time of the transaction and retains that revenue, even if it subsequently loses the customer. After the transaction, the brand may have no further contact with the customer.

From a consumer perspective, when a customer pays for the product, they own it. It is a single transaction that allows them to use the product as long as it continues to work. There are no additional payments to the brand. Regardless of how much the customer uses the product, sparingly or frequently, the price at the time of purchase is exactly the same. When the product no longer works, malfunctions, needs to be maintained, repaired, or even if the customer is unsatisfied with the product, the brand is under no obligation to resolve the issue. If the product is outside the return period and not covered by a warranty, and even if it is covered by the warranty, the burden is often on the customer more so than the brand.

Delivering Services

Services aren't just what brands offer beyond the sale, from troubleshooting and simple fixes to repair and replacement. They are an alternate form of the product, one that adds time as the most distinguishing feature. When brands decide to deliver services, there is a fundamental shift in business strategy and mindset that transforms the relationship from the manufacturer, product, and customer to provider, service, and subscriber.

In the services approach to delivering value, a subscriber pays a fee to the provider in intervals for the right to use the service for a period of time. Once the time period has ended, the user may no longer use the service until the next payment. The service is owned by the provider rather than the subscriber. If there is a problem with the service, it is in the provider's best interest to resolve the issue to retain the subscribers. If the subscriber continues to use the service, they will need to continue paying.

For the customer, there are multiple benefits to consuming services over products. There's a lower barrier to entry. The cost and risk to try the service is minimal. They do not need to commit to purchasing a product, they can just pay once to try the service, then decide after evaluating the experience if they wish to continue with their subscription. If the customer is dissatisfied with the service, they can simply stop using it by discontinuing payments or switching to another service provider. If the customer doesn't require the service regularly, they can choose to only pay the provider when they need it. Customers don't need to worry about repairing or maintaining the service.

There are benefits for the provider as well. The services approach maintains customer engagement with the provider, allowing for the continuous collection of data to improve the service offered. Unlike products, services can improve over time with the addition of new options and features. The subscription-based payment model provides a more predictable, reliable, and continuous revenue flow. Providers can direct a portion of the guaranteed revenue back into improving the service, which in turn helps with retention of existing customers and the acquisition of new customers. Providers can scale based on demand, committing resources when needed, and pulling back when necessary.

Service as a Product Extension

The transformation of a product into a service by taking the functionality of the product and offering it to consumers as a service for a fee is known as servitization. People will often use "as a service" or aaS tacked on to the end of the product category to note this distinction. The aaS terminology was made popular in the IT sector with applications becoming services in the cloud, Software-as-a-Service (SaaS). This is when software such as a word processor product, like Microsoft Word, versus a word processor service, like Google Docs becomes a service. The concept later expanded to Platform-as-a-Service (PaaS) and Infrastructure-as-a-Service (IaaS). Now the aaS model is being applied more broadly resulting in Anything-as-a-Service or Everything-as-a-Service (XaaS) (Figure 1.1).

Software -as-a-Service	Teambition (下载应用)	Microsoft Office 365	Adobe Creative Cloud		
Music -as-a-Service	NetEase Cloud Music (网易云音乐)	QQ Music (QQ音乐)	Spotify	SiriusXM	
Video -as-a-Service	Bilibili (哔哩哔哩)	iQiyi (爱奇艺)	Netflix	Amazon Prime Video	Hulu
Mobility -as-a-Service	China Auto Hire (神州租车)	DiDi (滴滴出行)	Uber	Lime	
Space -as-a-Service	Kr Space (氪空间)	Mixpace (米域)	AirBnB	WeWork	
Device -as-a-Service	Energy Monster (怪兽充电)	Apple iPhone Upgrade	AT&T Next		
Food -as-a-Service	Freshippo (盒马鲜生)	Blue Apron	Misfits Market		

Figure 1.1, *XaaS: Anything or Everything as a Service*

The process of servitization a product requires focusing on the needs of the customer and reimagining how to deliver your offering in the form of a service that they use rather than one that they own. A subscription-based revenue model providing predictable and sustained revenue flow.

The service economy has become increasingly significant in China's economy. It first exceeded the industrial economy in 2001, accounting for more than 50 percent of China's GDP, and has rivaled it ever since — despite China's enormous investments in infrastructure and urban growth. However, this transition was not uniform geographically. According to the National Bureau of Statistics, the value of the service economy in Shanghai exceeded that of the industrial economy as early as 1999, but economic development in Shanxi was still dominated by the industrial economy as late as 2018. China aims to increase the service sector's share of the GDP to 60 percent by 2025. [15] [16]

Digital Transformation

In the previous two trends, service economy and New Retail, you may have noticed there was a significant digital component to the execution and implementation. In some cases, the original business was a digital-native organization, where the use of technology was inherently part of their DNA. Most of these businesses were founded and grew in a digitally-enabled world — post Baidu, Alibabab, and Tencent (collectively referred to as BAT). These companies include DiDi, Freshippo, Weltmeister, and Xiaomi which not only incorporated the technologies pioneered by BAT, but also incorporated their processes and ways of thinking to disrupt established industries.

Traditional organizations prior to BAT, have their own established ways of working that were relevant in the previous era. But those that apply and leverage new technologies introduced by BAT to radically improve business performance have significant advantages compared to organizations that rely on legacy technologies, processes, and ways of thinking. Each new wave of innovations to the market requires incumbent organizations to undergo digital transformation.

In the current wave of digital transformation, organizations seek new ways to incorporate social networks, virtual and augmented reality, the internet of things, cloud computing, blockchain, big data, and artificial intelligence to enhance a brand's customer eXperience, operational processes, and business models.

One of the common missteps of digital transformation is emphasis on the word "digital." Focusing on the technological aspect can lead an organization down the wrong path. The key world is "transformation." Organizations need to understand how to adapt their business to align with the new reality before determining the technologies they need to adopt. Technology alone doesn't add value to organizations. The value of technology comes from its ability to enable a different way of doing business. Further, the end goal of the application of the technology should not be focused on optimizing the organization to do the same things better, faster, more efficiently, and more effectively; it fundamentally transforms the organization.

We'll discuss the process of digital transformation in detail in Chapter 6.

PEOPLE AS A SOURCE OF CHANGE

Why are these business trends relevant to brands at this moment in history? It is because they illustrate how consumers are changing in China. There are two significant trends in China which may predict the future of consumer behavior in the West: consumption upgrade and the rise of the post-90s generation.

Consumption Upgrade

Since China's economic reform in 1978, the country's economic growth has been unparalleled, matched by the increase in disposable income. Personal disposable income has increased from ¥343.40 RMB ($204 USD) in 1978 to an all time high of ¥36,396 RMB ($5,593 USD) in

2017. That amount of discretionary spending may sound minor, but only relative to the US cost of living, where some everyday expenses are up to four times higher. A restaurant meal in China that costs less than the equivalent of $4 USD would cost closer to $15 in the US. A one-bedroom apartment that costs the equivalent of $375 in China would cost $1,200 in the US. And as people have grown wealthier, they have sought out to improve their quality of life through the purchase of goods and services. Consumption upgrade is the phenomenon where Chinese consumer purchasing patterns shift from rational and practical needs to aspirational wants and desires. [17] [18]

The first consumption upgrade occurred in the 1980s immediately following the economic reform and the Opening of China where the country transitioned from a centrally planned economy to a market economy. Prior to this period, the availability of goods and services was largely controlled by the government. Once consumers were no longer limited by the scarcity of resources, people could freely purchase products based on their needs and income.

From the late 1980s into the early 1990s, the rapid development of the economy led to the production of industrial products that were previously in low supply. As incomes rose, increased purchasing power brought previously prohibitively expensive products, such as refrigerators, color televisions, and washing machines, within their reach.

The period from the early 1990s to the early 2010s were described as the "residents' consumption structure" because spending habits were no longer limited to daily necessities. People became aware that their quality of life could be enhanced through purchasing a home, car, and insurance.

In the past decade through the present, Chinese consumers are spending a lower percentage of income on basic needs, such as housing, food, and other commodities, and more on discretionary purchases to upgrade their lifestyle, in areas such as healthcare, education, travel, and entertainment. In addition to increasing income levels, another factor driving is government policy. The growth of the Chinese economy has been based on investment-led growth, based on the idea that investment creates new capacity, leading to more employment, and as a result, higher demand.

However, in recent years, the government has been transitioning to a consumption-led growth model. Consumption-led growth is based on higher consumer spending leading to higher demand, which leads to increased investment, resulting in economic growth. Consumption increases when incomes increase, or when the government decreases taxes. Through these policies, China's per capita income more than doubled in the past decade. [19] [20] [21]

What does this mean for brands? While commodity consumption is declining, service consumption and experiential consumption, or consumption driven by the desire for memorable experiences, has been steadily growing in China. New types of consumption have emerged during this period, such as gaming and online education. Additionally, consumers are beginning to purchase products that enhance their identity by selecting brands based on values and emotional appeals.

Unlike broad American demographic groups, such as millennials and baby boomers, generational divides in China are defined by decades. But like the US, political, economic, and cultural undercurrents manifest in ways that still defy even the most experienced market research. One group in particular that is driving the current upgrade consumption: the post-90s generation.

Post-90s Generation

In China, generations are referred to as "post-decade," referencing which decade in which they were born. The post-90s generation is a consumer segment in China that is growing rapidly in purchasing power and influence. According to a report by McKinsey, this generation comprises 16 percent of China's population today and by their projections, will "account for more than 20 percent of total consumption growth in China by 2030, higher than any other demographic segment." [22]

Born between the years of 1990 and 1999, at the younger end of the spectrum, they are still in college. At the older end, they're at an early stage of their career when their income will continue to rise over the next decade, along with their spending power.

What makes this particular generation unique from previous generations in China is their attitude and behavior. According to our research, we have found several distinguishing characteristics: they are optimistic about the future, they spend and save their disposable income differently, and they place and seek value in their lifestyle and diverse eXperiences.

While previous generations faced socio-economic and political uncertainties, this generation came of age during a time of stability and great economic growth. This has created a generation that is confident and has a more optimistic outlook. They live in the moment rather than worrying about the future. As a result, unlike previous generations that traditionally save more than 50 percent of their income, the post-90s are willing to spend more and save less. This mindset also affects what, where, and how they choose to spend their money.

Compared to prior generations who view saving for its own sake and consume luxury brands for the purpose of projecting wealth and status, post-90s view this approach as shallow and immature. Post-90s focus less on the price and brand name and more on experiential consumption and how a brand reflects their individual values and contributes to their lives. As a result, they place more value on quality and craftsmanship, on sentimental value rather than monetary value. They choose to consume in areas such as travel, entertainment, hobbies, sports, education, and health and wellness. Brands that stand for aspirational values and can deliver meaningful eXperiences connect with this generation.

Vanke, the largest real estate developer in China has been successful targeting the post-90s generation with their Li Xiang Jia sub-brand. The brand focuses on the unique housing needs of the generation and prioritizes an interior design tailored for their living situations and habits. The brand has won Vanke multiple awards and recognition since its launch.

When it comes to the purchasing process, a differentiated eXperience is also essential to post-90s. Because this generation is "digital native," where they grew up with digital technologies, their customer journey blurs the line between online and offline. They are a generation that prefers to learn and compare products both online and offline, purchase online, consume offline, and share online. Brands that can seamlessly bridge their eXperiences between offline and online touchpoints will have a significant advantage in attracting and capturing this generation compared to their competitors.

* * *

Summary

Consumers are changing and their purchasing habits are evolving. What once met the demands of previous generations is not sufficient for the new, young, rising middle class. Businesses are eager to transform. Some are looking towards the digital economy. Some are looking towards servicization. Others are proposing the next evolution of e-commerce in New Retail.

Each of these changes are complex and constantly evolving. They create a business environment that is unprecedented, unknown, and filled with uncertainty. How can businesses adapt and adjust to the unknown?

Section 2
PREPARING FOR THE FUTURE

Business isn't easy. In fact, it's quite challenging. Building, managing, and maintaining successful brands requires insights that often seem elusive. You need to see into the future, to effectively predict what consumers will need and want. You also need to be able to make the impossible possible, delivering what consumers will want AND have them pay for it. You have to do this before all of your competitors. And you have to keep doing all this time and time again. It's no small task.

Businesses are facing an unknown future, because the future is always uncertain. The future requires businesses to adjust and adapt to constantly changing contexts and emerging trends. Trends such as the service economy, New Retail, digital transformation, consumption upgrade, and the post-90s generation.

CONSTANT BUSINESSES CHALLENGES

While the future is always unknown, contexts continuously change, and new trends replace old ones. The times may change, but the types of challenges businesses face remain the same. However, there are three key challenges for businesses that remain constant: consumers are becoming more sophisticated, technologies are rapidly evolving, and businesses are having difficulty differentiating. The times may change, but the types of challenges businesses face remain the same.

Consumers Are Becoming More Sophisticated

With every new generation, with every year they come of age, with every new experience they have, consumers are becoming more sophisticated. There are three contributing factors: younger consumers have a higher starting point, exposure to more, and access to more.

Younger People Have a Higher Starting Point

With every new generation, consumers start with more. They start with what past generations leave behind: knowledge, technology, and resources. When basic needs are met, consumers are free to focus on higher needs, emotional needs, self-fulfillment.

Younger Chinese consumers didn't experience the same struggles of scarcity as their parents. They grew up during an era where China was open to social and economic development. And now their children live in the marvels of the modern world, one where they have the resources available to achieve what we never could.

Exposure to More

As the world continues to expand, it is simultaneously shrinking. People are traveling to the furthest corners of the globe seeking new experiences. People are also bringing foreign experiences home, making them local. Much like American millennials, Chinese post-90s have embraced coffee — with more than one in three preferring it over tea. [23]

The internet also makes the world smaller by giving people access to ideas, sights, and sounds. Trends and memes are no longer bound by regions, countries, continents, languages, or cultures; they are becoming global phenomena. And with the ubiquity of the mobile internet, people are sharing and learning new experiences anytime and anywhere, right in the palm of their hand.

Access to More

Since economic reforms and the Opening of China, Chinese consumers have also gained access to brands from around the world. As their own home markets have become saturated, Western brands see the Chinese market as an opportunity for continued growth.

With the advent of e-commerce, consumers are no longer limited to what is available locally. Goods can be shipped from anywhere in the world.

As consumers become more sophisticated, they demand and expect more value from brands. What satisfied previous generations, or even what satisfied the same consumers previously may no longer satisfy their increased expectations.

They're no longer persuaded by traditional branding, marketing approaches, and tactics. They're no longer comparing the experience with your brand to your competitors, but against the best practices from across all industries. Their expectations have been elevated, and they demand brands deliver more value.

If your brand is focused on satisfying your customers' every need, the depth and breadth are overwhelming. Competitors will drown you out due to your lack of focus. The challenge is determining who your brand should pursue, what experiences are they seeking, and how to go beyond the expectations of these sophisticated customers.

Technologies Are Rapidly Evolving

Technological advancements continue to transform humanity, helping people simplify tasks, save time, increase productivity, enhance communication, improve healthcare, enable education. Similarly for business, technology can offer a competitive advantage for businesses that are able to quickly adopt relevant, new technologies.

But technology is also a disruptive force for business, one that will continue to evolve at an exponential rate. This acceleration poses a risk to businesses that are unable to adapt. In fact, technology is changing so rapidly for businesses that the ability to adopt new technologies must become a core competency.

Which technologies should your business invest in and how should they be integrated? Which technologies are mostly hype versus those that will provide real benefits for consumers, and the businesses that serve them best?

Consider virtual reality (VR) as a cautionary tale. A few years ago, VR was everywhere and so were startups based entirely on the promises predicted by industry pundits. Oculus VR was acquired by Facebook for $3 billion USD in 2014. VR arcades were installed in shopping malls. But in recent years, the hype around VR has diminished those early expectations. At its most popular, VR was at the Peak of Inflated Expectation in Gartner's Hype Cycle (Figure 1.2), where consumers predict a technology is on the verge of widespread application and proliferation. Now it's in the Trough of Disillusionment where consumers have discovered that the technology isn't as spectacular as everyone thought it was. [24] [25]

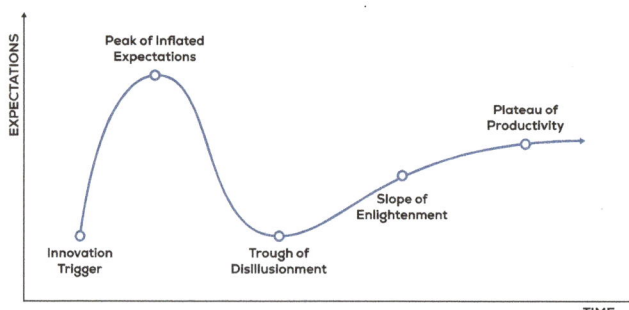

Figure 1.2, *Gartner's Hype Cycle*

Technology alone is of little value to brands and consumers. It is only of value when it can be applied in a meaningful way that changes the lives of consumers. Brands need to look beyond the technology itself and find the real world scenarios where the technology can empower business and consumers. Matching the right technology with the right scenarios is essential for brands to realize their digital transformation objectives.

Businesses Are Having Difficulty Differentiating

In any fast-paced society, competition is brutal, and businesses are seeking ways to gain an advantage over their competition.

Famed Harvard Business School professor, Michael Porter, wrote in his 1980 book, Competitive Strategy, that differentiation is one of three universal business strategies to gain a competitive advantage. (The other two are overall cost leadership and focus.) The strategy prioritizes offering consumers a clear value that competitors cannot. [26]

This competitive advantage helps brands break through the noise and stand out by offering something perceived as valuable and original. The purpose is to persuade consumers the difference the brand offers has more value than that of the competition.

If there is no discernable difference between competing brands, the choices become commodities, consumers choose the cheapest option, and brands end up competing exclusively based on the lowest price.

But suggesting a brand should differentiate is easier said than done (or in the case of businesses, it's cheaper said than done). Finding and creating that perceived difference in the company's product and service offerings requires time and money, research and development. And that still doesn't guarantee it's a difference consumers desire and value at a price they are willing to pay.

There are also subtle nuances to being different. There should be a perceivable difference, but not so different that the offering is unfamiliar. Brands should be first or early in introducing the innovation, but too early risks making the innovation ahead of its time and not ready for mass adoption. And even if the brand succeeds in creating an innovative differentiation that is widely adopted, no business idea is immune from imitation. A first-mover advantage for a new business, service, product, or feature is often short-lived.

Another approach to creating differentiation is through promotion. The key is perception. While there might not be an actual difference between two different brands, if people perceive a difference through how the brands promote their offerings, then how consumers value competing offerings changes. The positioning creates the difference.

Businesses must develop a sustainable strategy for creating a perceivable differentiation that consumers recognize and value.

TRANSITION TO THE EXPERIENCE ECONOMY

The increased focus on consumer experience as part of a larger evolution of the prevailing economic model is not a new or novel notion.

The idea was popularized by B. Joseph Pine II and James H. Gilmore in 1998 and published in the Harvard Business Review. Their book titled The Experience Economy was published the following year. In the book, economic history is divided into four stages: agricultural economy, industrial economy, service economy, and experience economy.

The emergence of the eXperience economy in China and the United States is not identical. China's adoption has been faster, fundamental, and transformational — not unlike countries throughout the world that moved through the four stages more quickly. The popularization of mobile payment platforms and the intersection of social media and consumer interactions has heralded a new age of constant connectivity that blurs the lines between traditional and online retail.

As mentioned earlier, the service economy has rivaled the industrial economy for the past two decades, but the emergence of the experience economy in China was almost simultaneous. Around 2000, the first batch of Internet entrepreneurs leveraging new technologies started a journey to create value for the masses. The Internet, and the mobile Internet that followed, changed the way people connected with others and the world. The rising Chinese middle class has thrived for decades that once struggled to satisfy material needs has now become more interested in experiences. But unlike previous economic eras, the experience economy is not limited by an exchange of goods or services for currency. It's based on value, which is not finite in the same way.

Net Gain: Integration Instead of Zero-Sum

The experience economy does not account for a new proportion of the economic aggregate. It doesn't replace or eliminate other economic patterns, but instead enables all of these economies to integrate with one another, pushing the overall economy forward. For the agricultural economy, industrial economy, and service economy, improvements and increases are measured by productivity and output capacity. These three account for a proportion of the economic aggregate. They wax and wane, but the sum of the proportions remains the same. In the experience economy, percentages become less relevant because the distinct economies that preceded it often overlap. For example, the concept of the so-called "sharing" economy isn't zero-sum. AirBnB is an example of how these economies often intertwine. Offering competitive rates to typical accommodation options, a key differentiator is the diversity of destinations and activities. A vacation to California's wine country is arguably more authentic and immersive when travelers can stay in Napa Valley instead of essentially commuting there from a hotel. AirBnB is a service, but the harvest of grapes is agricultural, and the process of winemaking is industrial — all of which are elevated by the experience.

With the integration of the experience economy, consumers gain improved experiences across these earlier economies. From traditional products and services to digital content, all are now interconnected (Figure 1.3).

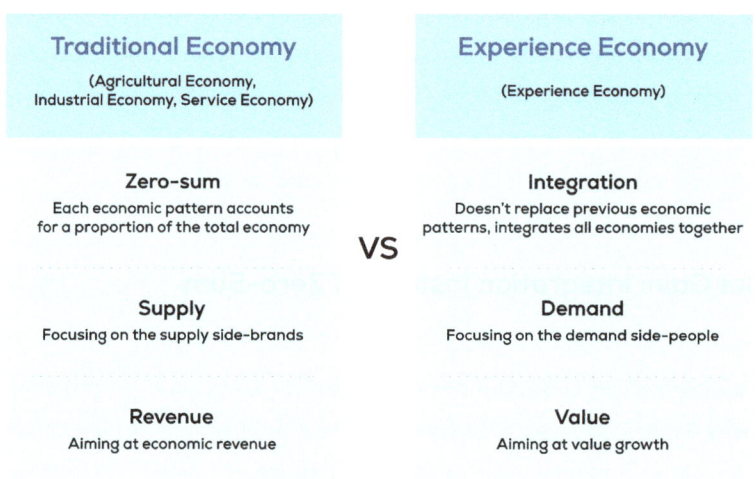

Figure 1.3, *Economies in Contrast*

Suppose you visit the same local restaurant for lunch everyday during the work week. The owner and wait staff know you by name, and your order, as soon as you walk through the door. In fact, the only time you're not there is when you're under the weather — and the restaurant knows that too. Sadly today is one of those days, so of course you order some comfort food from your favorite place. The delivery arrives on time, a porridge made from northeastern Wuchang rice, served with Tiger Bang Chili Sauce and Fuling pickles. Then you find a handwritten note that reads, "We hope you feel better soon." At that moment, you do feel better, even before the first bite.

Which economy is represented by this exchange? Wuchang rice is part of the agricultural economy, Tiger Bang Chili Sauce and Fuling pickles are from the industrial economy, and restaurants and takeout are the service economy. But it's the personal and unexpected note that integrates all of them organically. That's the power of the experience economy — combining elements of each of the earlier economies to create a net gain, one where simple percentages are unable to measure or express the overall impact.

Competition: Demand Drives Supply

Increasingly, brands in traditional industries have become frustrated — not by their competitors, but providers of new experiences. As noted in Liu Cixin's contemporary science fiction classic, The Three-Body Problem, the destructive potential of external forces is often ancillary. Such frustrations exist in every industry. The closure of Nikon plants was not caused by Canon, but Apple and Huawei, just as Alipay and WeChat undermined counterfeit currency by accelerating adoption of mobile payments.

The definition of competition is shifting from supply side to the demand side, as the original concept of competitors becomes increasingly disrupted. Cameras and cash weren't supplanted by typical competition. Both were replaced by smartphones. Competition in the experience economy is largely defined by whether the experience consumers demand is interchangeable with another, and how easily it can be replaced.

Luckin Coffee and Starbucks, both following a traditional economic approach, opened stores one by one selling coffee in cups. They certainly appear to be competitors. But in the experience economy, the two are not really head-to-head competition. Just like the US market, Starbucks offered a "third place" between home and office. So you'll find customers meeting socially, working, or doing homework at Starbucks. However, Luckin Coffee focuses on a carry-out coffee experience. By this measurement, coffee sold at convenience stores like ParCafé in FamilyMart or at 7-Eleven (which has been in China since 1992) might be the real competitors of Luckin Coffee — not Starbucks.

We'll discuss how Starbucks adapted their brand for China in Chapter 6.

Bottomline: Value Over Revenue

The concept of value isn't exclusive to the experience economy. But it is defined differently. In the experience economy, value is created as brands engage and interact with consumers, building a mutual relationship through meaningful experience. This intersection of value and experience isn't limited by the boundaries of the traditional economy, and defies measurement by revenues alone.

In some industries, customers view products and services as commodities, therefore the apparent value is easier to observe and understand. Take air conditioning as an example, with shipments across China in 2018 of more than 57 million units, up 1.6 percent from the previous year. The entire industry has reached saturation. When every room in China has been equipped with an air conditioner, the industry has little room for growth beyond replacing existing units.

Value created in the experience economy is more diversified by design. It includes people in the process in a way previous economies have not. In the three previous economies, value is more inherent. In the experience economy, consumers create value as well. But it's also not universal, because experience is subjective. Sometimes the most subtle differences have the greatest impact. Chinese smartphone maker Transsion dominates the African mobile phone market because it delivers a superior experience because their cameras more accurately capture a full range of skin tones than their better known competitors. Even if you find furniture at the same price point and quality as IKEA, you may still choose the Swedish brand because of the sense of involvement and accomplishment as you feel assembling it. Airports have also been known to intentionally place baggage claims farther from their terminals to relieve frustration of waiting for your luggage after the flight lands.

BUSINESSES NEED A NEW WAY OF THINKING

To address these three constant challenges of consumers, technology, and business differentiation, businesses look for different approaches to enhance understanding of their situation and discover a strategic competitive advantage. There are four key criteria for an effective new way of thinking for business: solid foundation, razor sharp focus, sustainable approaches, and connecting strategy to implementation.

Solid Foundation

When businesses are looking for a new way of thinking to guide their strategic decision making, the approach needs to be built on a solid foundation with a structure to expand for the future. There are two primary approaches: philosophy and theory, and real-world case studies.

Philosophy and theory provide a fundamental understanding of how the world works that can be applied to multiple opportunities and challenges. Grounding the thinking in philosophy and theory also allows the thinking to build on the "shoulders of giants", leveraging the experience and knowledge of history.

The second approach grounds the thinking in real world case studies. This approach ensures the thinking is proven and relevant. It works particularly well in situations that have no existing models and have not been previously explored by philosophy and theory.

In an ideal world, the foundation is built on a combination of philosophy, theory, and real world case studies. It provides a theoretical explanation to phenomena occurring in the real world.

Razor Sharp Focus

In today's fast-paced business environment, time is an invaluable resource. So any new thinking needs to have a razor sharp focus to address specific business problems. It would be best if the thinking went beyond a concept or an approach and provided a methodology, process, and tools that help brands perform specific activities towards achieving well-defined business goals. At the same time, the thinking also needs to be broad enough to adapt to multiple business scenarios.

Sustainable Approaches

When most people talk about sustainability, they refer to their commitment to reducing their impact on the environment through the use of clean energy and conserving natural resources. While we believe that everyone and every business needs to treat our environment responsibly, when we are referring to sustainability in this context, we are referring to the sustainability of their business.

The problem with many businesses is that they are often focused on short-term gains rather than the long term growth. However, when businesses don't consider how their actions impact their whole ecosystem, including their users, they are potentially jeopardizing their long-term viability. We believe that a new thinking needs to take a holistic approach that balances business perspectives and consumer perspectives, helping both achieve their short-term goals, and ensures the long-term sustainability of the business ecosystem.

Connecting Strategy to Implementation

Any new thinking that provides brands with an approach to defining strategy must also lead to actual implementation. One of the major challenges facing Chinese companies is having a strategy but not knowing what the next steps are toward implementing and executing the strategy. The new thinking needs to balance the strategic long-term with the practical short-term.

* * *

Summary

To address the constant challenges of consumer expectations, technology innovation, and business adaptation, organizations often rely on tried and true approaches. But for increasingly sophisticated consumers with an expanding set of options seeking improved experiences, traditional methods have become less effective in reaching new customers and maintaining existing ones.

Experience is a more comprehensive approach to understanding how consumers perceive value, both now and in the future. Compelling experiences create an impression that is the foundation of our memories. The experience economy effectively integrates the agricultural economy, industrial economy, and service economy. Incorporating the value of the experience economy into every customer interaction is a challenge and opportunity for all brands, regardless of industry.

Section 3
INTRODUCING X THINKING

With every new philosophy, there is a starting point. It may be a situation to understand, a need to address, a problem to solve. At this starting point, the existing ways we see the world are no longer sufficient. They cannot satisfactorily explain how the world works and how to navigate it — specifically the complex connection between consumers and brands, how their relationships evolve, and the needs, goals, and beliefs they share.

For X Thinking, this beginning dates back more than a decade, when TANG was founded by Jason Huang as one of China's first user experience (UX) consultancies. In those early years, what clients wanted was simple and specific. They were looking to enhance the value of their devices and software by making interfaces more attractive and intuitive.

But China was also transforming rapidly from traditional ways of conducting business, focusing on the creation of something new and innovative. Over time as China transformed, so did TANG's clients. Partnering with hundreds of clients and delivering thousands of real-world projects, TANG has also evolved and expanded its capabilities to help our clients deliver more value to customers through product innovation and a new approach to service planning.

During this time, we've come to realize that with China's unique business environment, Western mindsets, concepts, and tools could not, and should not, be directly applied here. There's an opportunity for something new to emerge from China, something derived from local and global culture and context.

It was with this premise that we began to question existing approaches. We weren't satisfied with what brands were doing, how they were doing it, and at times, why they were doing it. There had to be a different way, a better way. We started forming our own perspectives of why business exists, how it should be conducted, and what it should deliver.

The result is a philosophy, and an approach. We call it X Thinking.

CORE PRINCIPLES BEHIND BUSINESS INNOVATION

Every business must define a set of guiding principles that determine its priorities. The core principles of X Thinking are elemental: people, value, and sustainability. These principles are universal. Business innovation is a process, the application of these core principles and the search for solutions through continuous iteration and improvement.

People

Who are our ideal customers?
What expectations do they have, and why?

These are the two fundamental questions we asked ourselves when TANG was founded. But it's easy to overlook or even misinterpret the significance hidden in their simplicity. The experience economy in China illustrates that enterprises that respect, understand, and serve their customers are more likely to succeed than those that ignore, judge, and exploit them instead. Honest and genuine interactions with customers build authentic brands with the potential to revolutionize entire industries, inspiring the trends and opportunities for business innovation beyond China.

Consider the instant noodle industry as an example. For two decades, the instant noodle industry experienced reliable expansion and sustained growth. But from 2014 to 2017, the industry suddenly declined. China consumed 22.5 billion fewer packets of instant noodles in just three years. The reason had less to do with the product than the changing lifestyle of its consumers. Workers traveling from Beijing to Shanghai used to spend 15 to 20 hours aboard traditional trains, making instant noodles a convenient meal option. But with the advent of high-speed rail service, the same trip now takes only four to five hours, and travelers may be more likely to grab a bite upon arrival. Long nights and instant noodles used to be the standard, but now take-out has become far more typical. Many white-collar workers in urban centers are inclined to choose take-out meals three times a day during the week.

But, dire predictions that instant noodle sales would inevitably continue to decline were premature. They actually increased 4.5 percent between 2017 and 2018, only because the industry reconnected with their core customers through marketing campaigns that adapted to their change in lifestyle. Self-heating packages, appeal among single consumers, and a variety of new flavors also helped revive the product's popularity. Among the most notable was Master Kong. The preeminent brand in instant noodles, their 2019 sales led the industry with more than 43 percent of the market. [27]

The unanticipated decline in China's instant noodle industry stemmed from an insufficient understanding of rapidly changing demographics. The industry entirely overlooked the changing needs of their core consumers and the cultural context of their purchasing patterns. The rebound was the result of repositioning by leading brands to focus on core consumers and their needs consistent with a new cultural context. Understanding the changing demands of customers requires understanding the effects social structure, economic status, and lifestyle have on brand relationships. That's the origin point of business innovation.

Value

What values do customers need from my brand?
How does my brand distinguish itself from competitors?

Historically, consumer behavior has been driven by the desire to upgrade, while business development has focused on increasing value proposition. Brands tend to explore the needs of early adopters in business innovation, and then adapt. This benefits future customers by increasing overall value, further driving demand for improved products. In the past 20 years, the value expectations of early adopters have evolved through four stages: utility, appearance, efficiency, and significance. Thus, the evolution of value likewise aligns with these four stages (Figure 1.4).

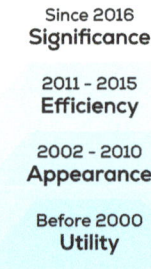

Figure 1.4. *Evolution of Value*

Utility

Before 2000, the value of a product or service was determined by its utility. This was still before the rise of the internet when computers were largely commodities. The determination of value depended on whether customers believed a product was more useful than a competing product.

From dandruff shampoo Head & Shoulders to the "shanghuo" (上火) reducing herbal tea Wong Lo Kat, similar products and brands were constantly emerging. Consumer demand for some products remains entirely dependent upon utility, seemingly immune to more contemporary market trends. The largest manufacturer of air conditioning systems in China doesn't need a more nuanced marketing campaign. Slogans that literally translate to "Gree Makes Good Air Conditioners" and claims of "one KWh a night" are enough to distinguish Gree as an industry leader. Another example of a similarly succinct slogan would be Campbell's "Soup is Good Food".

Appearance

From 2000 to 2010, value was increasingly determined by the visual attributes of a product. Home computers now had names — like Apple, Dell, and HP — as the internet increased access to information exponentially, including the comparison of products and services. With a seemingly endless inventory of otherwise identical items, industrial design became a distinguishing factor for recognizing brands and motivating purchases.

Inevitably, successful design trends became more uniform, if not pervasive. An industry of imitators, from nearly identical packaging to counterfeit websites, led business analysts to coyly brand 2008 The Year of the Copycat. Today, innovation has supplanted copycatting. Consumer tastes continue to diverge and aesthetics in turn are more diverse and increasingly integral to an item's overall value. Innovative eatery

Taoyuan Village redefined breakfast and kept things simple, serving only a handful of items: soy milk, deep-fried dough sticks, flaky flatbread, stuffed rice rolls, steamed buns, and iced desserts in the summer. Minimal menus, open kitchens, and free wifi were also growing trends in the US at the same time.

Efficiency

From 2011 to 2015, as focus pivoted to problem solving, the idea of variation as a feature was adopted throughout Chinese industry. With the advent of smartphones and mobile internet access, Chinese customer experience was constantly reinventing itself, creating new challenges to meet expectations for ease of use at a competitive price-point.

The rise of O2O (shorthand for interplay of online and offline) fueled by diverse product lines that addressed specific consumer demands still led to a vicious cycle that was ultimately unsustainable. Countless companies also found themselves facing the familiar struggles and predictable product development strategies that were no longer viable. Instead, brands that focused more intently on understanding their customers and embraced a more holistic approach thrived. WeChat became a pervasive and more robust alternative to text messaging. Yu'e Bao disrupted digital financial services with a small-scale investment app similar to Stash and Robinhood. DiDi offered ride-sharing at a lower price point for passengers than Uber, and with a higher percentage of the fare paid to drivers — and incorporated the existing taxi industry.

Significance

Since 2016, the concept of value proposition has continued to evolve. Customers more consciously consider their relationship with brands. Instead of simply choosing products based on utility, appearance, and efficiency, they've started to ask, "What does this brand mean to me?" and, "Does it match with my values?" Increasingly, customer behavior is informed by their measure of significance.

Answering these questions for core consumers, and expanding their ranks, is how niche brands emerged in recent years. NetEase's private-label powerhouse Yanxuan, online florist Reflower, and sorghum distillery Jiangxiaobai all launched brand campaigns highlighting the themes of affordable luxury, finding love, and everyday celebration focused on young adult, post-90s consumers. By contrast, traditional international brands like McDonald's, Watson, and Wal-Mart have experienced a steady decline in sales in China since 2015. They too found it necessary for their brands to adapt to these new consumer demands.

Over the past two decades, the progression from utility, appearance, efficiency, to significance reflects a shift in consumer expectations that continues to accelerate in pace. Every time a brand satisfies a new need, or introduces a new value, it reveals a path for the next iteration. Consumers now expect brands to create a world designed just for them. If companies commit to meeting these ever-expanding expectations, their brands are positioned to capture and retain more customers.

Sustainability

How do customers measure value over time?
How can my brand achieve and maintain sustainable growth and development?

Value is measured by perception, and therefore must be appreciated by consumers. The brand exists by observation. Let's take a retail grocery brand for example. When you use an app to place an order on your phone, which is delivered within 30 minutes, your experience is favorable. But if you have to wait in a long line at the store of the same brand, the opposite is likely true. Customers combine these positive and disappointing experiences together to form their perception of this retail grocery brand. This is brand perception. Unlike the abstract discussion of a brand in a corporate strategy meeting, the brand perception should be synonymous with the brand.

Consumer perception of brands is based on ongoing interactions with the brand through various touchpoints. A reciprocal relationship between brand and customer benefits both, serving as a means of achieving sustainable development. For example, the Chinese mobile phone brand Xiaomi has proven so popular with customers, it expanded into smart home solutions, including lifestyle products designed specifically for parents and pet owners. The company continues to create value by evolving with their core consumers and answering their needs. Increased customer loyalty has consequently changed their level of engagement with the brand. Instead of simply being consumers, they've become participants, sharing first-hand feedback, providing improvement suggestions, and collectively building the brand together.

As brands continue to create value for their customers, the beneficial relationship between them will also continue to evolve, from stranger to acquaintance, to friend, even family member. By better understanding the changing needs of customers, companies can continue to create perceived value, and contribute to the overall integration of customer-to-brand, customer-to-customer, also brand-to-brand relationships to achieve more sustainable development.

A PHILOSOPHY TO EMPOWER

X Thinking is our philosophy for how businesses can unleash their full potential to deliver value for consumers. It requires businesses to shift their mindset, to focus on forging long-term relationships with people of shared values and beliefs by creating experiences so that consumers come to know, feel, and believe in the value of the brand.

Create Value

Many believe the exclusive purpose of business is to generate profits. And while money is made by successful businesses, the activity of generating money is not the true purpose of business. The purpose is to generate value. Consumers purchase this value when they think it is worth more than the money they are paying. Profits are the reflection of successful businesses and losses are the reflection of unsuccessful businesses.

However, value is a very subjective concept. What is valuable to one person might be worthless to another. Ultimately, people assign value to something based on their own principles, perspectives, and contexts. This subjective nature of value and how it is perceived is a crucial concept for brands to understand. What a brand thinks is of value may be of value to some and not others.

We believe brands need to have a clear definition of the value they provide to consumers, and connect with those who share the same beliefs.

Forge Relationships

Many businesses view and treat customers as transactions. They focus on getting "the sale." They spend much of their energy establishing the brand and product to get customers in the store and make the sale. Some brands are even willing to mislead and deceive customers, just to get them to buy the product.

We believe that customers are not transactions, they represent long-lasting relationships. Brands that focus on treating consumers with respect and forging relationships will be rewarded with trust, loyalty, and advocacy. Customers who form deep bonds with brands will continue to patronize the brand over their lifetime, generating sales well beyond the initial transaction. Some consumers may not become customers, but still advocate the brand because they recognize the value the brand offers. These relationships are worth much more than a single transaction. Trust, loyalty, and advocacy can not be bought. They must be earned.

It's easy to use the term "relationship" to discuss the ongoing value customers associate with a brand. But building relationships isn't easy. All relationships take time and energy to build. Consumers do not become loyal fans of brands overnight. It's a process of getting to know the brand, helping customers understand the value of the brand through its products and services, and finally believing in the brand. It's not something that can be accomplished with clever slogans or manipulative marketing campaigns. People need to perceive the value of the brand over time.

We'll take a deeper look at the role relationships play and how brands should develop relationships with consumers in Chapter 2.

Define Customer Experience

Experiences are a formative part of people's lives. Consumers seek positive experiences and they avoid negative experiences. Experiences are how people understand the world around them by giving meaning to the things around them.

For consumers to recognize and understand the full value of something, it must be experienced. As part of that experience, they must be able to perceive the value. If consumers are unable to perceive and remember the value a brand offers, then it is essentially undifferentiated from the competition and invisible in the minds of the customer. It becomes a commodity.

Brands need to craft moments that are representative of the value the brand offers so consumers associate the value of the brand with the brand itself. These moments need to be distinct in a manner that can be identified and associated with the brand, and not confused with a competitor's experience. They need to be memorable in a way that consumers associate with the brand and how it contributes value to their lives. And there need to be multiple moments that reinforce the brand value over time. It's not enough for brands to shine one moment and expect customers to remain loyal indefinitely. There is too much distraction in the lives of consumers to undermine their attention. Brands need to reinforce their value repeatedly with multiple, distinctly memorable moments to remain in the minds of consumers.

We'll examine what makes an experience an "eXperience" and the concept of Return on eXperience (ROX) in Chapter 3.

AN APPROACH TO BUILDING RELATIONSHIPS

X Thinking is an approach for creating the optimal conditions for people to experience the value of the brand. Experiences, just like value, are subjective. They are unique to every person. No two people have identical experiences with any given brand, given their personal goals, values, and preferences. In addition, a person can have a different experience with the same brand at a later point in time.

For example, if your first experience with an Apple iPhone happened to be shortly after it was launched, you were probably overwhelmed with awe. But today, if we gave you the same iPhone to use instead of the latest model, you would probably be frustrated with the device's far more limited functionality. The device hasn't changed over time, but you have. Your expectations for a smartphone have changed, thus changing your experience.

Brands can't guarantee delivery of a specific experience to anyone, let alone everyone. But if brands can identify like-minded people who share similar values and beliefs, and understand the scenarios in which they desire the value brands offer, then brands can create touchpoints that maximize the possibility consumers will have a desired experience.

Simply stated, this approach helps brands better reach and retain consumers by identifying customers with whom they need to develop a relationship and prioritizing the touchpoint needed to create and deliver a desired experience. There are two main components to this approach: consumer insights and experience strategy.

Interpret Consumer Insights

All companies require insights from all aspects of their business to make informed, intelligent decisions. To create healthy relationships between your brand and customers, companies need actionable consumer insights that are timely, accurate, and contextually relevant to determine the correct course to create meaningful experiences.

Some businesses try to create a single, universal experience. This approach of prioritizing everyone often ends up satisfying no one. Other businesses might focus on identifying target customers for promotion and sales. Some might not be customers but influence potential customers on their purchasing decisions. Others may not be current customers, but may become future customers. Understanding the relationships between each of the different types of consumer, and with the brand, helps inform decision makers with the information they need to identify and prioritize those consumers who are most desireable for your brand to reach, manage, and maintain a relationship.

Customer insights can also provide the information necessary to understand what customers are trying to accomplish: what they need, want, and desire; under what context; and what they perceive as value. Understanding what they want to do, how they want to do it, where and when they want to do it, and why they want to do it, allows us to pair the right technology with the right scenarios to plan and deliver meaningful experiences that meet and exceed their expectations. It also establishes the criteria for evaluating relationships and experiences from their perspective.

By understanding real users, we learn who they are and what they want to achieve. We understand their journey with a brand and different scenarios interacting with the brand: discovering the brand, learning about its products and services, comparing the brand with competitors, purchasing and using these products and services, problems they may encounter, and resolving issues with the brand. We learn about how they think and feel during this journey. Only through connecting with real users and their journey can we uncover their goals, needs, pain points, attitudes, motivations, and expectations.

We'll learn more about how consumer insights benefit brands by identifying ideal customers in Chapter 4.

Develop Strategies

Brands use a combination of marketing, products, and services to realize the brand value. Marketing attracts consumers to the brand and communicates the brand's values. Products and services deliver value to consumers. Many brands segment these efforts into channels, such as traditional advertising, social networking, retail and online stores, and customer service and support. Channels are a means of delivering products, services, or information from brands to the consumers. Yet each channel is often designed in isolation from the other channels, creating separate and inconsistent experiences that can prove confusing, sometimes undermining the brand.

However, consumers don't experience a brand as just a single channel in isolation from other channels. People move from one touchpoint to another, regardless of channel, as they discover, learn, consider, purchase, and use products and services. They cognitively group all of these experiences with a brand into a collective experience that represents the value and meaning of the brand, and how it compares with competitors.

An experience strategy helps brands envision the experience, align touchpoints with scenarios, and prioritize tactical projects to deliver holistic experiences — from a customer's first interaction to their most recent, and across multiple online and offline touchpoints. This strategy integrates brand communications and delivers more personal experiences, resulting in enhancing brand perception. This leads to increased customer loyalty, increased value per transaction, and differentiates brands from their competition.

We'll share how brands can define, develop, and deliver "eXperiences" through the use of an "eXperience Strategy" in Chapter 5.

Drive Digital Transformation

Not all brands are built on the same foundation. Some are established, perhaps dominating their respective industries for decades. There are the startups that emerge with new ideas and offerings, the disruptors that challenge the status quo. Then there's everyone in-between with ties to the past and an eye on the future. Their journeys may have the same destination, but not the same path.

The origins of digital transformation in China and elsewhere likewise have similar starting points, but are not identical. Consumers and brands that are digital natives have expectations and advantages, those with longer memories and histories often face a steep climb to adapt existing business models into modern ones that turn data into intelligence. In the internet age, every consumer contact and customer interaction is personal, or should be.

Incorporating these concepts from traditional brick and mortar retail to integrated online stores that are consistent, intuitive, even predictive is the challenge ahead for all businesses, and those that do it best will survive and thrive.

We'll examine the intersection of online and offline experience, the necessity of digital transformation, and the steps to achieve it in Chapter 6.

Prepare for the Future

This is X Thinking, our philosophy and approach for businesses and brands. It's the collective knowledge and experience of TANG's history as China's leading experience strategy and design consultancy. Developed to answer the demands of China's emerging consumer markets, it has been shaped by tested strategy and tactical case studies, from real clients with real results. It has evolved to reveal new methods and novel approaches to solve the challenges brands face in China — and throughout the world.

It is our belief that delivering extraordinary eXperiences to customers will create deep, healthy, and meaningful relationships. It can directly help brands understand customers better and inform better decision making. It provides a strategy to deliver extraordinary experiences by leveraging an omni-touchpoint strategy. It helps brands develop new products and services that deliver value to customers. It has the approaches, processes, methods, tools, and activities to help brands do all this by creating better opportunities to deliver value to your customers, your brand, and the world.

We'll conclude our journey where we began, with our core principles, as well as and when and how organizations should incorporate them in Chapter 7.

* * *

Summary

X Thinking is built on the core principles of people, value, and sustainability. While business trends and technologies will always evolve and change, these three core beliefs won't. It's an approach that helps brands determine how to be the best possible version of themselves. It helps them transform from where they are into their ideal version from the outside in.

This transformation isn't just about how brands look, but also what brands value and how they behave. We've invested and built on the foundation of three beliefs to develop our philosophy and approach for X Thinking to address and prepare for the future of business and technology.

"A brand is the set of expectations, memories, stories, and relationships that, taken together, account for a consumer's decision to choose one product or service over another."

— *Seth Godin*

CHAPTER 2

The Relationship Between People and Brand

Understanding Connections

Applying the X Thinking Relationship Model

Case Study: Amway

INTRODUCTION

Relationships are one of the foundations of our common culture. We have relationships with family, friends, and co-workers, as well as with pets, places, environments, objects — and yes, even brands. So it's only fitting that relationships are one of the key concepts of X Thinking.

It's easy to presume a customer's relationship with a brand is transactional. After all, brands provide goods or services in exchange for money. In truth, consumer relationships with brands can be much more nuanced, complex, and meaningful. In Understanding Connections, we'll explore how enduring relationships with brands are less about transactions and more about trust. We'll examine why relationships are a fundamental aspect of the human experience, and how businesses that focus on relationships can improve their customer retention, reduce customer attrition, increase user activation, and ultimately supercharge customer lifetime value.

Relationships can also be complicated. They take time and energy to build and maintain, and they evolve as our needs and desires change. In Applying the X Relationship Model, we'll introduce our approach to simplify and focus your efforts for building better relationships with prospective and current customers. Through insights into beloved Chinese and American brands, we'll discuss how emerging consumer expectations and everyday interactions drive lasting customer loyalty — from Apple to Xiaoming Tongxue.

We'll wrap up with a reintroduction of Amway, an American brand that required more than a little reinvention to reach Chinese consumers. The entrepreneurial roots of the company run deep, but combining both physical and digital stores with their novel approach to personal selling made their health and beauty products one of the most popular brands in China.

Section 1
UNDERSTANDING CONNECTIONS

Some brands inspire fierce loyalty. Apple is among the most notable. Passionate customers pore over the latest news and rumors, stream every live product launch, and line up outside of their flagship stores for days just to be the first to buy the latest device. They're the urban legend of brand loyalty that turns out to be entirely true.

But Apple's retail destinations are also brand showcases, providing both a hands-on experience and assurance of service that extends beyond the store to their online retail strategy.

The same is true of Freshippo, the rapidly expanding Chinese grocery chain launched in 2016 by e-commerce giant Alibaba. As introduced in the previous chapter, imagine if Amazon had created its own grocery experience rather than simply buying Whole Foods. But instead of premium brands and well-appointed stores, the retail environment more closely resembled ALDI. The comparison, however, ends there. Grocery stores are among the most challenging retail experiences to replicate online. Picking out produce and protein is a personal preference that comes down to trust, a relationship Freshippo has built by creating a network of traditional brick and mortar stores where 60 percent of sales come from mobile orders. Fresh seafood was an early draw for curious customers, but a strategic one for Alibaba. By demonstrating high quality and preparation of premium items like Alaskan Golden King Crab and Boston Lobster, customers were quick to place that same trust in Freshippo to fulfill online orders for pickup and delivery. Not unlike Apple, the store is also a showcase, an experience that broke down the walls that define traditional retail and created an immediate and enviable loyalty among its customers.

Why are some brands loved by consumers with such passion and devotion? Why are others seemingly so invisible, unable to attract their attention? How do brands capture customers' minds and hearts? What prevents brands and consumers from getting closer?

One of the principles of X Thinking is belief in the value and importance of human connections. In China, deep, lasting relationships hold great cultural significance. We believe strength comes from community. We believe that meaningful, harmonious relationships create wealth, and not exclusively in an economic sense. Relationships instill the confidence we all seek to thrive in the modern world.

Customer relationships should be no different. While brands are inherently an abstract concept, they are ultimately human constructs and an interface between individuals and businesses.

CLOSING THE RELATIONSHIP GAP

To bring people and brands closer together, we need to close a metaphorical gap between them. But before we do that, it's essential to understand why the gap exists: because consumers and brands are inherently different, with their own objectives and perspectives, their own paths and journeys.

People

Humans instinctively seek happiness and purpose, and avoid pain and suffering. We aim to improve our own lives and the lives of those close to us. This is why the consumption upgrade phenomenon is so significant in China. Consumers are enhancing their abilities with access to new information, making more mindful decisions about their health, buying high-quality foods, enjoying creature comforts, traveling to new places, embracing new cultures, and expressing themselves in new ways.

Brands

Businesses exist to create value, and for customers that value is measured by improving their lives through products and services. For employees, businesses also create value through opportunities that directly improve their own lives and those of their customers. For shareholders, businesses generate both financial value and lasting value, a legacy that endures over time.

The Gap

Consumers and brands are on separate journeys, represented as two paths. Because their objectives and perspectives are never entirely aligned, these two paths never intersect (Figure 2.1). When brands and their customers share mutually beneficial objectives and perspectives, the gap between them shrinks, bringing them closer together. The less aligned their objectives and perspectives are, the gap between them grows wider, driving them further apart.

Consumers interact with brands at touchpoints. A touchpoint

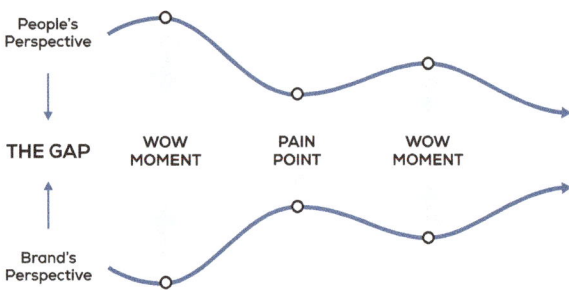

Figure 2.1. *The Relationship Gap*

can be a product or service offering, an employee representing the brand, an advertisement or similar form of communication, or even an environment. They can include television commercials, print ads, social media, messaging and mobile payment apps, retail stores and online outlets, and, of course, the product itself. Brand touchpoints are where brand actions and consumer actions meet. This is where experiences are established, the point where relationships are either strengthened or diminished.

When a customer has a negative experience at a touchpoint, it creates a pain point. Brand pain points drive these two paths apart and widens the gap. When people have an extraordinary experience, known as a WOW moment, it brings objectives and perspectives closer together. The more positive experiences consumers have with the brand, the closer the two paths become. The narrower the gap, the stronger the relationship.

A transaction-based relationship focuses on the purchase of products and services. Transactions are a foundation for how society exchanges value between parties and are fundamental for trade, commerce, and economic development.

When the relationship is transactional, businesses tend to focus on features and price. Yet, in every product category, most product and service offerings are fairly uniform, with feature parity and similar price points. Without a differentiating feature, brands begin competing predominately on price — an inevitable race to the bottom.

However, when a brand defines its relationship with consumers based on the exchange of products and services for money, the business views people as little more than a means of revenue. And this can diminish or even damage the potential for experiences. Such businesses easily become obsessed with increasing the number of transactions and the amount per transaction instead of meeting the needs, wants, and desires of customers. The key performance indicator (KPI) for the business becomes transactions. Whether intentional or not, KPI often favors organizational priorities, activities, and structure while undermining customer relationships.

Relationships are more than a series of transactions. They're about connections, meaning, and loyalty. Brands should view their relationships with customers as much more than just a means of making money. Instead, businesses should view customers as an opportunity for building lasting meaningful relationships. — an opportunity to fulfill the needs, wants, and desires of their customers. We believe the value of the relationship is greater than the value of the transaction.

HUMANS SEEK RELATIONSHIPS

Imagine what life would be like if we had to make everything we consume, entirely on our own. How much time and money would it take? Journalist Andy George explored this very idea in his Emmy award-winning series How to Make Everything. In the first episode of the series, he attempts to make a sandwich from scratch, only from raw ingredients that are found in nature. He harvested his own wheat, ground it into flour, milked a cow, churned his own butter, made his own cheese, collected honey from bees, produced salt from seawater, baked his own bread, grew lettuce and tomatoes, and even slaughtered a chicken, all by himself. Six months of hard work and $1,500 USD later, George could finally eat his chicken sandwich. So how did it taste? "It's not bad," George said. "That's about it. It's not bad. Six months of my life is not bad. Yeah."

After creating the sandwich, George created a suit, a book, a bottle, and other everyday items from scratch. His series showcases not just the skill, effort, time, and money required to create the inconspicuous items from our daily lives, but also how dependent we've become on one another for our survival. It is the relationships we have with each other — how we cooperate and collaborate with specialists, companies for mass production, and countries for international trade — that allows society to enhance the convenience and quality of our lives.

Without Relationships, We Have Nothing

Our social tendencies are more than just a practical and impersonal means of increasing productivity and improving our quality of living. According to Matthew Lieberman, Ph.D., Director of the Social Cognitive Neuroscience Lab at University of California Los Angeles (UCLA), our brains are biologically wired for social connection. In his book Social: Why Our Brains Are Wired to Connect, Lieberman explains how the brain is innately inclined to "care about social pains and pleasures in much the same way it cares about physical pains and pleasures."

Using fMRI, Lieberman's research reveals our brains react to social pain, like grieving over the death of a loved one or being treated unfairly, in the same region and manner as physical pain, like breaking a leg. Similarly, social pleasures, such as professional recognition and being treated fairly, are also processed in the same region and manner in the brain as physical pleasures, such as eating a favorite food.

The biological need for humans to connect, as well as our sense of pain when we don't, is what motivates us to interact — to live, work, and play together. Understanding these universal, biological needs and emotional instincts is crucial to many experience principles. Without social connections, even the greatest ideas can go unheeded or undeveloped.

Objects of Affection

The human imperative to connect is so strong that we not only form relationships with each other, but also with animals, inanimate objects, and even abstract concepts. Have you ever associated a human emotion with a pet? How about a natural phenomenon, like a furious thunderstorm, or a beloved car that tends to be temperamental? Anthropomorphism is the innate psychological tendency to ascribe human-like characteristics, emotions, and motivations to non-human entities.

It's quite common for children to anthropomorphize their toys. The emotional attachment a child feels for a favorite teddy bear or stuffed animal is real. They assign mental states, such as happiness or love. When the child goes to school and leaves the toy at home, they often say the toy was lonely at home by itself. If the toy loses an eye or becomes damaged, the child believes the toy was hurt and that it needs to see a doctor.

We continue to anthropomorphize as adults. We tend to treat our pets as if they are human. We give them names, groom them, talk to them, share our homes with them, even dress them up for Halloween.

And this tendency isn't limited to affection. How many times have we cursed at a computer when it crashes? Or given our cars a name, talking about how it behaves on the road, getting angry at it when it breaks down, and begging it to go a bit farther to make it to the next gas station?

Through work with our clients, we've observed how customers often develop friendships with their cars. One interview subject purchased a Jeep as his first vehicle, which he regarded as his best friend.

They would go on adventures together, taking road trips to distant places, sharing the experiences. His second car was a Mini Cooper. He also perceived the Mini Cooper as a friend, but different compared to the Jeep. The Mini Cooper was a friend that connected him to those with similar hobbies and lifestyles. Both brands were considered close friends by the owner, but their relationships with him served different roles —just as our human friends aren't uniform and tend to reveal different values.

Anthropomorphizing also extends from the objects people use to the brands that create them. Consumers attach personality traits to the brands they love: responsible, trustworthy, caring, innovative. They may describe brands they hate as evil, greedy, heartless, and shameless.

So why do humans anthropomorphize? Nicholas Epley, Ph.D., a professor of behavioral science at the University of Chicago Booth School of Business and an expert on anthropomorphism, suggests the psychological mechanisms are the same as those used for human-to-human social interactions. As the most social species on the planet, humans "build and maintain the intimate relationships that make life worth living." These relationships are often between people and other people. But they also extend to non-human entities, including brands.

BRANDS CREATE MEANINGFUL RELATIONSHIPS

According to a 2014 global study by Edelman, 87 percent of consumers want more meaningful relationships with brands, yet only 17 percent of brands deliver. Two-thirds of consumers felt that their brand relationships were one-sided, offering limited value, and 70 percent of consumers believe the only reason brands interact with them is the desire to increase profits.

"Consumers are sharing content and information about themselves, making purchases and recommending brands, but don't feel they are getting much in return," noted Michelle Hutton, global chair of Consumer Marketing at Edelman. "Consumer expectations have become much higher for brands and people expect to get more out of these relationships than they're currently receiving."

While brands serve as a construct to help customers identify and differentiate between similar offerings, they've come to encompass so much more. Brands can embody specific qualities and values. Sometimes these are values people want to associate with themselves. Brands can elicit memories from a time when we were younger, a sense of nostalgia. And brands can foster the emotional connections that establish relationships. Meaning has become more than just an abstract metric, and these values have become a deciding factor for an emerging class of consumers (Figure 2.2).

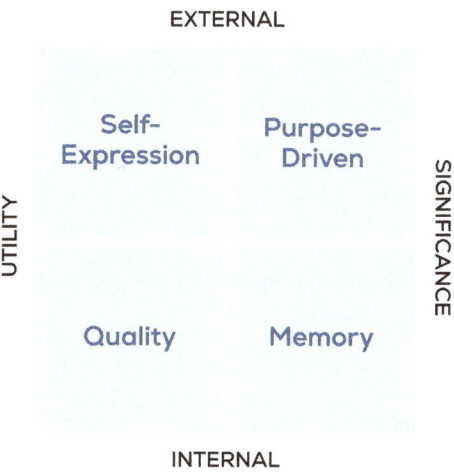

Figure 2.2, *How brands create meaningful relationships*

Quality

Consumers often associate low cost with low quality, hence the phrase, "You get what you pay for." And when consumers consider private label brands (products that are sourced and branded by the retailer, to compete directly with national brands in their stores), they're often seen as an excellent value compared to their brand-name competitors —but perhaps not as good. But that's notably not the case with Costco's high-end private label brand, Kirkland Signature, sold primarily at their membership-only warehouse clubs. Yes, Kirkland Signature products are less expensive than brand-name products. But many customers think they are actually BETTER than their brand-name counterparts.

Kirkland Signature products are perceived to be so good, they've developed a cult following for their consistent quality. It isn't an accident. When Costco introduces a new product, it's created entirely from scratch. The scale of the company allows them to choose materials and ingredients that add what Costco refers to as "hidden quality" — from the cotton used in their sheets to the wheat used in their macaroni and cheese.

Kirkland Signature also doesn't advertise, or need to, allowing Costco to invest instead in improving quality and reducing costs. When customers see the Kirkland Signature logo on a product, they recognize it as a mark of quality. Lower cost may be the reason consumers first try Kirkland Signature, but the quality creates brand loyalty. Annual sales of Kirkland Signature products exceed those of Kellogg, Hershey, and Campbell's Soup combined.

Self-Expression

The clothes we wear, the car we drive, the things we use, and the food we eat are all a reflection of who we are. The choices we make regarding things we surround ourselves with are a form of self-expression that communicates different aspects of our identity to the people around us. We use the distinct characteristics of these objects, their form and color, to express our personal style and taste.

In some cases, we can also use the attributes and status associated with a brand to represent our identity. Just like in high school, some students would hang out with the cool kids hoping their popularity would somehow rub off. They too would become cool by association. Consumers use brands the same way.

Wearing Supreme is street smart and subversive. Driving a BMW is a conspicuous reflection of social and economic status. Wearing a Rolex symbolizes your success, perhaps influence. Each of these (and we didn't even need to name the products, just the brands) embodies these traits, and by associating with these brands by purchasing and showcasing their products, these traits are transferred to your own identity. The brand becomes a relationship.

Purpose-Driven

Some brands stand for something greater, something more than premium merchandise or profit margins. They have a vision for the future. They plant a figurative flag and dare to lead the charge into that better world, recruiting the rest of us to join their movement.

One such brand is Patagonia. Their purpose and mission: "Build the best product, cause no unnecessary harm, use business to inspire and implement solutions to the environmental crisis." In pursuit of their purpose and mission, they've aligned their products, business practices, and other initiatives with it. Their products use organic cotton, traceable down, and responsibly-sourced Merino wool. They have implemented fair trade, certified wages, and created a used clothing market called Worn Wear. They've even created one of the largest private nature reserves in the world, Patagonia Park.

They also aren't afraid to call out those whose words and actions undermine their purpose and mission — even if it's the President of the United States. On December 2, 2017, President Trump ordered the reduction of two national monuments in Utah by nearly 2 million acres. The very same day, Patagonia updated their homepage to one with a black background and stark white letters reading: "The President Stole Your Land."

The company has even gone as far as telling customers not to buy new products, including their own jackets, in a Black Friday ad in the New York Times in 2011. The anti-consumerist message resonated with customers. The more they pushed the message, the more concerned customers connected with their brand, contributing to a sales increase of roughly 30 percent the following year.

Patagonia CEO Michael Crooke, PhD, summed up the strategy: "Customers become advocates of brands because they develop an emotional connection with their core purpose.… Customers see this association as something that makes their world a little bit better and, in so doing, creates satisfaction and motivates them to take action. It turns out that customers want to be part of something bigger than themselves, to help achieve something that they can't necessarily achieve on their own. When this relationship is found, consumers move beyond being casual customers and become advocates."

Memory

Brands are more than a window to the past. Sometimes, they're a time machine. They create a relationship with specific memories that customers can revisit over and over again. For one of our good friends, Peter Chan, PhD, an accomplished brand strategist and Associate Professor of

Design at The Ohio State University in Columbus, Ohio, Coca-Cola is more than a soft drink; it is an emotional connection to his past.

Peter grew up in Hong Kong, known for its sweltering heat and humid weather. Whenever Peter received high marks on a school test, his parents would reward him with an ice-cold bottle of Coca-Cola, a rare treat in his modest household. Memories of the satisfaction, celebration, and sharing of joy and love stay with him to this day. Those memories created an enduring association, a bond between Peter and the Coca-Cola brand, which continues to represent a reward for a job well done. In fact, when Peter conducts "ice breaker" exercises with clients or students, he asks them to share brand stories that are particularly special to them, Coca-Cola is always his go-to example.

Brands can also represent generational values, those from another era projected into modern times. Warrior, an established Chinese shoe brand, has seen a recent resurgence in popularity among Chinese youth. It echoes a nostalgic connection to the passion of being young shared among today's youth, and a brand worn by their parents. It's the difference between being dated versus classic. The brand transcends a generational divide, worn today as vintage-inspired fashion that pays tribute to an earlier age.

RELATIONSHIPS BENEFIT BUSINESS

Building and maintaining brand relationships isn't easy. It requires time, energy, and investment. But the benefits are also measurable, increasing user activation rates, reducing customer attrition, increasing customer retention, and, ultimately, creating greater lifetime value for customers.

Many businesses focus their relationship-building on branding and marketing efforts that capture customer attention, pulling them in and persuading them to make a purchase. But as competition increases and markets become more crowded, the amount of money your business needs to spend to persuade one person to become your customer — the new customer acquisition cost (CAC), — also increases. Studies suggest the costs for acquiring one new customer can be anywhere from five to 25 times more expensive than retaining an existing one.

Brands also need to embrace efforts that appreciate and prioritize existing relationships, such as after-sales service, and creating communities for customers to connect with the brand and each other. Looking past the initial transaction and developing sincere relationships built on trust generate loyalty and advocacy, leading to repeat sales and testimonial marketing. One study by Frederick Reichheld at Bain suggests improving customer retention rates by 5 percent can increase profits from 25 percent to 95 percent.

The longer and more often a customer remains engaged with your brand, the more value they add back to your business. The metric that helps your brand assess the financial value of each customer during their entire relationship is the customer lifetime value (CLV)

Another benefit of brands developing relationships with consumers is getting to know and understand their needs and expectations to serve them better. This too can improve user activation rates. In addition, brands can expand beyond delivering just one offering to developing an eco-system of interconnected offerings built around customer lifestyles. Brands can venture into new industries by delivering new value, identifying new scenarios by leveraging the knowledge and understanding gained from interactive customer relationships.

All these benefits can increase the CLV of every customer, ultimately creating increased revenue and profits for the business.

* * *

Summary

Humans don't simply desire connections, they require them. It's hardwired. We seek them out to satisfy innate needs for safety, belonging, assurance, and affection. Brands can satisfy these same needs. It's not the products and services they offer that fulfill these essential requirements, it's the relationships they represent. They add meaning to our lives in ways that may be more intuitive than articulated.

Businesses that satisfy these needs well, predict them, and build meaningful relationships around them achieve measurable success by caring about their customers and the value their brand creates for more than just the last or next transaction.

Section 2
APPLYING THE X THINKING RELATIONSHIP MODEL

The series "Friends" quickly became one of the most beloved shows in modern television history. It follows a group of six unlikely friends in their 20s, their triumphs and hardships, set against the backdrop of New York City. Though Ross and Rachel's on-again off-again relationship is maybe more iconic, the romantic journey of Chandler and Monica is perhaps more typical and relatable.

At their first meeting, Monica develops a crush on Chandler, but overhears Chandler candidly comment about her weight, and in a revenge plot to humiliate him, accidentally cuts off one of his toes. Needless to say, this isn't a great start to a relationship.

But eventually, they do become friends as part of a group. They become closer, support each other in times of insecurity, and share secrets and vulnerabilities which no one else in the group knows. Then their relationship takes the next step at Ross' rehearsal dinner. Monica laments that she's still single, and Chandler consoles and confides in her that she is the most beautiful woman in the room, which finally leads to them becoming a couple.

At one point, the couple keeps receiving signs that they should get married. But they feel they aren't ready and agree to move in together instead, matching their commitment level at the time. As expected, living together is difficult. They fight about what belongs in the apartment, and end up accepting the items that are important to one another, despite their disagreement. They also make space for something both of them will enjoy.

RELATIONSHIPS AS A PROCESS

After living together for a year, Chandler believes he is finally ready to propose, but being an episode of "Friends," it didn't turn out the way he hoped. Drama ensues and he doesn't get a chance to propose. Unbeknownst to him, Monica surprises him with her own proposal back at their apartment.

Their relationship isn't any less complicated after they are married. Chandler and Monica struggle through a long distance relationship and one of Chandler's colleagues tries to seduce him. Chandler responds that though she is attractive, he loves Monica, deciding to return to New York for Christmas and quit his job.

In the end, they adopt a pair of twins and move to the suburbs seeking more space for their new family. They both give up many things along the way as they grow together, from strangers to friends, partners to parents. Their move is a metaphor for the transition from one stage of their lives to the next, the series finale of their decade-long relationship — and as an audience, our relationship with the show. Even 17 years later when the cast gathered for a reunion to reflect on the lasting impact of the series, it was their actual relationships that were every bit as compelling as their fictional ones.

There are many types of relationships. And while they are not all like Chandler and Monica's, they all share similar characteristics. They're even seen in the relationships between brands and consumers.

Relationships Are Dynamic

Relationships are never static. They can grow closer together or further apart, or they may evolve into something completely different. Relationships are constantly changing, just like those involved in them. As people change, so do their needs, wants, and desires. Certain needs are fulfilled over time, and new needs arise. Existing relationships will evolve and new relationships will be created.

Different Perspectives

Everyone comes into a relationship with their own unique perspective, and everyone's perspective includes objectives for the relationship and associated behaviors in pursuit of those objectives. The closeness of a relationship can affect the various roles we play, our interactions, our expectations for these interactions, and the resulting experiences. Successful relationships require communication and understanding of intent to achieve individual and mutual objectives.

Relationships Need Nurturing

As Chandler and Monica demonstrated, relationships don't just happen overnight — they take time and effort. The relationship must fulfill everyone's needs. When a relationship becomes one-sided by primarily meeting the needs of one party while ignoring the needs of another, it becomes strained. Healthy relationships need to be mutually beneficial for all parties involved, and that takes work all around. But after a relationship has been established, it can't be neglected, either. It still needs attention and care, or it runs the risk of regressing. Maintaining the relationship requires time and effort to continuously meet the evolving expectations and objectives of everyone involved.

Relationships aren't easy. This is true for all types of relationships, including those between brands and consumers. But there is a predictable pattern to how relationships begin and evolve.

THE X THINKING RELATIONSHIP MODEL

While many brands look at people in binary terms, as simply prospective customers or existing customers, we've developed a model that more accurately represents the relationship with more subtlety and insight. Our X Thinking Relationship Model helps brands examine the various aspects of their relationship with consumers at an elevated level: how the relationship evolves over time, how customers and brands perceive the relationship, and the activities necessary to continue nurturing the relationship.

So how do consumers form relationships with brands? It's actually similar to how we form relationships with one another. While there are many types of relationships, our concept of the relationship model is based on the process of moving from stranger status to that of a family member — from no relationship at all, to the closest kind you can have.

Relationships between brands and customers have four stages: Strangers, Acquaintances, Friends, and Family (Figure 2.3). In every relationship, the customer and the brand start as strangers. As the customer and brand advance through each of the following stages, their objectives and behaviors evolve.

CHAPTER 2: The Relationship Between People and Brands | 83

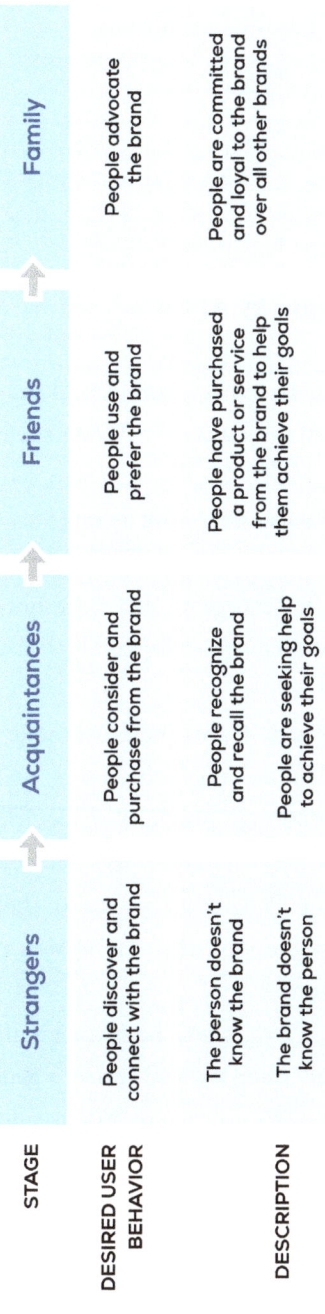

Figure 2.3, *X Thinking Relationship Model*

Strangers

Every relationship starts out in the Strangers stage. There are many strangers in our lives. We pass by them every day — the nameless people that surround us. We live our lives while they live their lives. Never connecting. Never interacting. A stranger can also be someone that you may only know by reputation, but have never met or interacted with in person.

The same is true between consumers and brands. There are many brands that remain unfamiliar to us. We see their ads on TV; we pass by them in shopping malls. We browse them on supermarket shelves. Our friends and family use them. But as much as they surround us, we don't acknowledge them in passing. We may have heard of the brand before, but they remain strangers. They have not made an impression on us. We don't know what they offer and how they may help us satisfy our needs, wants, and desires.

The goal for businesses at this stage is to take that first step, to introduce themselves to prospective customers, and to create a positive impression. Consumers may not have a specific expectation of the brand at this stage. They may have a need or objective the brand can fulfill, or they may not. Whatever the reason, the brand wants to connect with potential customers. This connection could be initiated by the brand or by consumers.

Nao Bai Jin (脑白金), a Chinese healthcare brand, makes quite an introduction to potential customers and creates a generational first impression. Their brand name literally means "just as valuable as platinum and good for your brain." They're perhaps most familiar for their pervasive advertising during primetime television. The commercials feature an animated, elderly couple dancing in various distinctive styles, from an Egyptian dance to a Hawaiian hula. They're fun and playful, with a memorable jingle and a catchy slogan, "We refuse any gifts for this festival, except for Nao Bai Jin." (今年过节不收礼, 收礼只收脑白金). Gift giving is an integral part of Chinese culture, a celebration of holidays and personal milestones much like the West, but one also involving specific traditions and etiquette. So when this adorable couple rejects any alternative gift for the Spring Festival (Chinese New Year), it resonates with audiences as intended. It makes such a lasting impression, even children easily recognize the brand name. It's also not a coincidence that when those same children become adults and are purchasing healthcare products for their aging parents, Nao Bai Jin is the first name that comes to mind.

First impressions matter because they have the potential to change the course of the relationship. They're the determining factor between remaining strangers or becoming something more. This is true in personal relationships and professional relationships, from first dates to job interviews. The same is true for relationships between brands and consumers. Brands want people to remember them in a positive light so that in the future, they may remember and reconnect with the brand.

Acquaintances

When two strangers meet and create a connection, but are not quite familiar, they move on to the next relationship stage: Acquaintances. In interpersonal relationships, an acquaintance is someone you know, but not that well. You know their name; they know yours. They may be colleagues or classmates. They may be friends of friends. You may spend time with them in a group, but not individually. Even though you spend time with acquaintances, you don't feel completely comfortable with bringing them closer.

When we view brands as acquaintances, we recognize and recall them and some of their offerings. We include them in our consideration set, or a subset of brands we consider when making a purchase decision. We interact with them to learn more about them by browsing their website and online stores, visiting traditional retail stores to try out products, engaging with employees and social network presences. But we may not yet be comfortable enough to commit to making a purchase or subscribing to the brand's services.

From the brand's perspective, when you begin interacting, it creates an opportunity. They know you're considering them. They may begin to get to know you better and try to understand your needs, to ensure they can provide the best possible products and services for your needs, wants, and desires. They're also trying to help you get to know them better, so you have the information you need to make an informed decision.

The ultimate goal during the Acquaintance Stage of the relationship is to convert potential customers into actual customers by building meaningful connections.

Xiaoming Tongxue (小茗同学), the popular tea drink for children, teenagers, and young adults in China, is a relatively new beverage brand with a novel approach to connecting with China's "Post-00" generation. The brand places interactive vending machines in high-traffic locations frequented by prospective customers, such as subway stations and universities. Interactive digital screens on vending machines invite passersby to play short, fun mini-games. Those skilled enough to score well on the game are rewarded with a free bottle of Xiaoming Tongxue. The brand also holds competitions on social media platforms such as Weibo, often described as the Chinese version of Twitter, to impersonate the comical faces of their cartoon namesake mascot, Xiaoming. These activities have actively engaged countless consumers, building buzz around the brand and meaningful connections with customers by creating shared eXperiences.

Acquaintances need to build understanding and feel comfortable with one another to reach the next relationship stage. This requires trust and reliability in meeting the objectives and needs of one another. For customers, this means ensuring the brand can provide the product, services, and experiences to reach their objectives and satisfy their needs, wants, and desires. For brands, it involves determining whether consumers are the right customers for their offerings. They don't sell products and services to those who don't need them. Both need to be comfortable before moving on to the Friends stage of the relationship.

Friends

When acquaintances begin to know each other at a personal level, they become friends. Friends are those you view as reliable and looking out for your best interests. These feelings and behaviors become reciprocal, and you prefer spending time with them over other acquaintances. How do you become friends? You bond over shared experiences, through participating in activities together. These experiences help you get to know each other better because they create opportunities to exchange personal information and insights about one another through authentic interactions.

When we become friends with a brand, we prefer it over other brands. We demonstrate this distinction by choosing their products and services. We share similar values and believe they offer a better fit for our needs than their competitors. Their offerings support us by helping to achieve our objectives. When we use their products and services, we're spending time together, an experience that creates a deeper understanding of one another. We view the brand as reliable, and we expect the brand to be there to support us, even if we have trouble with one of their products and services.

From the brand's perspective, their customers are their friends, too. They value their customers over non-customers. They focus on helping their customers achieve their objectives, fulfilling their needs, wants, and desires through their products and services. They appreciate the thoughts and feelings of their customers.

During this stage, the objective is to turn their customers into their advocates. They want to develop a deep, emotional connection. They want existing customers to become recurring customers. And they want repeat customers to recommend the brand to family and friends.

We've mentioned how customers tend to develop a relationship with their cars. Though less well-known than industry titan Tesla, NIO is among the most notable Chinese names in electric cars for reinventing every aspect of the traditional sales and service model. Their electric vehicles are more than the sum of styling and engineering. Though based in Shanghai, NIO relies on a global presence, from product design in Munich to autonomous driving development in San Jose. By foregoing dealerships and referring to associates collectively as "fellows" instead of competitive "salespeople," the shift toward a consistent and centralized point of contact with customers fostered an affinity among early adopters. Charging stations remain the sticking point for most customers considering electric cars over their hybrid counterparts, and NIO's strategy of building the largest, fastest network (including a fleet of mobile charging vehicles) reveals a focus on creating a legion of loyal advocates, then building a car company around them that serves customers better beyond the initial sale.

The interactions between customers and brands during the Friend stage of the relationship is based on the personal use of products and services. Positive experiences from these interactions create an interdependence between the customer and the brand. When customers encounter concerns, these are opportunities for brands to prove they are reliable and helpful. These crucial interactions are known as moments-of-truth, because how the brand responds will demonstrate to customers how the brand values the relationship. Successfully delivering exceptional experiences allows brands to take the relationship with customers to the next stage.

Family

There are some relationships that develop so deeply and friends become so close that they view one another as family. Even though two people may not be biologically related, they feel so close that they call each other "xiongdi" (brother) or "jiemei" (sister). Similar terms of affection and trust exist in English, varying along cultural and generational lines. But the implications are the same; close friends are more like family.

In Family relationships, you're committed to one another above all others. You prioritize their needs above the needs of your other relationships, possibly above your own. Your support for one another is unconditional. Likewise, you can turn to family in times of need. They are someone on which you can always depend, someone you feel you could talk with about anything, from your deepest secrets to the most mundane of topics. You develop a shared language based on mutual references and inside jokes. They just get you, and care about you deeply. There is a history and longevity in the relationship that endures, in both good times and bad times. You have developed a common value system through shared history, objectives, accomplishments, and experiences. Ultimately, you want to spend time together because it is someone you love.

When we view a brand as family, we are committed and loyal to the brand over all other brands. When the brand releases a new product or service, we want to be the first to buy it. We recommend the brand to our friends and acquaintances, noting its virtues and persuading them to also purchase from the brand. We defend the brand from its critics, and forgive the brand when it releases a less-than-stellar product. We develop a history with the brand. The brand has always been there to help us achieve our objectives. It's there to provide the support when times may be tough. You've come to trust and depend on the brand through its ability to deliver consistently.

From the brand perspective, the customers in the Family stage of the relationship are the most loyal and dedicated. The brand is closest to these customers. They involve them in major milestones for the brand. They value the opinions and feedback of these customers. They celebrate together the accomplishments of the brand as well as those of the customers. They bring the customers in on special events and occasions. They prioritize these customers by going the extra mile, especially during times of need.

The Family Stage is the final and closest stage between brands and customers. The focus for brands during this stage is finding ways to grow together. Customers grow and change over time, and brands need to adapt to grow and change with them.

As the closest relationship between brands and people, this final stage is what both desire most in their relationships with one another. They're seeking a relationship where they feel understood and valued. For customers, they can depend on the brand to be reliable and always deliver extraordinary experiences. And when things don't work out, they can expect the brand to be supportive and work to make things right. For brands, their dedication has earned the trust and loyalty of their customers, and they're rewarded with recommendations and customer advocacy.

The Family Stage of the relationship is extremely relevant for large enterprises in traditional industries that have reached market saturation. When growth is no longer dependent on reaching new customers, and is only achievable through acquisition of customers from competitors, brands should work to develop Family relationships with existing customers. By treating customers as family, brands can reduce customer attrition rates, increase customer retention, and maximize CLV.

Deterioration

There is one more stage that is not part of the relationship model, but is an important one to discuss: the Deterioration stage, when things begin to unravel in the relationship.

Not all relationships end happily ever after. Relationships also thrive or fail based on fit. When two people do not share similar views and values, or worse, don't respect and accept one another for their differing perspectives, it's hard for them to develop a close and healthy relationship.

But even if they seem to align, there are other reasons a relationship may deteriorate. If the brand keeps disappointing you with their products and services, or if they let you down when you need them to resolve an issue, these behaviors can lead to customers distancing themselves from the brand, regardless of the stage of the relationship they are in. The closer people are to the brand, the more forgiving they may be, but every relationship has its breaking point. Even the closest relationships can end.

But there is also a fate worse than a relationship ending. When a brand betrays customer trust, such as selling private information, a brand can actually create the opposite of an advocate. They can create enough hostility for their brand that former customers actively campaign against the brand and its efforts.

DEVELOP RELATIONSHIPS

The X Thinking Relationship Model provides a guide to help brands build and maintain sincere relationships with customers. It can help guide the conversation on how to build and maintain the relationship between your brand and customers at each stage.

We acknowledge that not all interactions will lead to a friend or family relationship. There are additional types of relationships: teacher/student, mentor/protege, master/apprentice, idol/fan... Each of these may also serve as a potential relationship model, depending on the brand. However, we believe the core concepts of our relationship model, multiple stages of bringing people closer to the brand, apply for each of the additional types of relationships.

The underlying lesson is that there are different stages of relationships between brands and customers, which evolve over time. This affects expectations of the experiences brands must deliver and the types of activities needed to continue building and maintaining these relationships.

Brands also evolve, and certain stages are particularly important for different types of companies at different stages in their own evolution. For new brands and startups, when time and money are in short supply, they should focus on the Acquaintance stage — converting potential customers to actual customers for the sustainability of the business. They can best achieve this by building meaningful connections with prospective customers.

For larger enterprises and traditional industries with an established customer base, the path for continued growth is focusing on the Family stage by growing with existing customers. This will lead to increased loyalty and advocacy, resulting in higher CLV that is more easily measured in the bottom line.

* * *

Summary

Relationships define us, and the journey from strangers then acquaintances, friends to family is similar to the relationships consumers have with brands. These stages parallel the familiarity, trust, and intimacy we have with one another, and with product and service offerings. We are enamored, and sometimes disappointed. The connection is never static, constantly recalibrating, often subconsciously.

Not all relationships follow this pattern in a single direction of progression, they may move forward and backward at times. But brands that engage with prospective and established customers to build and improve these relationships grow closer to consumers in a way both recognize as beneficial.

Case Study
AMWAY

Who Are They?

Amway is among the first and most familiar brands in the world in the health, beauty, and home care industry. Founded by Jay Van Andel and Richard DeVos in the 1950s, Amway's development is fundamentally built on relationships, an organizing insight gleaned by the two founders through door-to-door sales of Nutrilite vitamins. That understanding is still the organizing principle of Amway's development, that the relationship between people is the foundation of any business. Where there is the continuous trust of customers, there is a constant increase in success.

Amway entered the Chinese market in 1992 and quickly acquired a significant market share with consistent quality and novel sales methods. The Chinese market was Amway's 97th overseas market, but soon became their largest. In 2010, Amway's sales in China generated revenue of almost ¥22 billion RMB ($3.3 billion USD), and maintained a strong momentum with a steady annual growth rate of 10 percent until 2014.

The business environment in the digital era was changing rapidly, which made Amway's incumbent advantages less competitive. Micro Retail Enterprises, or MREs, are often overlooked by the West as overwhelming contributors to the Chinese economy. From street vendors and specialty service providers to small scale retail establishments, MREs now account for a significant portion of China's GDP. In 2013, the total sales of MREs in China was less than ¥10 billion RMB ($1.65 billion USD), yet in 2014, the sales exceeded ¥60 billion RMB ($9.67 billion USD). These rising MREs posed a huge threat to the direct selling industry. Since 2014, Amway's sales growth had ground to a halt, and so had Amway's development.

What Did They Need?

For Amway, the concept of family is one of the original values and principles established by their founders more than 50 years ago. But like Tupperware and Mary Kay, the brand has sometimes struggled to reinvent itself in the evolving US market. Adapting their longstanding, direct sales, business model to China was even more challenging.

Generations raised in the Internet era inevitably became consumers, and though their size and impact were significant, they were not concentrated in any geographic region. Amway's offline sales experience, refined by its Amway Business Owners (ABOs) over the years didn't translate to China's rapidly changing economic landscape. They were underprepared for digital contact and data accumulation, which became the biggest bottleneck for Amway's transformation.

In addition, new brands rapidly taking shape in the Internet era were also diminishing market share from Amway that relied heavily on ABOs for offline business expansion, lacking the agility to adapt to consumer expectations. Amway didn't know which groups of customers were attracted to competitors, nor could it enable ABOs nationwide with efficient digital tools to serve a large number of customers.

What Did We Do?

TANG helped Amway create an immersive brand experience that builds an authentic relationship between their customers and ABOs. When customers are invited by ABOs to a new experience journey, they receive a digital invitation which will guide them to the nearby Amway Experience Center (ACE). Customers visit different brand centers, from testing physical health attributes and receiving a detailed digital report to playing VR interactive games in the virtual farm, or even exploring a 3D environment to learn the scientific principles of a water purifier.

The interaction between customers and ABOs as well as Amway strengthens customer understanding and recognition of the brand instead of aiming solely for a sales target (Figure 2.4). During the entire experience journey, ABOs accompany customers, and at the conclusion, they can share a cup of coffee and chat about their impressions and preferences.

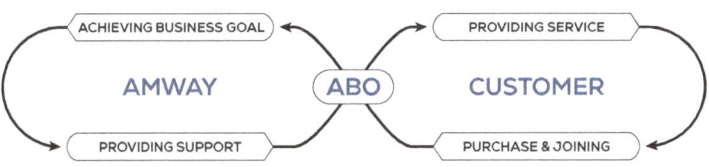

Figure 2.4, *Interaction between Amway, ABOs, and their customers*

Industry Context

Digital connectivity has changed the way people interact, creating both opportunities and challenges for many brands. Population convergence and frequent interactions are two distinctive features among generations of the Internet era. The emergence and rapid development of social commerce benefited from mutually-beneficial interpersonal relationships. Social commerce upholds three core elements, namely, trust, products and relationship monetization, all of which are in line with Amway's business approach. However, the major difference was that Amway relied solely on offline contacts, while social-commerce companies leverage the mobile internet for more interactions with customers.

In an online channel, the number of potential customers a brand can reach and influence is several times more than in the traditional offline channel in which an ABO on average could only get into contact with six customers per day. In a brand event, an ABO may meet about 20 customers at most. However, with the advent of social networks, an ABO can reach more than 1,000 new customers in one day, and a product community can send production introduction and promotional materials to more than 200 potential customers.

At the same time, transactions are no longer restricted by channels. As consumers become more comfortable placing orders online, the offline store gradually becomes the center to showcase brand experiences, while the online platform is for remote brand communications and real-time transactions. Both online and offline channels represent new functionalities. ABOs can initially reach and filter customers using WeChat and Weibo, then establish user communities for corresponding product segments to further impress and attract them by sending targeted information.

Establishing trust is a prerequisite for any successful sale. As the way people communicate is changing, the way Amway builds up trust is also changing. Social networking in the digital era is mostly online, which means ABOs also need to adapt to better cater to customer behaviors and preferences.

Direct selling is one of the most classic and straightforward business models. Amway's sales representatives don't need to go through a dealer to promote and sell products to customers. ABOs are often converted from the customers of Amway products or services. Amway sells products, provides services, and achieves business targets through its ABOs. For this reason, Amway needed to offer efficient and agile sales and management tools to over 3 million ABOs worldwide.

In the face of more divergent customer bases in the digital age, ABOs adopt a different way of communicating. Data shows that among Amway's active ABOs, about 40 percent are under the age of 35; among newly hired ABOs, half are under the age of 35. They are digital natives, with the lifestyle and the social style significantly different from the previous generations (Figure 2.5).

To convert young Internet natives into its customers and ABOs, Amway launched its experience strategy in 2014 to speed up the transformation and upgrading of the traditional direct selling model. To attract young customers, Amway started to rejuvenate its products, marketing, and business forms. In September 2017, Amway introduced a series of products, including energy beverages, facial masks and cosmetics, with slogans to attract young customers. Low-sugar and low-calorie foods and beverages quickly became popular among fashion-sensitive and sports-loving customers. In 2018, Amway also introduced the Artistry Makeup Collection, which tripled the number of Artistry customers under the age of 35.

Distinct from the separation between customers and sales representatives in other industries, Amway's ABOs are all developed and converted from customers. It normally takes more than five years for a new ABO to become a team leader of Amway. Considering most ABOs started as Amway customers, the ABO may actually know about Amway for a much longer time. This led to a very wide age span of ABO team, ranging from the young post-90s to the mature post-70s. In addition to the age, ABOs are also much different in region, habits, and educational background.

NEW GENERATION ABO

"A friend of mine works for Amway. I admire the fact that she doesn't have to work nine to five. I want to know more about her."

BASIC INFORMATION

Age **25**

Family Unmarried

Career Not selling business, occasionally buying Amway products

CAPABILITY RADAR MAP

- Internal Ability
- Digital Ability
- Input Level
- Social Sales Resources
- Values
- External Ability

EXPERIENCE PREFERENCE

- Contact and understanding phase, doesn't want to be frequently disturbed
- Understand Amway brand and product strength
- More product experience opportunities
- Simple and direct way to join
- Smooth and consistent social selling experience

CONTACT AND UNDERSTANDING

Amway's Official Website

 WeChat

 Search Engine

Figure 2.5, *Amway's ABOs in China are Distinct*

Amway has paid continuous attention to young people and hopes to encourage better teamwork by offering them more targeted tools. For the core needs and social patterns of young people, Amway designs and provides differentiated tools. Young ABOs want attractive product pictures to post in their WeChat Moments, while established ABOs prefer meeting customers in person to introduce products and share product videos.

In response, Amway introduced the Entrepreneur 2.0 program, centering around the concept of starting a business with a mobile phone, one interest, and a group of friends (Figure 2.6). Entrepreneur 2.0 satisfies beginner entrepreneurs' need for lite entrepreneurship, and also increases its own attraction to the internet natives. Young ABOs enjoy tasty food and promote Amway's products on Amway Weigo while traveling. Amway Entrepreneur 2.0 converts loyal customers of Amway to future business partners of Amway.

By planning the entire journey for customers to grow into ABOs, Amway could revisit its previously fragmented experience from a more consistent and unified perspective, which has allowed the experience fragments to reflect its value, and facilitated a better cross-departmental cooperation in Amway. Based on the insights into customers and their journey, Amway could also enable ABOs at different stages more specifically. In the process, Amway's digital capability and experience have been constantly iterating, allowing Amway to further enable ABOs with the powerful digital tools and services.

Business Objectives

In the digital era, people's real life and virtual life are intertwined. Therefore, brands need to create an omni-channel digital experience for both online and offline. ABOs are Amway's most valuable asset, and their efficiency and capability determine the value they create. Amway

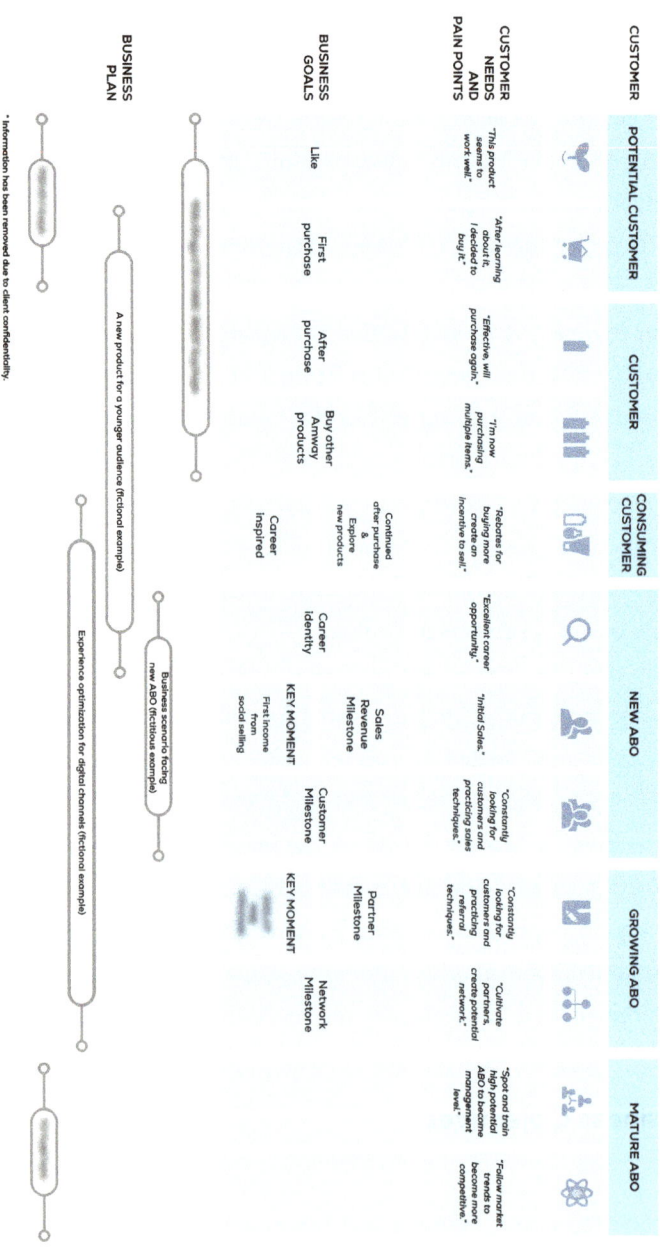

Figure 2.6, *Amway's Entrepreneur 2.0*

needs to empower young ABOs by integrating them into the direct selling system quickly and seamlessly so they can expand the system and create more brand value. To continuously enable ABOs, Amway and TANG designed a digital transformation strategy focused on relationship building to:

- **Reduce sales channel fragmentation and the resulting burden on ABOs.** Unify offline tasks with digital tools that allow ABOs to manage sales and grow relationships.

- **Extend digitization to datatization to improve ABO performance.** Create cross-compatible opportunities to understand customer needs and expectations.

- **Provide personalization and intelligence gathered from digital transformation to ABOs.** Convert experience and customer data into meaningful guidance for continued growth.

The Solution

Although an increasing amount of the customer experience can be completed online, the offline store is still a necessary touchpoint to build a relationship with customers. Though the emergence of VR and AR technologies is breaking the boundary between the two-dimensional world and the three-dimensional world, and to some extent, is filling up the experience gap between online and offline.

The Amway Experience Center (ACE) is Amway's physical store offline, a destination to build trust (Figure 2.7). In the past, when Amway only relied on their offline channel for business expansion, ABOs often invited customers to their homes for dinner to build

104 | X THINKING

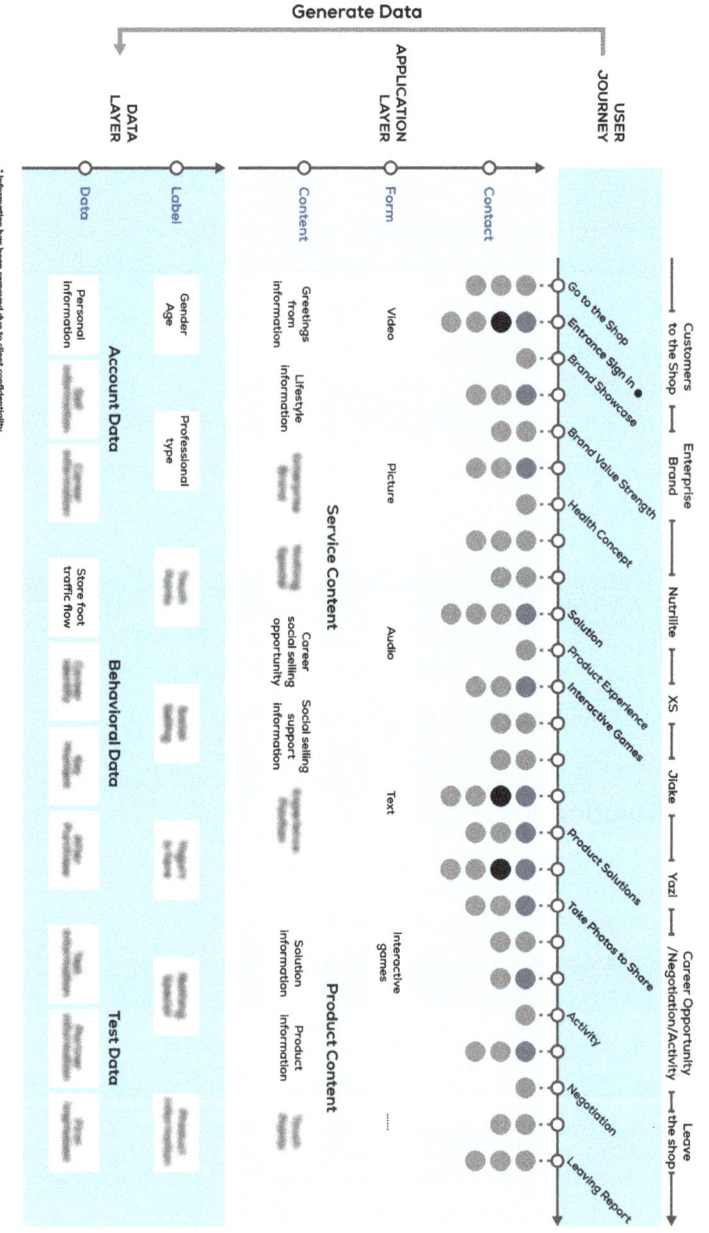

Figure 2.7, *Amway Experience Center (ACE)*

trust and promoted products to the guests. Compared to rigid door-to-door sales, scenario-based communication can create more trust and intimacy between ABOs and customers. Therefore, Amway opened many offline spaces, including stores dedicated to selling products and experience stores for showcasing. ABOs could always find a convenient space to communicate with customers.

Amway is renovating these experience stores to seamlessly connect online and offline by offering a consistent and holistic brand experience; on the other hand, these stores are renovated into a space that is more in line with the Internet era, which can help Amway eliminate people's stereotype and quickly build up the connection with customers offline.

The reason AECs offer a seamless front-end experience is because it is supported by multiple digital touchpoints along the entire experience journey. In an AEC, customers are connected with Amway's data center via various wearable, smart monitoring devices. Immersive, interactive displays present brand and product information, in addition to conventional video, audio, image and text. Amway also enriches the visit with interactive games and testing services.

The mobile internet helps customers obtain and share real-time information. Custom apps and WeChat mini programs are critical to connecting customers, who can scan a QR code to connect their account to obtain information like personal reports and product recommendation. With all the touchpoints connected, people can easily share or repost any information to social media.

Digital touchpoints are designed around the customer eXperience journey. Amway also made the services behind these touchpoints modular, so they can be configured to provide flexibility for AECs in a different region. With touchpoints connected, the underlying information can be commonly shared across different platforms and cities; with content modularized, the brand and product information shared by ABOs can have a good quality and also a consistent brand image of Amway.

In the digital era, the brand-people interaction is bi-directional. The digital touchpoints in AEC are not only sharing information about Amway, but also collecting information about its customers.

For brands, all customer information and behavioral data is valuable. Brands need to collect and incorporate multidimensional customer information, including gender, age, region, as well as qualitative behavioral preference and value orientations. Such insights will complete the digital persona helping Amway to provide younger products, as well as more personalized and intelligent services. ABOs will not obtain customers' private information, but will receive more information about customers preference and suggestions to provide better tailored services to customers.

Result

In 2018, after going through three years of sales decline, Amway China achieved a 3 percent sales growth, contributing 30 percent of Amway's global sales. In 2018, over 80 percent of Amway China's revenue was from online channels. In November of the same year, Amway China established the Amway Global Digital Innovation Center which would introduce Amway China's digital solutions and practices to the rest of the world.

Amway's evolution in China also tapped into the company's origin, one that turns relationships into entrepreneurship, now adapted for the digital age. They consider every customer a member of "Amway's Global Family" and encourage MREs to build communities around their brand. These communities help one another, exchange information, and develop business together.

"Exceptional customer experiences are the only sustainable platform for competitive differentiation."

— *Kerry Bodine*

CHAPTER 3

The Value of eXperiences

Understanding eXperiences

Defining Ideal and Holistic eXperiences

Measuring Return on eXperience (ROX)

Case Study: Xiao Guan Tea

INTRODUCTION

In Chapter 2, we looked at how relationships are one of the foundations of humanity, and one of the foundations of X Thinking. In this chapter, we'll look at another essential aspect of being human: eXperiences — the origin of the X in X Thinking.

Experiences are a fundamental part of social development. People learn and understand the world around them through experiences; they influence our behaviors and the way we think. In Understanding eXperiences, we'll dive deep into what experiences are and the role experiences have had on humanity as individuals, as a society, and as a species. We look at how experiences affect the relationships that consumers have with brands.

In Defining Ideal and Holistic eXperiences, we'll introduce the concepts of both Ideal eXperiences of Holistic eXperiences: their similarities and defining characteristics, the power of perspective, and how brands help consumers achieve their goals.

But as important as eXperiences are for people and for the relationships between people and brands, they must also deliver value to businesses in order for them to be sustainable. In Measuring Return on eXperience (ROX), we'll propose that companies should change their focus from Return on Investment (ROI) to ROX. We'll discuss how eXperiences contribute value to businesses through competitive strategy, higher revenues, lower expenses, and higher stock valuations.

Then we'll talk tea, Xiao Guan Tea — a Chinese startup that transformed what many consumers considered a commodity into a premium brand and retail destination, reinventing tea drinking as an entirely new eXperience.

Section 1
UNDERSTANDING EXPERIENCES

One summer, as a young child, Mike and his family visited Los Angeles to see their relatives, including his maternal grandmother, who was a smoker. A curious child, Mike was fascinated by this narrow, white cylinder that his grandmother would put to her lips at one end, emitting a beautiful orange glow and smoke at the other. His grandmother told him smoking is bad, and that she developed the habit when she was young and living in China. But Mike remained intrigued.

So his grandmother tried another approach to dissuade him from the habit: she let young Mike try for himself.

The story could have gone two ways from here: Mike enjoyed that first taste of smoke from the cigarette, or Mike hated it. The latter happened. He remembers the intense cough after inhaling and a disgusting aftertaste left in his mouth. That meaningful event, that moment, has stuck with him for years — among the first experiences he can remember.

From that point on, smoke has always represented pain and discomfort for Mike. And subsequent encounters with smoke have yielded similar experiences for him.

One that reinforced his prior impression of smoke happened during another family reunion cookout in Los Angeles. Mike was chatting with his uncles and cousins when his uncle opened the grill lid, releasing a massive cloud of smoke. Mike, standing a bit too close to the grill, breathed in a lungful of smoke that triggered an asthma attack.

These experiences, and others like them throughout Mike's life, reinforced his connection between smoke and discomfort. Moments like these often define how we interpret and understand the world around us, and can affect future behavior.

EXPERIENCE AS PART OF HUMAN DEVELOPMENT

Experiences are fundamental to human development. We use experiences to grow and develop as individuals, as a society, and as a species.

Experiences for Individuals

At the most basic level, individual human behavior can be explained based on the pain-and-pleasure principle. Why do we eat cake? Why do we avoid the dentist? What prompts us to exercise, or not? Why do we go on vacation? Or, in Mike's case, why does he detest smoking? Our motivations for these behaviors can be explained by the Freudian principle: people avoid painful experiences and seek pleasurable experiences. What a simple concept!

Some believe, however, that Mike did not actually learn from the experience itself. According to influential American philosopher, psychologist, and educator John Dewey, "We do not learn from experience… we learn from reflecting on experience." Dewey suggests that when we have an experience, we do not automatically gain new insights and learning. We need to pay attention to it; we need to see connections between what we do and the consequences of our actions. It is only then that we learn.

So the act of smoking, the coughing that followed, and the resulting discomfort wasn't how young Mike learned. It was the act of reflection that created the connection between the actions and the consequences that resulted in Mike's growth and development.

These concepts also apply to experiences with brands. We've already discussed how when customers interact with brands, they can have negative experiences known as pain points, or extraordinarily positive experiences, known as WOW moments. When customers encounter pain points with a brand, they try to avoid them. These pain points may include difficulty finding information about an offering, being pestered by salespeople and excessive unwanted marketing, undisclosed costs, and difficulty repairing products. When consumers begin to identify a pattern of pain points with a brand, they associate the pain with the brand and avoid not just the pain points, but also the brand in the future.

But when a brand delivers a WOW moment, such as helping a customer in a time of need or despair, extending VIP treatment, an unexpected discount, or any other better-than-expected experience, customers associate these pleasurable moments with the brand and will develop a connection with the brand.

As pervasive as the Apple brand is today, there was a time not so long ago when the company was all but absent from traditional retail. Before launching its own flagship stores, retail partnerships had withered for decades. The only way to buy a Macintosh was through a handful of resellers or their obscure online store. Like many brands, Apple has since closed that gap with customers, seamlessly integrating the efficiency of online purchases with the immediacy of in-store pickup. But the Apple experience remains a personal one, ensuring orders are ready, customers are satisfied, and the full suite of services and workshops are open to everyone — regardless of where or whether they've already purchased an Apple product. It's an approach that doesn't simply serve existing customers, it creates and retains them.

Experiences for Society and Species

Human experiences are not just for the development of individuals, but also for our society and our species as a whole. German statesman Otto von Bismarck once noted, "Only a fool learns from his own mistakes. The wise man learns from the mistakes of others."

One of the things that makes humanity unique is the ability to pass our experiences from one individual to another, from one generation to those that follow — like Mike's grandmother's initial attempt to teach him that smoking is bad. Unfortunately, young Mike still needed to learn from his own experience.

Prior to the ubiquity of the mobile internet and social networks, consumers were more reliant on traditional advertising and marketing approaches to learn about brands. The means of communicating personal experiences were limited by the technology of the time. People primarily shared their experiences personally with family, friends, and acquaintances around them. As a result, brands could afford to spend more money and energy focusing on converting strangers to acquaintances, and acquaintances to friends.

But in today's mobile information age, good and bad experiences can spread farther and faster with the touch of a screen. The ubiquity of high-speed wireless networks, smartphones equipped with cameras, and social networks enables customers to share experiences as they are having them. It also empowers consumers through access to a global community of past and present experiences.

Today, when consumers have a bad experience with a brand, it can be live-streamed not just to family, friends, and acquaintances, but to millions of people around the world. The negative publicity for the brand can be harmful to the brand's image and reputation, its revenue, and share price. Likewise, when someone has an extraordinary experience, they too can share their story with the world and bring awareness and advocacy to the brand. This type of viral positive word of mouth is invaluable to the brand, because the most credible form of advertising comes from people we know and trust. According to a 2015 Nielsen Global Trust in Advertising Report, 83 percent of consumers say they trust the recommendations of friends and family and 66 percent of consumers trust consumer opinions posted online. Both are higher than the 63 percent of consumers who trust television advertising and less than 50 percent who trust online advertising.

This incredible ability to access and share experiences allows us to learn from past experiences across great distances as well as across time, and also to pass on our own knowledge and wisdom to future generations.

WHAT IS AN EXPERIENCE?

We keep talking about experiences and how they are valuable for us as individuals, for us as a society and species, and also for brands that want to create deep, long-lasting relationships with customers (Figure 3.1). But what are they? What makes an experience an eXperience? We need to know what an eXperience is before we can create them for customers. So, what is an eXperience?

An eXperience is a Series of Memorable Events

Consumers experience (lowercase X in this case) many things over the course of our lives. Most of what we experience is not memorable. For

Figure 3.1, *What is an eXperience?*

example, can you remember what you had for dinner three weeks ago? Probably not. Most people can't. We all experienced eating dinner three weeks ago, but it wasn't memorable enough to be an "eXperience" for you. However, the romantic dinner at L'Ambassade D'Auvergne that you enjoyed with your spouse in Paris during your honeymoon several years ago was an eXperience you will never forget.

When customers describe eXperiences, they often talk about them as singular events. However, eXperiences comprise multiple events rather than just one moment in time. These can occur relatively quickly, such as the romantic dinner, where multiple events happen one after another during the duration of the dinner. Other eXperiences can have a course of many events separated across time. An eXperience of attending the World Series would be such an eXperience, where the eXperience happens one game at a time, separated across multiple days, and in two cities.

An eXperience is Connected to a Brand

Because an eXperience consists of multiple elements, they require a brand to connect them. The brand binds the elements of the eXperience together in your mind. Themes also help connect brands to a person, object, place, time, activity, or purpose.

In the dinner example above, there could be multiple themes that classify the experience: romantic dinner, dinner in Paris, or honeymoon dinner. There is no right or wrong way to label the event in your memory; how you classify these events, and how they're connected, is up to you.

But when the theme is a brand (in this case, L'Ambassade D'Augergne) all the memorable interactions serve as the events of your eXperience with that brand. These may include the first time you were introduced to the brand (referral from a friend), to learning about the brand on a website (reviews), to placing a reservation (their website), to arrival (greeting by maître de), to service (the server), to the food itself. In a traditional shopping example, it includes an introduction to the brand, exploring the product at the retail store, the purchase process on their online store, receiving the delivery at home, using the product, servicing the product, contacting customer service, having the product repaired, and so on.

These events don't happen all at once. They also aren't limited to a single channel or touchpoint. Sometimes there may be days, weeks, months, or even years between events. But they are still connected by the common theme of the brand.

An eXperience is Perceived through the Senses

You experience each event through your five senses of taste, sight, touch, smell, and hearing. Back to the restaurant example. You can see the cozy traditional decor of the restaurant and the friendly staff. You can smell the aroma from each course as the server places it in front of you. You can taste their famous, deliciously creamy aligot. You can touch and feel the quality of the materials, from the softness of the seat, to the sturdiness of the table, to the smoothness of the silverware. You can hear the delightful sounds of the music playing in the background. Together, all these sensations contribute to how you perceive the eXperience.

When brands create eXperiences for consumers, they need to engage as many of the five senses as possible to help create a lasting impression.

An eXperience Leaves an Impression

Before every eXperience, you may have an expectation for what may happen. This expectation is based on your previous eXperiences and is also informed by the eXperiences of others.

As each eXperience unfolds, you evaluate what you perceive through your senses against your expectations. This evaluation creates your impression. Initially, this impression comes in the form of thoughts and emotions. When part of the experience is perceived to be much worse than your expectations, that moment is a low point. And when parts of the experience are perceived to exceed your expectations, those moments become high points.

Upon conclusion of the events, you reflect on what's transpired and assign your own personal meaning to the eXperience. Your thoughts, emotions, and meanings associated with the event become your expectations for future eXperiences. The impression forms how you see and understand the world around you and influences your future behaviors, actions, and decisions.

With eXperiences, advertising and marketing play a major role in setting expectations. They make declarations about why you need the brand's product or service offering, how it can help solve your problem, what their product and service offering is, and who they are as a brand. They position themselves by stating they may be better, faster, and/or cheaper than their competition.

The execution of the brand's products and service offerings, environments, communications, and employee behaviors are critical for meeting expectations created by advertising and marketing. Customer eXperiences demonstrate whether or not the brand lives up to its claims. Impressions from the eXperience help consumers define the relationship they have with the brand. Later, we'll examine in detail how eXperiences can be used to achieve stronger brand positioning.

Let's take a look at Mercedes Benz. They adopted founder Gottlieb Daimler's, motto, "The best or nothing," as their brand slogan. It sets a standard for the eXperience that customers should expect from the brand. The cars, the dealership, the staff, the purchase process, the warranty, the car maintenance — all need to be the best.

The Mercedes Benz eXperience is considered so superlative, if it falls short in any way in the opinion of their customers, it adversely affects their perception of the brand position.

THREE TAKEAWAYS REGARDING EXPERIENCES

eXperiences Change People's Understanding of the World

As humans, we learn by reflecting on the experiences we have. By having new experiences, people can change their preconceived notions about the world and redefine them based on their reflections to the new experiences. Existing relationships can be changed, and new relationships can be forged.

Every new eXperience is an opportunity for brands to change the status quo and create new relationships with customers — eXperiences that have the power to determine brand positioning. Shouting into the world that a brand is better or faster is not enough. The brand needs to find ways to make people believe their positioning by executing their communication, offerings, environments, and behaviors in a manner that fulfills its promise.

eXperiences Change People's Behaviors

When people have a new understanding of the world, they no longer act and behave in the same manner; they react and adapt. People seek out pleasurable experiences and avoid painful ones.

When brands deliver WOW moments, it attracts customers to the brand and changes their preferences and consumption behavior. When brands eliminate their pain points, it removes the reasons consumers would avoid the brand and move toward a competitor's offerings.

Delivering extraordinary eXperiences improves customer acquisition while reducing customer churn.

eXperiences Change People's Thinking

If you're able to change the world someone lives in and the way they see it, and you are able to change the way someone behaves in that world, you're ultimately changing the way they think. If you are able to persuade someone that there is a better way to live and to think, then you are passing your worldview on to them. eXperiences have the ability to change the way people think.

* * *

Summary

Experiences are as much a part of being human as relationships. They rely on our senses and build memories that define how we see the world. But eXperiences are more specific, and defy expectations by design. We use the term as a noun, not a verb, because eXperiences aren't something we or brands do. They are the result of a shared interaction that benefits both the consumer and the brand.

They're intentional, extraordinary, and always associated with a brand. Therefore, our earlier example of the Apple experience is more accurately an eXperience. It's the culmination of memory, connection, perception, and impression that make it an eXperience.

Section 2
DEFINING IDEAL AND HOLISTIC EXPERIENCES

The human experience is more fundamental than the consumer eXperience, but the former offers keen insights into understanding the latter. How we see ourselves in the world, how we measure our contributions, and how we respond to challenges define who we are. This is not unlike the standard we use to define brands and the value they present.

- How do they fit into our world?
- What contributions do they make to our lives?
- How do their products and services solve problems we have?

Answering these questions is essential to understanding Ideal eXperiences.

IDEAL EXPERIENCES

Ideal eXperiences are shared between consumers and brands. The greater the overlap in customer goals and the business objectives of the brand, the more valuable the eXperience and the relationship become.

When consumers interact with a brand, they both come in with expectations. However, that perceived eXperience is not always an ideal one. Pain points for consumers take away from the maximum value possible for the brand. Energy spent developing solutions consumers don't readily recognize as valuable are also a loss for brands. Reducing and eliminating such pain points and prioritizing efforts benefit the brand by minimizing the value lost in a less than Ideal eXperience. But brands also benefit by exceeding expectations, and fulfilling needs consumers may not even realize exist until brands offer a solution (Figure 3.2).

Whether it's the complicated, less intuitive interface on an app, the gap between an online store and a traditional retail shop, or the unrealistic expectations that come from a product that overpromises and underdelivers, the perceived eXperience for consumers and for brands is the starting point for creating Ideal eXperiences (Figure 3.3).

Perception Becomes Reality

Consumers think they know what they want, just and much as brands think they know what their customers want. Yet both are often wrong, or at the very least, their understanding is incomplete. A desired eXperience has a set of known needs at the core, but inevitably includes unknown needs as well. These may be features or attributes of a product or service consumers subconsciously expect, but may not always recognize or articulate. These are the unspoken expectations that undermine an Ideal eXperience. Brands may deliver exactly what customers say they want, but that may only include known needs, because customers often don't know what they want — because the status quo is sufficient or no brand offers a product or service that meets the needs they don't yet realize exist, or in fact may not exist.

This creates opportunities for brands that understand consumers at a more thoughtful and personal level. In the next chapter, we'll exam-

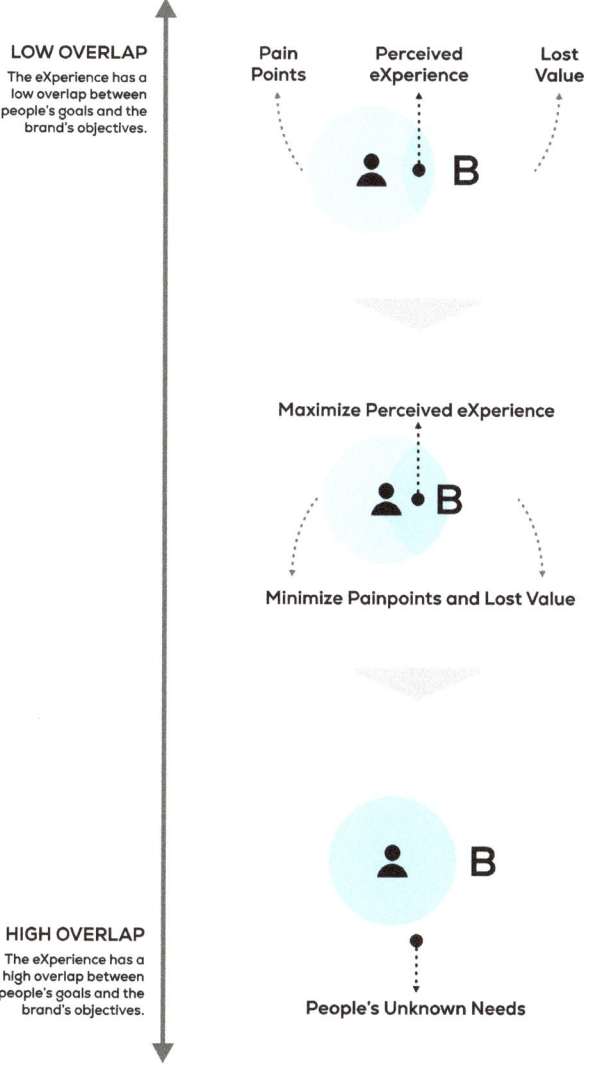

Figure 3.2, *Perceived eXperience*

MAINTAINING IDEAL EXPERIENCES

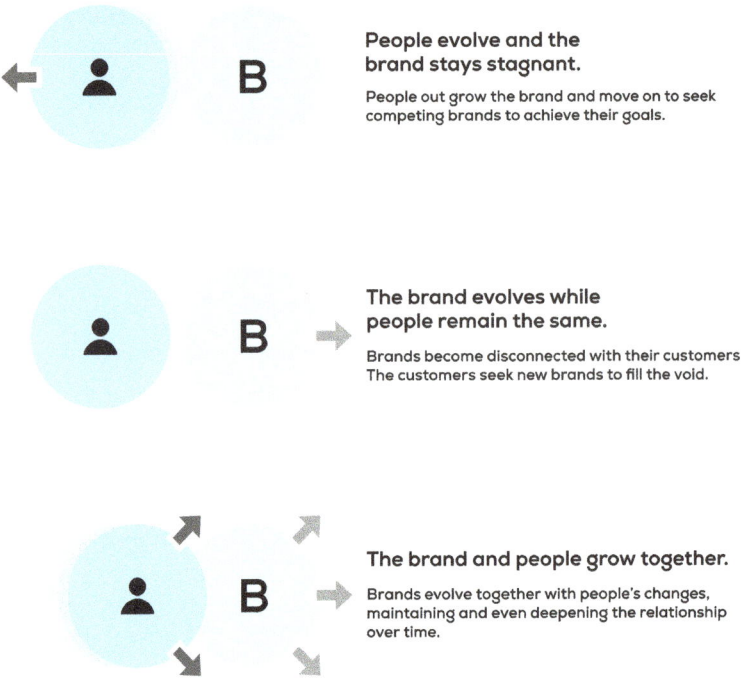

Figure 3.3, *Maintaining Ideal eXperience*

ine how personas and scenarios can help identify the needs of different kinds of customers. But for now, it's sufficient to know that brands that satisfy the unspoken and unrealized needs of customers significantly increase the value customers associate with these brands, forming the basis of a relationship built on exceeding expectations.

But this value is not exclusive to the consumer. By exceeding expectations and delivering value to customers by satisfying previous unknown needs, the brand generates value as well through recurring sales, recommendations, and loyalty that last far longer than an individual transaction. It becomes an ongoing relationship that increases in value over time.

THERE'S A DISCREPANCY BETWEEN HOW BRANDS THINK PEOPLE PERCEIVE BRAND VALUE VERSUS HOW THEY ACTUALLY DO

For brands to remain competitive, their value must be perceived. Value that cannot be perceived is value that does not exist. It's essential to understand how consumers perceive the value of a brand before you determine the essential business activities to deliver value that people can eXperience.

How Brands Think People Perceive Value

The way brands typically think about how people perceive the value that brands deliver is outdated. Brands approach the delivery of value starting with marketing. Traditional advertising is used to pull people into the brand by piquing their interest, leading to a purchase. Once people buy the brand's products, they receive the core value the brand delivers. In addition to the product offerings, brands also sell services so customers can receive the full value of the brand.

Many brands believe this sequential progression from marketing to the purchase of products to services, consumers perceive the brand's value proposition. The problem is that they are approaching how they provide value to customers, and the eXperiences associated with them, from an inside-out perspective (Figure 3.4).

Figure 3.4, *Inside-Out Perspective of Brand Value*

People Perceive Brand Value Proposition Through eXperiences

Understanding how people actually perceive the value of a brand requires an outside-in approach. From this perspective, you'll see that consumers don't always discover or learn about the product from advertising and marketing. Nor is the path consumers take to perceiving the brand value proposition always the sequential progression that brands plan.

How people actually perceive the value of a brand is through the eXperiences they have with the brand. What actually ends up happening is that people begin with a goal and seek a means to achieve their goal. The goal may be a problem that needs to be solved or just something they desire. They may reach out to their friends in real life and on social networks for ways to achieve their goal. In the process, they discover new brands that offer potential solutions. They might visit a website to learn more about the products and services; they could visit a retail store to see and touch the products. Upon making a decision, they can order the product from their phone and have it delivered to them at home.

Through this journey, consumers experience the brand through many interactions at multiple touchpoints (Figure 3.5). Some of these touchpoints are deployed by the brand, while other touchpoints are not under the brand's control. The touchpoints with which people interact depend on the goals, needs, and contexts of the consumer. At the end of each interaction with a touchpoint, they have the freedom to decide their path forward: choosing to continue their eXperience at the touchpoint, continue their eXperience through another touchpoint, or suspending the eXperience until a later time and/or location. Rather than brands crafting the narrative in which the brand is at the center of the story, consumers create their own story where they are the hero plotting their own path forward. The result of their eXperience with the brand determines how people perceive the value of the brand.

Figure 3.5, *Outside-In Perspective of Brand Value*

HOLISTIC EXPERIENCES

Brands create Holistic eXperiences to ensure consumer interactions are comprehensive, with a smooth transition between touchpoints over time throughout their relationship.

For example, imagine finding a product you like through a brand's mobile app. You read about the product in the app, but want to try it out in person. Later in the week, you go to the physical retail store and try it out in person. The salesperson shows you how to use the product and also shares that there is a new promotion on the product. You decide to purchase the product, but rather than taking it with you out of the store, you decide to have it delivered to your home. When you check out at the register, the cashier notices that you have some other products in your virtual cart, and asks you whether you would like to purchase those items as well. You do, but would like to have them shipped together with what you are buying in the store today. You're able to pay for all the items with the mobile app. The app already has your home address from previous purchases, so you don't need to supply any shipping information at the store. Once you arrive home, you open the app on your phone and check on the delivery status of your purchases.

In this experience, you can see how you are able to transition smoothly back and forth between the touchpoints, regardless of their location or whether they are online or offline.

Interaction with the Brand Is Integrated

Consumers interact with brands based on the ability to help achieve their goals. Every time they interact with the brand, they expect to make progress toward those goals.

For example, if you're having computer trouble, you call technical support for help. You spend the time explaining everything that is wrong, and the customer service representative recommends that you try some procedures to see whether they resolve the issue. Unfortunately, none of his advice solves your problem, resulting in the recommendation to take the computer into the store for further troubleshooting. At the conclusion of the call, the customer service representative says everything you discussed and attempted will be documented. You take the computer into the retail store for service, and they are already familiar with the problem you are having and the solutions you have attempted with the customer service representative over the phone. They are able to take your computer and investigate further.

Though this is a simple set of interactions, it is quite difficult to implement. Many brands stumble between touchpoints, such as the phone and retail store in the example above. For many companies, the same scenario at the retail store would have played out quite differently. It would start with you needing to recall and repeat everything you told the customer service representative because the store technician has no information from the call you made to customer service, followed by the frustration of watching the technician try all the same solutions you already completed with the customer service representative. Then finally, the service technician takes the computer for service.

Every interaction at every touchpoint should bring consumers one step closer to achieving their goals. Though every relationship will encounter bumps in the road, brands must do their best to ensure customers don't need to repeat undesirable and avoidable interactions, ones that potentially place customers no closer, if not further away, from their goals.

Transition between Brand Touchpoints Is Frictionless

With the advent of new technologies, brands have created new ways to interact with consumers and deliver new types of eXperiences. But often, these new technologies are introduced as separate channels with eXperiences that are isolated from existing eXperiences.

For example, when e-commerce was introduced, shopping online was a separate eXperience from shopping at a brick-and-mortar store. When you buy a product from the online store, often you cannot return it at the retail store. They operate as two different stores with their own processes, inventory, and management. But from a customer's perspective, you bought the product from the brand, so you should be able to return it to the brand, regardless of which channel you used to purchase it.

Brands should not offer an online eXperience and a separate, offline brand retail eXperience that compete with one another. They should serve one brand eXperience in which customers can transition between touchpoints painlessly and frictionlessly.

Reflection Reinforces the Positioning of the Brand

Marketing and advertising is a double-edged sword. In one respect, it broadcasts statements out into the world to attract people to the brand to purchase their product and service offerings. At the same time, it needs to fulfill the promise made in those same statements. It needs to live up to or surpass customer expectations established by the brand at every interaction and touchpoint.

If a brand positions itself as the fastest and most efficient, then you would expect its products and services to be faster and more efficient than competing brands. You would expect the purchase process at their physical store and online store to be faster and more efficient than competing stores, and you would expect employees working for the brand to be faster and more efficient than competing brands.

When brands fail to deliver on the brand promise, consumers view the brand as unreliable. When brands fail to deliver consistently across all touchpoints, customers won't consider the brand dependable. Businesses need to ensure every touchpoint is aligned to the brand positioning by creating an eXperience that represents the brand's value.

An understanding of Ideal eXperiences is essential for our discussion of personas, scenarios, and prioritizing the right consumers for your brand in Chapter 4. But because Holistic eXperiences are interconnected we've introduced both concepts together here, with detailed discussion of touchpoints, how to ensure they are aligned, and their future in Chapter 5.

* * *

Summary

Ideal and Holistic eXperiences are interconnected, but not synonymous. Ideal eXperiences reduce potential pain points and are defined by how well interactions with brands exceed customer expectations and generate WOW moments. Holistic eXperiences are a measure of how integrated interactions are with brands, whether they are consistent and comprehensive.

Though both depend on perception, consumers rarely think of their brand interactions in these terms. Creating interactions that help customers achieve their goals and offer frictionless transitions between touchpoints is the responsibility of the brand. Consumers will recognize the ease and efficiency of these interactions, but the complex mechanisms necessary to deliver Ideal and Holistic eXperiences are often invisible.

Section 3

MEASURING RETURN ON EXPERIENCE (ROX)

Brands today are delivering Ideal and Holistic eXperiences to build relationships with consumers. But how do eXperiences contribute value to the business?

One of the traditional metrics to evaluate the success of business activity is Return on Investment (ROI). ROI is often used to measure the results of specific short-term business strategies by comparing how much money was invested versus how much profit was generated. In other words, ROI metrics look at how much profit can be gained directly from a short-term investment. If a business initiative has a negative ROI, or lower ROI compared to other initiatives, this is often an indicator to terminate the initiative or to pursue alternate options.

MEASURING EXPERIENCES WITH ROI IS INSUFFICIENT

While ROI is a universal metric that isn't complicated and is easy to understand, it doesn't tell the full story when evaluating eXperience initiatives. There are several factors to consider in deciding whether

ROI should be used to evaluate the value eXperiences contribute to the brand.

Short-term VS Long-term

The very nature of ROI focuses on a business activity's short-term financial benefits. However, relationships between brands and consumers take time to build and grow; they do not develop overnight. It is a process that takes the relationship from Strangers, to Acquaintances, to Friends before the brand finally sees the ROI. As the relationship moves between the stages of Strangers and Friends, there are multiple activities that deliver extraordinary eXperiences to the potential customer that are not focused on generating money. How should these business activities be evaluated? ROI also does not consider how eXperiences contribute to the CLV that occurs over the whole relationship versus a single transaction.

Sum Is Greater than the Parts

People evaluate the relationship holistically across all interactions of the brand eXperience, not as separate individual interactions with the brand. These eXperiences are delivered through multiple touchpoints across online and offline environments, product and service offerings, communications, and employee behaviors. As a result, the sum total of the interactions working as a Holistic eXperience is greater than any individual touchpoint working alone.

Humans Are Complex

While businesses may be structured as channels such as retail stores, websites, e-commerce, and social media, consumer behavior is not restricted by channel. They bounce between channels, performing certain tasks in each channel. Customers delay their decisions. They compare different brands and different offerings, and ask for advice. They may also repeat these tasks over and over again before they make a purchase. And where they purchase a product or service may not be the same place where they first saw it.

Here's an example. One night, you and your significant other are out on the town. On your way to dinner, you pass by a Nike store and see a beautiful new display for a shoe that launched that very day. You've been looking for a new pair of runners for the past three months, but nothing seems to match your style. Unfortunately, you have to make your dinner reservation so you can't stay to try on the shoes. At dinner, you visit the Nike website on your phone to learn more about the new shoe. You like the look of the shoe, but your feet are finicky and you're afraid to make the purchase, fearing the shoes won't fit. So after dinner, you and your significant other head to the flagship Nike store nearby to try on the new shoe. It fits great. You share a few pics of you wearing the shoes on Instagram so your besties can offer some second opinions. They love it! They look great, they feel great, and people love them. You've decided; you're getting them. You go to Nike's app on your phone and make the purchase. You even scored a discount! Booyah! They'll be delivered to your home the next day. You complete the purchase before you even take off the shoes at the retail store. You leave the Nike store with your significant other and enjoy a romantic stroll to finish the evening.

In this example, you made your purchase on Nike's app. But that does not mean the website or the two retail stores didn't contribute to the overall eXperience. In fact, it was the final fitting at the flagship store that convinced you to buy the shoes. The fact of the matter is that all of the touch points contributed to your eXperience, and ultimately to the sale. Just because someone went into a retail store, tried the product, but left the store without making a purchase does not mean that they had a negative experience at the store. And purchasing the shoes online also does not mean that the online store is better than the retail store. They serve different purposes in the customer journey. The retail store may allow you to experience the product in real life; buying the product on Nike's online store doesn't require you to carry the product home.

What we need to do is understand the scenarios and behaviors of people to understand the role these touchpoints play in the process of building the relationship between brands and people. The ROI of a touchpoint is not representative of the contribution the touchpoint made toward the eXperience, and ultimately the sale.

A NEW CONCEPT FOR EVALUATING THE BUSINESS VALUE OF EXPERIENCES: RETURN ON EXPERIENCE (ROX)

When brands focus on delivering extraordinary eXperiences, they need a new approach to evaluate how the delivery of eXperiences contributes value to the business. Rather than focusing on the amount of money that goes into creating an eXperience and the amount of money that is generated from that eXperience, brands should focus on the impact created from connected eXperiences. We call this concept Return on eXperience (ROX).

ROX is a comprehensive approach to measure the entire eXperience and its long-term impact. While relationships are intangible and difficult to quantify, changes in consumer behaviors serve as indicators of the type of relationship and eXperience people have with the brand. These behaviors include increasing interest in the brand, saving and sharing of the eXperiences, and recommending the eXperiences to others.

So how does ROX contribute value to a business? Four ways: as a competitive strategy, higher revenues, lower expenses, and higher stock valuations.

ROX as a Competitive Strategy

In a highly competitive market, businesses are looking for strategic advantages over their industry rivals. Some brands focus on developing new technologies, but new technologies can be copied. Same for new products — competitors can easily copy them. Just look at how quickly smartphone companies copy the newest innovations from one another every year.

However, interconnected eXperiences across multiple touchpoints create a more defensible competitive strategy against copying. Why? Because an eXperience is unique to both the brand and those it serves.

An eXperience requires deeply knowing the customers the brand serves and their needs, wants, and desires. It requires understanding the brand's promise to them, and knowing their journey with the brand, and where and when the brand must deliver on that promise. The brand must align all of its internal processes to deliver on the promise. The challenges of this alignment were clearly illustrated across the retail sector with the migration to online shopping.

About a decade ago, China's e-commerce industry was booming as a result of the large number of Chinese consumers turning toward online shopping. During this time, many brands in China focused their efforts on new customer acquisition and improving transaction rates. And many of these brands profited from this approach during this period.

However, Jingdong (京东), better known as JD, took a different approach. They focused their efforts and resources on delivering a better eXperience for their end users. While customers may have a good eXperience shopping on e-commerce websites, their eXperience deteriorated after their purchase during the shipment of the products from the warehouse to the customer — where packages were often delayed or lost. So rather than relying on third-party logistics services, JD decided to build out a first-party logistics system where they could manage every part of the package's journey to the customer, including the last mile, where other e-commerce companies were facing significant challenges.

This investment in logistics resulted in an overall improvement in the online shopping eXperience by increasing the service quality and reducing shipping times to customers. While the investment in logistics did not initially yield much gain in revenue and stock valuation compared to their competitors, customers gradually gravitated toward JD due to their superior delivery eXperience. Today, JD is one of the leading e-commerce sites with record profits and stock valuation. This is the long-term strategic benefit of delivering extraordinary eXperiences for customers. [28] [29]

To do all this requires an eXperience Strategy and an implementation plan to deliver these types of eXperiences.

We'll discuss how brands should develop an eXperience Strategy in Chapter 5.

We should take a quick moment to clarify that we are not advocating for brands to focus on eXperiences in place of developing new technologies or developing new products. Rather, we believe focusing on eXperiences will amplify your product and technological innovations. Leveraging eXperiences as a strategic advantage allows you to plan for the future while protecting your investment in your existing products and technologies.

ROX Contributes to Higher Revenues

There are multiple ways that delivering better eXperiences to people will lead to higher revenue.

Increased Customer Retention Rates

As we discussed earlier, delivering extraordinary eXperiences can improve customer retention by creating closer relationships between the brand and consumers. People in deep relationships with brands prefer and depend on the brands to consistently deliver extraordinary experiences that surpass the competition. As a result, they have no reason to seek alternatives.

Higher Share of Wallet

Another contribution to higher revenues is through higher wallet share. Where market share focuses on acquiring more customers, wallet share focuses on the percentage of a customer's expenses that go to a particular brand. Customers who have a close relationship through one offering are more likely to purchase other offerings from the brand. This is because they already have a relationship with the brand that they know. They prefer the eXperience the brand delivers and expect a similar eXperience from the brand's other offerings. It is a lower risk for customers to purchase from a brand they already trust versus a competing brand without any relationship.

Increased Customer Lifetime Value

The combination of increased customer retention and higher wallet share leads to increased CLV. The more consumers spend on the brand

and the longer they stay with the brand, the more revenue the brand brings in over the lifetime of the relationship.

Positive Word of Mouth

Great eXperiences also lead to positive word of mouth. Customers naturally want to share their good eXperiences with their friends and family. And with today's social media, these eXperiences can go viral, spreading to millions of people around the globe. This type of publicity is priceless. As mentioned earlier, over 83 percent of people believe suggestions from friends and family more than they do from advertising. [30]

And word of mouth marketing doesn't just come from customers; it can also come from people who have never purchased the brand's product. In our research, we have found that often consumers who have a positive eXperience with a brand, but ultimately decide the brand wasn't a fit for them, would still recommend that brand to friends and family if they felt the brand fit their needs.

ROX Contributes to Lower Expenses

Higher profits do not come from just increasing revenue, but also from lowering expenses. ROX can help with that in two specific areas.

Reduced Customer Acquisition Costs

With increased customer retention, brands do not need to work as hard to find new customers to replace the previous ones who leave the brand. In addition, word of mouth marketing of the exceptional eXperiences customers are having are much more effective than any advertising. As a result, brands that invest in eXperience often spend less on traditional advertising and marketing for the purposes of acquiring new customers.

Fewer Customer Complaints

Brands that focus on delivering great eXperiences are inherently delivering fewer disappointing eXperiences. This means customers have fewer pain points with the brand and the brand's offerings. This leads to fewer complaints, which requires fewer customer-support resources to field them.

ROX Contributes to Higher Stock Valuations

Back in 2006, Teehan+Lax, a leading digital eXperience agency in Canada, tried an experiment. They believed, "Companies that focus on delivering great user experiences will see it reflected in their stock price." To test this assertion, they formed what they called the "UX Fund" and invested a total of $50,000 CAD (roughly $44,000 USD) in 10 companies — $5,000 CAD ($4400 USD) each, which they thought delivered excellent eXperiences (Figure 3.6). The companies included: Apple, Google, JetBlue, Netflix, Nike, Progressive Insurance, Target, Yahoo!, RIM, and Electronic Arts.

Remember, these companies were picked more than a decade ago. This was before Apple announced the first iPhone, before Google released the Android operating system, and before Netflix announced streaming video. These companies were all leaders in delivering the best eXperiences of the time prior to many of the products and services they are known for today.

George Teehan, one of the co-founders, conducted a retrospective on the experiment and shared the one-year and ten-year performance of the UX Fund, if they held onto the assets for the whole time. (They ended the experiment after one year, selling all the assets):

Figure 3.6, *Teehan + Lax "UX Fund"*

The UX Fund revealed that overall, during both a one-year and a ten-year period, companies that focused on delivering great eXperiences out-performed the NASDAQ. In a ten-year period, 9 out of 10 stocks had gained and the fund increased by more than a staggering 450 percent compared to NASDAQ's 93.2 percent. (Note the actual rate of return was calculated in Canadian dollars, as the variable exchange in currencies over the course of a decade makes comparison in American dollars problematic.) [31]

So how do great eXperiences contribute to a brand's stock market value? The value of a stock is the reflection of its future cash flow. As illustrated earlier, eXperiences can help grow revenue while shrinking expenses, thus generating positive cash flow.

While eXperiences are not physical in nature and may be difficult to quantify in financial terms for the business, they still have value — intangible value. Items of tangible value are concrete and easily quantified, such as cash flow, revenue, and profits. Items of intangible value are things that cannot be touched, such as intellectual property, brand, eXperiences, and relationships, and therefore much more difficult to assign a financial value. Intangible value is determined by the market's perception of whether the business will fulfill its projected growth.

LOOK OUT FOR KEY BEHAVIOR INDICATORS (KBI) FOR ROX

As brands begin to focus more on ROX, they will need to find ways to identify and measure changes in consumer behaviors. Earlier we talked about how there are different changes in behavior that serve as indicators for ROX: increasing interest in the brand, saving and sharing of the brand eXperiences, and recommending the brand eXperiences (Figure 3.7).

Figure 3.7, *Return on eXperience (ROX)*

Increasing Interest

When customers have repeat visits to multiple touchpoints, it's an indication of interest in a brand. Each touchpoint provides a different eXperience and provides different information. Visiting different touchpoints is a sign that consumers are still seeking out the brand as they are considering their purchase decisions. This can include visiting the website, opening an email, adding a WeChat official account, browsing a TMall store, clicking an advertisement, or downloading and using an app.

Saving and Sharing eXperiences

These days, people love taking pictures of their eXperiences on their phones. These are indicators that they may be having a memorable eXperience. Sharing these eXperiences with others through social networks, messaging apps, or just old-fashioned face-to-face communication is also an indicator that consumers had a memorable eXperience.

But a word of caution: memorable eXperiences can be both WOW moments and pain points. Not all publicity is good publicity.

In Chapter 4, we will look at how pain points are used to identify opportunities for innovative new eXperiences.

Recommending and Advocating

Consumer willingness to recommend an eXperience is another indicator of ROX. One metric used to evaluate this is Net Promoter Score (NPS). The metric is used by more than two-thirds of Fortune 1000 companies to evaluate customer's loyalty. It's based on a consumer's answer to the question, "How likely is it that you would recommend our company/product/service to a friend or colleague?" [32]

Another way consumers recommend eXperiences is through posting online reviews of the offerings they use. Of course, this too is a double-edged sword, where people can post positive and negative reviews.

* * *

Summary

Delivering great eXperiences leads to closer relationships with customers, who will reward brands with their patronage and loyalty. Though there are additional indicators of ROX, the key is for brands to begin paying attention to these indicators, understand their meaning, and measure how they contribute to their ROX.

Investment in eXperience increases revenue while simultaneously decreasing expenditures. Investors will also recognize and reward brands for the financial performance resulting from the delivery of extraordinary eXperiences. This is the measurable value of ROX.

Case Study
XIAO GUAN TEA

Who Are They?

Xiao Guan Tea (小罐茶) is a modern Chinese tea startup launched in 2014. Founder and CEO Du Guoying set out to change the Chinese tea industry by integrating the best-sourced tea in China with new, innovative technologies. The brand is renowned for their high-quality loose-leaf teas packaged in their namesake "Xiao Guan" or "small capsule," and are a top selling tea brand in China.

The company started by collaborating with eight expert "Tea Masters" to source some of the best high-end tea trees in China. Each tea is created through the mastery of the traditional craft of growing, harvesting, and producing. High-quality tea was combined with new proprietary technologies for preserving the taste, from production to the tea cup, setting a new elevated standard. Xiao Guan Tea also sought to change how the ancient cultural heritage of tea integrates with contemporary lifestyles.

What Did They Need?

Taking advantage of China's commoditized tea industry and the recent consumption upgrade trend, Xiao Guan Tea worked with TANG to develop a new brand eXperience and flagship retail store.

What Did We Do?

TANG helped Xiao Guan Tea uncover how consumers connect brands and eXperiences within the concept of a high-end lifestyle. By developing an eXperience strategy that shifted the focus from the physical quality of the brand's products, TANG focused on an emotional connection with the brand through the development of a flagship retail presence and a new approach to selling tea by creating meaningful moments.

Industry Context

As we discussed earlier in Chapter 1, the era of consumption upgrade is affecting traditional industries. Consumers are no longer content with the status quo; quality products and services at a great price point are not enough to ensure brand loyalty. Consumers, particularly in first-tier and second-tier cities, are upgrading to brands that deliver eXperiences that reflect their individual tastes, and they're willing to spend more to do so. Brands that understand this trend and take advantage of this opportunity are disrupting established brands in their industry. The Chinese tea industry is no exception.

China has long been recognized as a global producer and consumer of tea. Since the tea plant Camellia sinensis was first harvested in China more than 4,600 years ago, it has become the world's most-consumed beverage. [33]

Globally, there are some industries consumers often associate with a region or country, and in turn with specific brands. Among technology innovators, brands such as Microsoft, Google, and Apple represent the United States. Perfume is often associated with Europe, specifically France and Italy, with standout brands such as Chanel, Dior, and Gucci. But unfortunately, though consumers may associate tea with China, the tea brands that easily come to mind are not Chinese.

Even within China, there isn't a Chinese tea brand, company, or product that rises above the competition. Though consumers may recall Chinese tea brands, they primarily think of the brands as categories, such as Oolong tea, green tea, and black tea, or the origin of the tea, such as Longjing Tea from Longjing Village in Hangzhou, Zhejiang province and Huangshan Maofeng Tea from Huangshan Mountain in Anhui province. What China lacked were tea brands that stood out in the minds of consumers.

Though China's tea market was then valued at over ¥360 billion RMB ($58 billion USD), the top 100 brands represented less than 10 percent of the market. It was highly commoditized and extremely fragmented with no brands achieving notable market dominance. [34] [35]

Business Objectives

Commoditization and a lack of dominant brands in China's tea industry, combined with the new era of consumption upgrade, Xiao Guan Tea identified a prime opportunity to disrupt the industry with a differentiated premium tea eXperience, having already sourced premium teas and developed an innovative new packaging technology.

Consistent with their vision of "Creating a globally recognizable Chinese tea brand" through its mission of "Making great Chinese tea. Making China's tea great," previous projects with TANG helped Xiao Guan Tea identify opportunities for innovation by understanding their users and defining the brand's target audience. Xiao Guan Tea and TANG focused on developing a new brand eXperience to:

- **Attract curious 30 to 40 year old consumers to create premium customers**
  Target first-time customers and position the brand for high-end business tea drinking and gifting.

- **Reinvent the modern expectation of how tea is sold**
  Leverage the opportunity to break through traditional tea thinking and create a new retail tea culture.

The Solution

When Xiao Guan Tea first partnered with TANG, one of the greatest challenges the brand faced was that only the most perceptive and knowledgeable tea experts and connoisseurs could easily differentiate teas. Most consumers couldn't distinguish a high-end tea from an average tea.

Before TANG and Xiao Guan Tea could develop a strategy for positioning the brand eXperience, we needed to understand the type of eXperiences target customers associate with a "high-end lifestyle." Common themes emerged: eXperiences needed to be exquisite, unique, stylish, novel, exclusive, and personalized. But it was also important for these eXperiences to integrate their work lives and their social lives. The eXperience should result in customers feeling knowledgeable and refined (Figure 3.8).

The problem was that the existing perception of tea among younger generations was old and traditional. The culture around tea had not been updated and adapted into a more updated context. How can Chinese tea be integrated into a modern high-end lifestyle in the same manner as cigars and wine have become synonymous with high society? What TANG and Xiao Guan Tea needed to do was create a new Xiao Guan Tea culture that combined traditional Chinese tea culture with modern lifestyles, connecting consumers at a psychological and emotional level.

Figure 3.8, *Integrating Tea into a High-End Lifestyle*

Xiao Guan Tea needed to be more than just a high-quality beverage that people drink and enjoy. It needed to become a tool that allowed customers to express their identity and values.

Based on our understanding of eXperiences, we co-created a vision of the ideal Xiao Guan Tea brand eXperience and how it would change the way consumers think and feel about the brand. Customer interactions with each of the different types of touchpoints would result in an eXperience that changes their understanding of Xiao Guan Tea (Figure 3.9).

The eXperience Vision is an ideal result when people have an eXperience with the Xiao Guan Tea brand. Through this vision, we defined a new meaning consumers should have of the brand after eXperiencing it. To increase the possibility that customers would have this preferred eXperience, TANG and Xiao Guan Tea created a series of memorable moments guided by the brand principles on how brand value should be expressed through each of the touchpoints.

156 | X THINKING

BRAND VALUE PROPOSITION		
PHYSICAL LEVEL:	Convienient	Carefully selected	Premium quality tea of many different flavors
PSYCHOLOGICAL LEVEL:	A tool that allows to our target customer to express their identity, perspective, and value

	OFFERINGS	COMMUNICATIONS	ENVIRONMENTS	BEHAVIORS
	Balance between technology and art	Xiao Guan Tea tone of voice	Sensory experience	Stories
	A-must-have for a modern luxury lifestyle	Connect emotionally	Experience the ritual of tea	Deliver premium experience
		Stories that highlight the skill and craft of tea masters	Natural and real materials to reflect Chinese heritage	Generosity
		Connect the modern lifestyle with the ancient heritage of tea	Layered spaces to create sense of discovery	Relationships not transactions
EXPERIENCE PRINCIPLES	Move from a commodity to something people love	Position as luxury	Contrast between the environment and product	Master of trade
				Empathy
OUTCOMES	Appreciate Tea as an Essential Part of Life	Inspire and Inform	Experience the Process	Tea Enables Relationships

Figure 3.9, *The Ideal Xiao Guan Tea Brand eXperience*

Many traditional Chinese tea shops look like they haven't been updated in several decades. We wanted the Xiao Guan Tea retail store to make a statement; it needed to communicate the traditional, high-quality nature of the product combined with today's modern luxury lifestyle.

When customers visit a store, as they approach the storefront, they are greeted by captivating, revolving glass doors that serve as both the store's entrance and a product display. Inside, through the use of rich bronze and brushed steel finishes accented with natural wood grains, the space expresses a distinct sense of modern luxury. The openness and layered nature of the store invites people in to explore, linger, and discover tea.

An essential part of the Xiao Guan Tea eXperience is helping consumers learn about tea and discover their own personal preferences. We developed two features in the store that provide customers with an immersive tea discovery eXperience: the Tea Vault and the Tea Bar.

The Tea Vault houses and showcases each of the teas curated by the Tea Masters. The teas are set out on display so customers can touch and smell the tea leaves. Customers can watch videos on screens placed just above the tea display to hear the Tea Master's story and the process for creating the tea featured in the display. This is also where the store host introduces the brand story and technology behind the tea capsules to the customer.

At the Tea Bar, customers can sit down and enjoy a sample of the tea of their choice as part of a Chinese tea ritual. The store host helps visitors understand how to drink and appreciate the teas. Through the eXperience, customers can discover their personal favorites.

The tea discovery process utilizes all five senses of sight, sound, touch, smell, and taste for customers to perceive the Xiao Guan Tea eXperience. Together, they help immerse the customer into the Xiao Guan Tea culture, building trust in the process.

The highlight of the eXperience is when customers choose the teas that they would like to purchase.

The traditional approach to buying tea in China involved choosing either a disc of tightly compressed tea leaves or loose leaves in foil packets in beautiful canisters. For both approaches, customers need to commit to buying a large amount of tea at a time, enough to steep multiple pots (from 30 to more than 100). And once opened, the tea is exposed to the air and moisture that can begin to affect the tea's quality over time.

At Xiao Guan Tea, customers can select from a variety of single-pot tea capsules that the store host places in a beautiful box, perfect for setting out for display at the office or at home or as an elaborate gift box.

The customized tea gift box connects with the customers at two levels:

1) The majority of the Xiao Guan Tea's customers are not experts who have a clear preference for a specific type of tea. Instead, they prefer eXperiencing multiple types of tea to match different moods and settings.

2) The ability for customers to customize their tea selection allows them to express their own personal style and create something that is distinctly their own.

Because the capsules are for steeping a single pot of tea, customers are not locked into buying a large quantity of a single tea, but can mix and match based on their personal preferences. Involving the customer in the process of selecting their own personal or gift box of tea elevates the eXperience and develops an intimate relationship between Xiao Guan Tea and its customers.

Xiao Guan Tea's tea capsules are made from aluminum and house one pot of loose-leaf teas in nitrogen gas, protecting the tea from moisture, oxidation, age, and crushing. This ensures it remains as fresh as the day it left the production facility. The tea is sealed with peel-off aluminum foil, easy to remove but secure enough not to come off accidentally.

Compared to traditional tea packaging and inconsistent preparation, the Xiao Guan Tea capsules are much more suited to our modern lifestyle. Because each Xiao Guan Tea capsule is premeasured for a single pot, it ensures that the rest of the tea purchased isn't exposed to air and moisture every time you make a pot of tea. It's also an ideal size for travel without the hassle of preparing another container to hold loose tea leaves.

The tea capsules are beautiful objects with excellent functionality. They modernized the traditional Chinese tea ritual for today's business and social context. The capsules also serve as a subject of conversation between people as they share a pot of tea, promoting the brand and generating future sales.

Result

The new brand eXperience and retail store were an overwhelming success for Xiao Guan Tea. The first retail store was opened at Parc 66 in Jinan, China in November 2016. Over 210,000 people watched the opening via livestream. Soon after the launch, Xiao Guan Tea was sold out everywhere, exhausting their entire inventory and requiring the expansion of their supply chain. By the end of 2018, Xiao Guan Tea had opened more than 500 offline retail stores. With sales exceeding ¥2 billion RMB ($290 million USD), it remains a top-ranking brand in China's tea industry.

Xiao Guan Tea initially approached TANG to help develop a new brand and retail store that would attract premium customers and sell tea in a new way. By turning transactions into memorable moments, the company transcended the physical value of their product and created an emotional connection through eXperience. But in the process, X Thinking helped Xiao Guan Tea develop a new culture for tea based on lifestyle — one that will redefine more than what tea means to China, but also to the rest of the world.

"Get closer than ever to your customers. So close that you tell them what they need well before they realize it themselves."

— *Steve Jobs*

CHAPTER 4

The Source of All Change

Understanding Consumers

Identifying Meaningful Opportunities

Prioritizing the Seven Types of Consumers

Case Study: China Merchants Bank

INTRODUCTION

Now that we understand the value created for consumers and brands by Ideal and Holistic eXperiences, and how to measure their benefits, let's look deeper. What motivates consumers and how do their goals align with the eXperiences brands offer?

People are the source of all change, and eXperiences are where consumers and brands both find value, from a one-time interaction to an ongoing relationship. But if consumers don't recognize the increased value in the brand, and brands miss the opportunity to foster future interactions with the consumer, is it really an eXperience?

In Understanding Consumers, we'll learn that knowing your customers is more than just a list of transactions and purchasing patterns. It requires knowing them at a more thoughtful and fundamental level — their needs, desires, and aspirations. We'll introduce personas, complex consumer profiles created to appreciate and anticipate the appeals and activities of actual customers, and how they can help identify ideal customers.

We'll combine this understanding with practical examples in Identifying Meaningful Opportunities. Scenarios will help us apply perspective, to consider the functional, emotional, and identity needs all consumers have. We'll examine eXperience maps to help refine existing products and services and introduce new ones. Then we'll apply these insights to actionable strategies — all while remaining focused on the overall eXperience.

Targeting the right customers is crucial to meeting and exceeding their expectations. In Prioritizing the Seven Types of Consumers, we'll examine the roles different kinds of consumers play as businesses evolve, from seed users to "wanghongs," China's own distinct brand of highly-influential internet celebrities.

Then, we'll look at China Merchants Bank, a company that pioneered the industry in China as the first to create a customer call center, provide online banking, and offer wealth management products. But they eventually struggled to differentiate themselves from competitors, requiring a shift to a mobile-centric approach and individualized eXperiences for customers.

Section 1
UNDERSTANDING CONSUMERS

As we learned from our case study on Xiao Guan Tea, gift giving reflects a deep cultural symbolism and significance in China. But gift giving is also a universal custom. Imagine the process of selecting a gift for a close friend named Ben. We start by asking ourselves a series of questions.

What is the purpose of the gift?
Does he have a goal or dream that a gift can help fulfill?
Is there something he wants but has not purchased for himself?
What would fit his personal tastes and lifestyle?
What is something uniquely personal that only you can give that reflects your friendship?

The challenge with gift giving is determining the answers to these questions without saying, "Hi Ben. I'm going to buy you a gift. What do you want?"

What we can do instead is create an imaginary version of Ben in our minds. We imagine giving him each of our gift options and picture how he might react based on our real-life eXperiences with him. The more you know about him (who he is, how he thinks, his lifestyle), the easier it is to put yourself in his shoes and imagine how he would react to receiving each gift, and the easier it is to give him something that he will appreciate.

The same is true when brands create eXperiences, ones that connect to people by creating value. The more the brand knows about its customers and their expectations, the easier it is to create an eXperience that exceeds their expectations.

CONSUMER CRITERIA FOR EVALUATING THEIR EXPERIENCES

What brands really want to know is how customers will likely behave when they interact with the brand and its touchpoints. To help guide brands during this process, X Thinking helps brands create and maintain relationships through the criteria consumers use for evaluating their eXperiences based on three aspects: who they are, what they want to accomplish, and how they want to do it.

Who They Are — Attributes and Capabilities

The attributes and capabilities help us understand who the customer is. These are defining characteristics. Do they have any special skills or strengths? Do they have any particular limitations or weaknesses?

If the customer was a baseball player, some of these attributes and capabilities would be highlighted on their trading card, such as their height, weight, batting average, hits, home runs, stolen bases, etc.

Time and place are also tied to who customers are. A little too early, a little too late, and you've missed your opportunity. What additional contexts define who they are and the decision? What influence does age or life stage have on these?

Through our work with our clients, the attributes and characteristics we understand of those who have a relationship with their brand vary on a project-by-project basis. They should pertain in some manner to the goals of the customer and the objectives of the brand. Some of the attributes we consider include customer spending potential, openness to trying new things, risk aversion, expertise, and ability to influence other people.

What They Want to Accomplish – Goals and Fears

Brands that can uncover how consumers think can get a peek into their minds and begin to understand why they do what they do. X Thinking leverages key concepts from psychology to help companies view their brands from the customer perspective. We break down how consumers think into goals and fears.

Goals are what people strive to achieve and accomplish. They give us direction in our endeavors. They help people, as well as our society and humanity, grow and advance. They provide a purpose that guides our work and actions. Brands that understand customer goals know who they are trying to become and where they are trying to go. These brands can then create connections with them by helping them reach their goals.

The counterpoint to goals are fears. For example, if people are afraid of failing in a new endeavor, they may never get started. Consumers are attracted to brands that can help them reduce, avoid, or overcome their fears. Fundamentally, fear is about safety and security. Automakers often note their performance on safety testing. Retirement accounts and health insurance also assure customers that as they age, they're families won't face financial hardship.

For brands, goals and fears explain the motivation for consumer behavior — why someone is doing what they are doing. Needs provide insights into the criteria they will use to evaluate their eXperiences. We break down consumer needs into three categories: functional needs, emotional needs, and identity needs.

FUNCTIONAL NEEDS are the practical benefits consumers expect and desire from an eXperience. For example, functional requirements for food include satisfying hunger, healthy, organic, appearance, etc. Functional requirements are logical and rational in nature.

EMOTIONAL NEEDS are how eXperiences should make consumers feel. If consumers face a stressful and confusing situation when they are investing their hard-earned money, they may desire a product or service eXperience that makes them feel safe, secure, and confident about their financial future.

IDENTITY NEEDS are how an eXperience helps define or redefine consumer identity. For example, when they go to a grand opening of a new eXperience center, they may have a special invitation that allows them to skip the line at the exclusive event. This redefines their identity as a VIP.

How They Want to Do It – Values

How people choose to live their lives doesn't always align how they actually live. It is the result of choices they have made, manifested in the people and objects with which they surround themselves, environments they inhabit, and the brands they consume. But the aspiration is still there, and affects their priorities that they apply in daily life.

When we talk to customers to better understand them, we also ask about some of the other brands they consume in addition to our client's brand. With this information, we hope to identify the connection between these additional brands and how they help balance their aspirations and priorities, which sometimes conflict. Often, we find that the criteria people use to evaluate their eXperiences with other brands are the same criteria they would use to evaluate their eXperiences with our client's brand. So we dig deeper, to uncover the perceived differences and how our client's offering can align their expressed values and purchasing decisions.

Values are a set of beliefs that guide everyone in how they live their lives. Values are concerned with the manner of our actions, rather than the consequences or performance. They provide guidance on how to act in a variety of situations we encounter in our daily lives. [36]

- How we treat people (with compassion, honesty, and humanity)
- How we act (with energy, passion, and humility).
- How we approach situations (with curiosity, strategy, and flexibility).
- How we keep things (simple, sharp, and sustainable).

Here are some of the values that we have revealed through our project work:

Work/Life Balance Values
- Pursuit of prosperity
- Balance career and family
- Focus on hobbies

Consumption Values
- Spend the lowest amount for acceptable quality
- Choose the best quality that money can buy
- Improve perception by others

Social and Environmental Responsibility Values
- Leave a better world for our children
- Make sustainable choices
- Live for today, as well as tomorrow

Reconciling these competing values is challenging for both consumers and brands. A contemporary example of this delicate balance is Li Ziqi, whose internet celebrity is as impressive as it is unlikely.

Orphaned at a young age, Li was raised by her grandparents in rural Sichuan province in southwest China. When her grandfather passed away and her grandmother was unable to afford her education, she dropped out of school and eventually moved to the city, working for more than a decade as a waitress, a singer, and even a deejay. But as her grandmother grew older, Li returned to a more traditional life in the countryside of Mianyang — one she started to chronicle through a series of immersive videos initially shot on her smartphone.

The videos are visceral and voyeuristic, underscored to the sounds of nature with only the occasional conversation between Li and her grandmother. From creating her own clothes to preparing regional cuisine, Chinese audiences were immediately enamored by the simplicity and authenticity. A video on the process of making peach wine proved so popular, it was featured on the video platform's front page. With billions of views across China's robust social media networks, Li now has more subscribers than any other Chinese YouTube channel. Her most devoted followers are actually young, urban Chinese viewers drawn in by "fugu" (复古), or the vintage appeal her videos evoke.

Before becoming a household name, Li used to sell agricultural products on Taobao. She has since tapped into the popularity of her recipes and cooking demonstrations by launching a branded line of prepared foods distributed throughout China. When asked why she started sharing her daily routine online with the world, she replied, "I simply want people in the city to know where their food comes from."

Li Ziqi's success illustrates this often elusive balance, one that reflects her values, resonates with audiences, and attracts customers to her brand.

PERSONAS – REPRESENTING THE CUSTOMERS

At the beginning of this section, we examined the hypothetical situation where we were selecting a gift for our friend Ben. Instead of directly asking Ben what he wanted for a gift, we created an imaginary version of him that embodied everything we know about Ben: who he is, what he wants to accomplish, and how he wants to do it.

Back to our baseball card analogy, what if you could represent all of those player attributes and capabilities in a format that made predicting their behavior and performance possible?

Similarly, brands also need to create an imaginary version of their customers that can embody all that they know and understand about them. We call this imaginary version of our customers a persona (Figure 4.1).

A persona is a representation of users that captures their essence in the form of a fictitious character. While a brand has too many customers to create a persona for each and every one of them, personas are created to represent a group of customers that share common attributes and characteristics, such as who they are, how they think, and what type of lifestyle they have. Personas help us understand customers, not as part of a group or demographic, but as an individual with history, goals, interests, and relationships.

Origin of Personas

Personas are created by combining characteristics gathered from a number of real customers. The data is generated using a variety of user research methods, both observing their behavior and conducting interviews. Each piece of information in the persona helps communicate something that contributes to their overall story and their significance to the brand.

Each persona is given a name to make the fictitious character feel more real.

Information such as age, gender, relationship status, and whether they have children help communicate the persona's current life stage. The persona's location of residence, education, career, and income level can be used to provide some insight into the persona's personality and capability.

But personas are more than their demographic information. What

174 | X THINKING

BRAND APPRECIATOR
"PURCHASES reflect our VALUES"

Miranda, 35 years old, Actuary

| First-Tier Cities | Married No Children | Financially Independent | Socializes with Acquaintances and Those with Shared Interests |

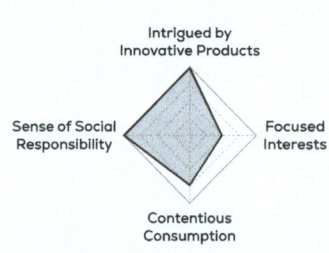

Intrigued by Innovative Products
Sense of Social Responsibility
Focused Interests
Contentious Consumption

Demand for New Brand
- Quality details
- Common values

Service Experience Preference
- Courtesy; Respect
- Clear communication of Brand Value
- Exclusivity creates a sense of belonging

Focus of Current Life Stage
Simple and comfortable

Consumption Values
The purchase of new products is part of a trendsetting lifestyle.

Relationship with the Brand
Embracing the brand through meaningful interaction reinforces shared values.

New Consumer Preferences
Health and household

Figure 4.1, *Example of a Persona*

is most important in crafting personas is communicating who they are, what are their goals , and how they want to accomplish them. This information is what helps brands understand how personas will evaluate the eXperiences that we will create for them.

Range of Personas

Much like baseball teams consist of multiple types of players who each have different strengths and weaknesses that complement one another, a brand should also consider all the different consumers who come together to help them reach their goals. When crafting personas, brands should consider what kinds of characteristics make up these different types of consumers and how they work together.

For example, someone looking for a new car may have a high budget, but doesn't trust advertising and marketing. However, they look to expert influencers who may have a lower budget but who are highly knowledgeable about cars and able to influence others. A brand needs to recognize the relationship not only between their brand and consumers, but also among consumers independent of the brand.

Benefits of Personas

The benefit of personas goes beyond simply being a means for brands to document their understanding of the customer — it makes the customer tangible and relatable for the people who are creating eXperiences for them. It brings them to life rather than existing as market statistics.

As a document, personas help organizations align and establish a common understanding about who their customer is and what they know about them. It allows them to have constant awareness of the brand's target customers and to develop empathy and compassion for them. Personas serve as a reminder of who the organization is serving as well as a reference point to test new eXperiences against.

PERSONAS AND MARKET SEGMENTATION ARE DIFFERENT

Many brands use market segmentation to identify distinct groups of existing or potential customers. The practice involves dividing a large market into smaller groups, known as segments, based on quantitative research of shared characteristics such as demographics and purchase behavior. Brands can then prioritize segments that have the highest probability of profitability or that have the most growth potential.

Segmentation is a great way to get a high-level understanding of the customer landscape and generalized characteristics of each segment. Segmentation research often includes statistics that highlight and breakdown percentages of the target market each segment represents. However, segmentation does not provide the actionable insights X Thinking requires to identify the consumers brands should pursue. You have to step back and start with a more purpose-driven approach. Personas are more than statistics. They reveal the relationships that help brands better understand their customers.

Personas are most valuable as a decision-making tool that helps brands prioritize whom they should target, as well as whom they shouldn't. Consumers who are more likely to share their eXperiences with friends and family may prove more valuable than those who are just as satisfied, but less active on social media. The use of personas may also identify market vacancies, serving consumers whose needs aren't satisfied by any brand's products or services. They help brands capture and create new customers.

X THINKING PERSONA LIBRARY

Over the past decade, TANG has generated more than 500 personas that make up our Persona Library. These personas feature the most relevant target audiences for brands in China today. We use these personas as a starting point for discussion to help our clients understand who their users might be and their needs, pain points, attitudes, motivations, and expectations. The benefit of personas is that many brands share similar customers, so insights aggregated over time increase the value of the persona library. Additional client research can then provide an even more complete picture of how these common personas interact with specific industries, offerings, and brands.

* * *

Summary

By identifying people's goals, fears, and values, brands gain insight into the minds of their customers, and begin to understand the reasoning behind their behaviors, decisions, and choices. Brands need to ensure the offerings they develop create value, helping customers achieve their goals, and manage their fears, in a manner that aligns with their beliefs.

However, these insights are often abstract. Creating personas that represent various prospective and current customers helps brands develop Ideal eXperiences that are appropriate for who they are, what they want to do, and how they prefer to accomplish their goals. Using personas reveals opportunities to narrow focus on specific consumers, to serve needs competitors aren't, and build relationships with new customers.

Section 2
IDENTIFYING MEANINGFUL OPPORTUNITIES

"If I had asked people what they wanted, they would have said faster horses."

This quote (erroneously attributed to Henry Ford) is often invoked to debate the value of user research and the origins of understanding consumers and their behavior. This assertion argues the outside-in perspective is not the source of understanding consumers — that if brands ask them what they want, they will lead brands astray and not toward a greater appreciation of their motivations. [37]

Understanding consumer desires and delivering Ideal eXperiences are inherently linked (Figure 4.2). Insights reveal opportunities to create something new. It is an opportunity to help consumers achieve their goals in a new way, a way that they prefer over the status quo. If understanding consumers is all about identifying opportunity, what is opportunity? Simply put, opportunity is a set of circumstances that makes it possible to do something. It's when all the conditions are aligned: the right need, the right location, the right time, and the right eXperience delivered by the brand.

Then how do we find these opportunities? How can we find the right need, the right location, the right time?

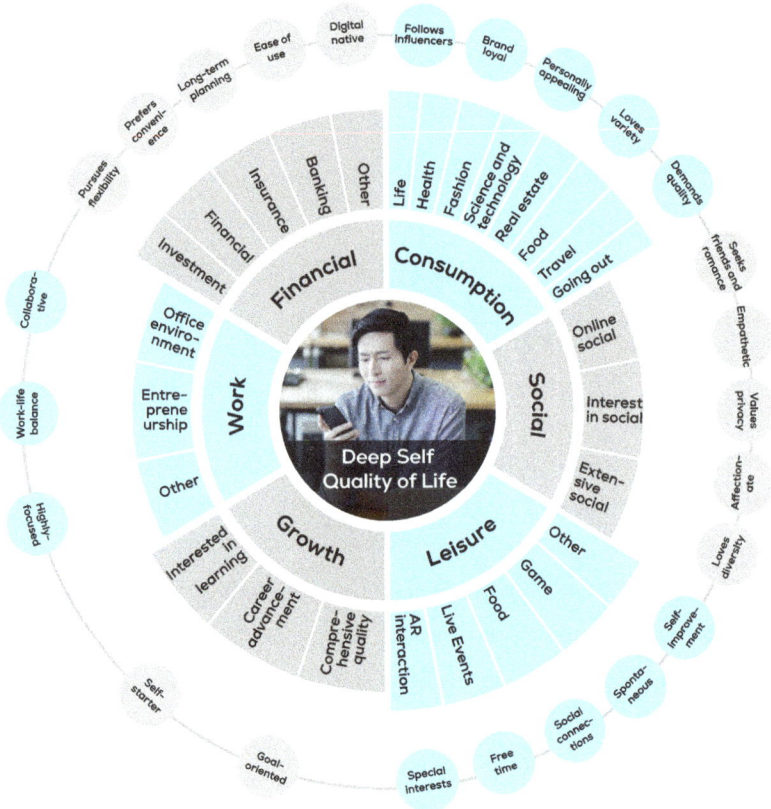

Figure 4.2, *Understanding Consumer Desires*

SEARCHING FOR OPPORTUNITIES

One night, Batman was out on patrol in Gotham. Perched on top of a building in The Narrows just after midnight, he saw the Bat-Signal shine across the night sky. He thought to himself, "Gotham is in trouble, Commissioner Gordon needs my help! I need to get across town to him ASAP and find out who is threatening our city."

But on this particular night, the circumstances were not in Batman's favor. The Batmobile had broken down, and his grappling hook was malfunctioning. The Batboat, Batcycle, Batcopter, Batwing, and all the other Bat-vehicles were out of commission. In addition, Alfred had the night off and was unavailable to chauffeur Batman personally.

He thought about hailing a taxi, but there were none around. And the nearest subway station was quite a hike away.

He saw several cars passing by with empty passenger seats, so he tried to hitch a ride, but no one would stop for the mysterious man dressed in black in this dangerous neighborhood. He also saw many bicycles parked on the sidewalk, chained to bike stands, but none he could use. He could always steal a bike or carjack an innocent bystander, but that wouldn't exactly be on brand for a crimefighter.

Frustrated and feeling defeated, he realized he needed to go on foot to meet up with the commissioner across town. So our hero flew into the night, hopping from one rooftop to the next. Jim Gordon was going to be waiting for a while.

Let's do a quick analysis of our little Batman story…
Who is the story about? Batman.
Where is his location? The Narrows.
When is it? Just after midnight.
What is his goal? Save Gotham from its latest threat.
What is his first activity toward accomplishing the goal? Travel to Jim Gordon.
How does he do this? Running on foot.

Poor Batman. Things weren't going so well for our vigilante billionaire. He was having a bad moment, or a pain point, where the situation was worse than he expected. He had a problem finding transportation from The Narrows at midnight. While this was a bad situation for Batman, we've uncovered an opportunity. We found a specific need at a particular time and location. What led to finding this opportunity? We observed the scenario from a consumer perspective.

SCENARIOS

Searching for opportunities requires finding little stories, or what we call scenarios. A scenario is a sequence of events from the human perspective that helps us uncover the context and requirements for the opportunity. In order to do so, each scenario must contain information that leads to insights.

> Every scenario should include key pieces of information:
> Who is in the scenario?
> When and where does the scenario take place?
> What do they want to accomplish?
> What activities are required to accomplish these goals?
> What additional support do they need for each activity?
> What do they think and how do they feel about their eXperience?

As we learned in the previous section, identifying who your customers are, the context of where and when they interact with your brand, and what they want to accomplish can be aided by the use of personas — detailed representations of various potential customers. But actually helping them achieve these goals, ensuring they have the additional support necessary to do so, and understanding the thoughts and feelings of their eXperience require scenarios.

A scenario's ability to provide insights into opportunities for Ideal eXperiences depends on how well it can answer these questions.

What are the Activities and Actions Required to Achieve their Goals?

Most goals require more than one step to complete. We can break down goals into smaller activities that consumers need to perform to accomplish specific goals. For example, if a goal is to acquire a car for transportation needs, activities for achieving this goal may include researching car brands, comparing car models, selecting a car model, and purchasing the selected car.

Each activity can be broken down further into a series of actions. Continuing the example above, researching car brands includes actions such as visiting websites for prospective car brands, asking friends for opinions, browsing discussion forms, and visiting dealerships.

Activities and actions help us understand the efforts consumers make in pursuit of their goals. Which activities and actions do consumers want to perform? Which activities and actions can brands offer to replace with a product or service? Identifying the activities and actions that consumers don't want to perform are opportunities for Ideal eXperiences.

What Additional Support Do They Need to Accomplish Them?

Are there any people, objects, products, or services that support consumers in achieving their goals? These are the things that are currently being used, but have the potential to be replaced with a new product or service offerings if they can help consumers achieve the goal in a more preferred manner.

If another brand's products or services are required, perhaps your brand could offer the same support or a collaboration to provide customers an improved eXperience. If the lack of support suggests an unnecessarily complex or cumbersome process, creating one that better serves customers turns an oversight into an opportunity.

What Are They Thinking and Feeling?

How successful were consumers in achieving their goals? Did they require additional support? How did they think or feel about the eXperience? What they are thinking explains their logic, while their emotions reveal the quality of the eXperience. Was it a WOW moment, or was it a pain point? Remember, understanding how consumers think and feel are key to understanding how they will evaluate future offerings and the eXperience the brand delivers.

EXPERIENCE MAP

Scenarios contain lots of information, as illustrated in Figure 4.3. And as consumers pursue their goals, their eXperiences may consist of multiple scenarios spread across different locations and points in time. It can become difficult and overwhelming to manage all the information gathered from scenarios as we search for new opportunities to deliver eXperiences. One of the tools we use to manage and analyze all the information is eXperience mapping.

An eXperience map documents customer activities as a journey in pursuit of their goals. It provides a structure that helps brands organize the key moments of an eXperience, what people are doing, and what they are thinking and feeling across the whole journey. By visualizing the information, it makes the intangible nature of customer eXperiences tangible.

Origin of eXperience Maps

An eXperience map begins earlier than most might expect. It's not when the customer engages with the brand for the first time. It also includes the path along the way. Selecting a brand as the provider of products or services has become more time consuming as the depth of offerings has increased and the number of competing brands has as well.

When a customer researches a brand to determine whether it can help accomplish a particular goal, it could include word of mouth, influencers, and negative experiences with competing brands — as well as advertising, touchpoints, and ancillary eXperience with the brand. Direct interaction is part of eXperience mapping, but it isn't necessarily the beginning.

Range of eXperience Maps

While personas are used to represent a group of consumers who share common attributes and characteristics, an eXperience map is a representation of their common eXperiences. They're created by combining the shared aspects of actual customers' real-world eXperiences to depict typical eXperiences in pursuit of their goals.

An eXperience map visualizes the key information from the scenarios to draw attention to the insights discovered from these eXperiences. It breaks down an eXperience into multiple stages based on the major activities performed in pursuit of their goals. The persona's needs, behaviors, what they are thinking, and what they are feeling are recorded at each stage.

186 | X THINKING

Figure 4.3, *Scenarios are the Basis of an eXperience Map*

CHAPTER 4: The Source of All Change | 187

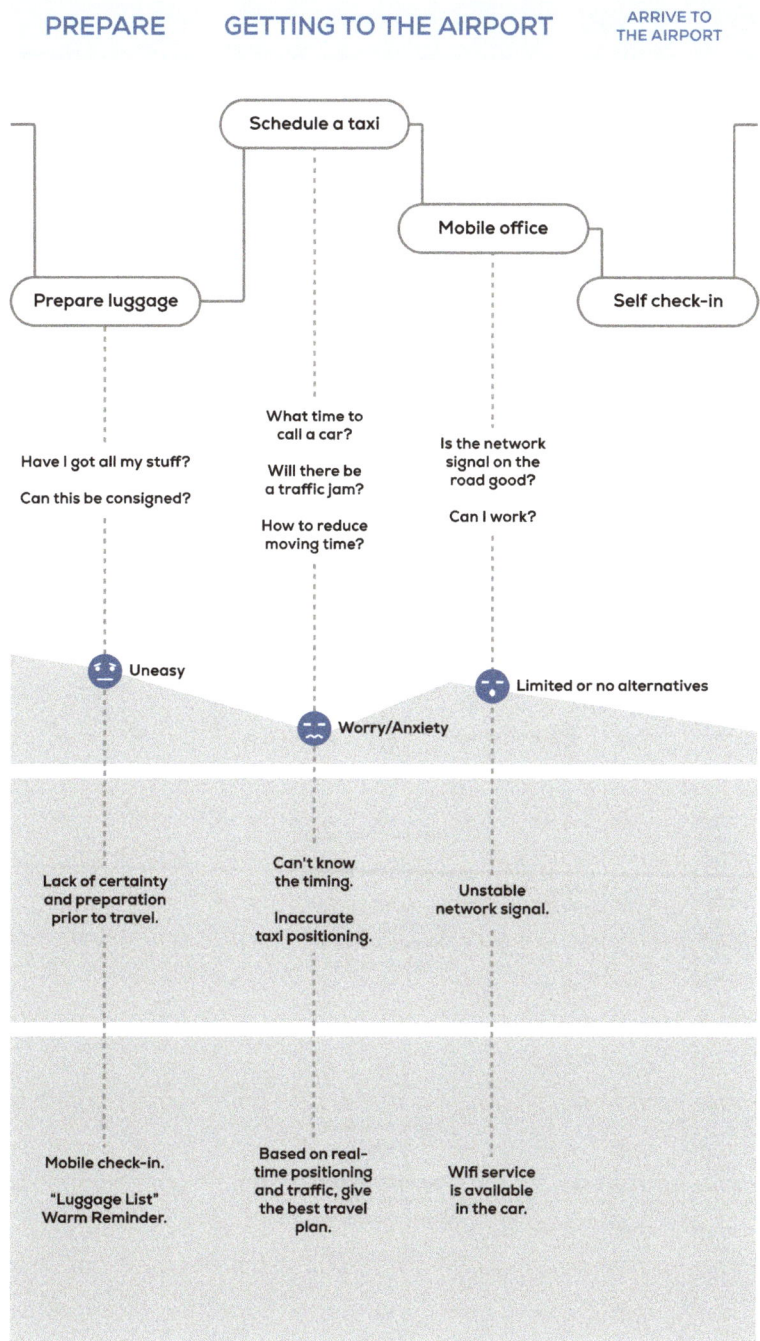

Figure 4.3, eXperience Map, Continued

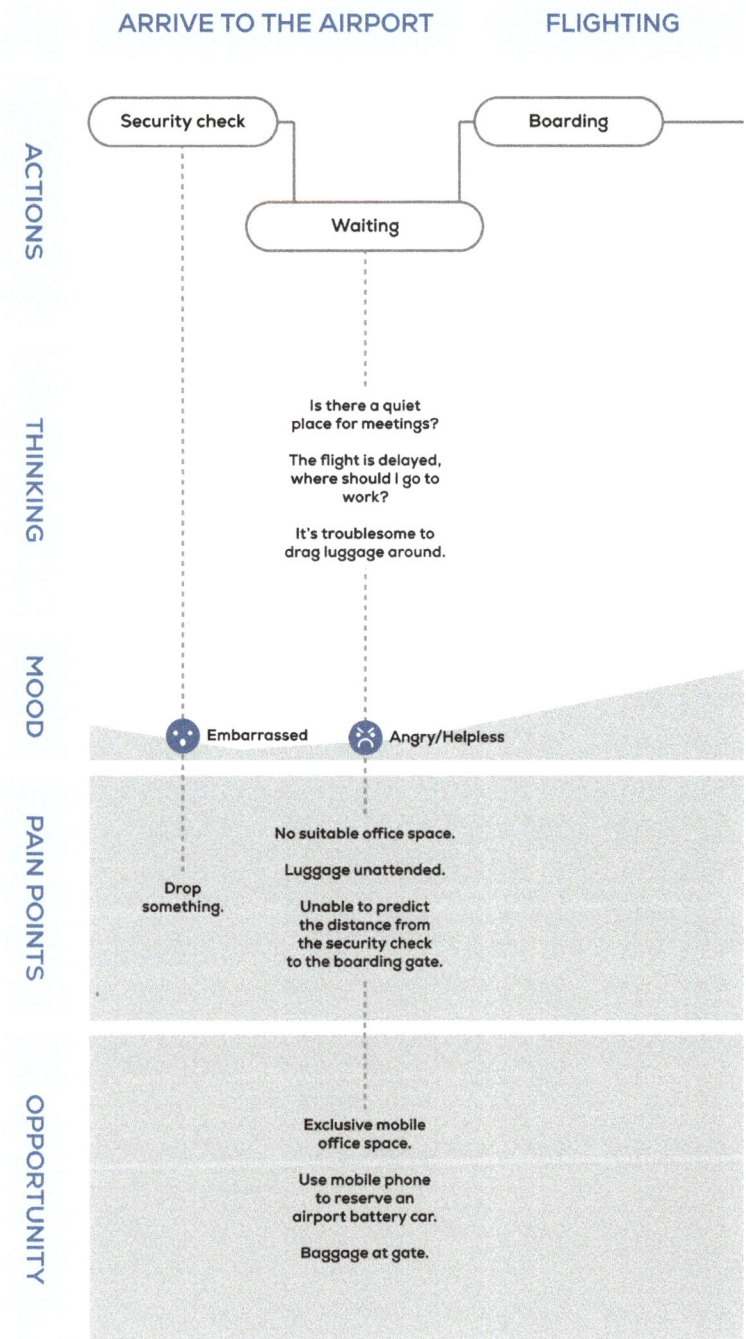

Figure 4.3, *eXperience Map, Continued*

CHAPTER 4: The Source of All Change | 189

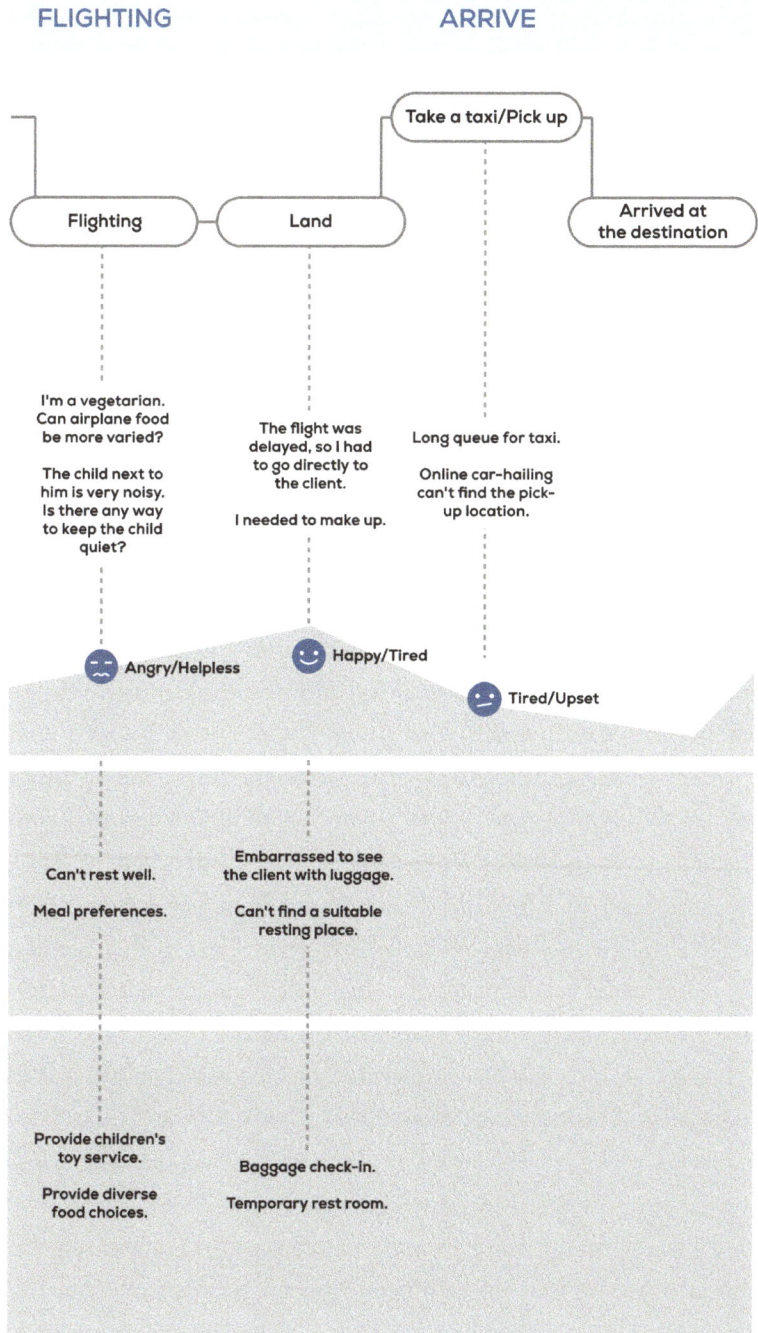

Figure 4.3, *eXperience Map, Continued*

Benefits of eXperience Maps

eXperience maps are an extremely powerful tool for helping brands understand a customer's complete eXperiences, how their behaviors are related to their context, what they are trying to achieve, and how the brand fits into the picture.

They help brands understand how customers move across different touchpoints, when they do so, and for what reasons. This helps brands find opportunities to deliver eXperiences that can deepen the relationships between brands and consumers.

eXperience maps also illustrate the interconnectedness of the different touchpoints of a brand. While departments within an organization are responsible for a set of particular touchpoints, and other departments are responsible for other touchpoints, an eXperience map highlights how they are all connected and play a role in delivering the eXperience to consumers.

InterContinental Hotels Group, better known in the hospitality industry as IHG, isn't necessarily a name as well-known to consumers. However, their 16 brands representing 6,000 destinations worldwide reveal the depth and breadth of their reach. From family-focused Holiday Inn and business traveler friendly Crowne Plaza to their signature InterContinental Hotels & Resorts, each offer accommodations intended to meet the distinct needs of specific customers.

But an abundance of options doesn't necessarily translate to a wealth of insights. Like any eXperience, a hotel stay rarely starts when a customer walks into the lobby. The days of choosing the next roadside motel that once dotted western highways in the United States as the sun fell below the horizon have evolved into complex comparisons from exhaustive online searches long before anyone boards a plane or train, or even hops in an automobile. That's why eXperience maps encompass every potential touchpoint.

When IHG stepped back to see the larger picture, the details of the decision-making process, booking, confirmation, and check in were just the beginning. Robust amenities have long been points of differentiation. But what about spontaneous sightseeing, an unexpected culinary excursion, or even the ease with which these adventures can be shared on social media or in-person with family, friends, and colleagues after the trip has concluded? The eXperience isn't just the stay, it's everything related to the stay — from the idea to the memorabilia.

Even the largest hotel company in the world had room to grow, and ultimately decided to create the first upscale international hotel brand specifically for Chinese travelers. HUALUXE (华邑) Hotels and Resorts takes its name from "Hua"(华) or "Majestic China, and "Yi"(邑) for "Urban or City". (For many Chinese professionals, the amenities and convenience of urban living are synonymous with luxury living.) Featuring refined design including the finest tea, premium fare from their own Fu Lin restaurant, and a more casual late night noodle bar, IHG recognized destinations deeply-rooted in Chinese culture offered a consistent eXperience their competitors couldn't match. Twelve current locations are exclusive to China, with an additional 26 in development. International expansion would serve the exponential rise in Chinese business and leisure travel abroad, which increased from 50 million trips annually to 170 million in the past decade.

Four Things to Remember When Using eXperience Maps

Experience Maps Focus On The Goal, Not Just The Brand

An eXperience map does not just concern the journey with the brand or a specific product. The best eXperience maps are focused on a journey in pursuit of a goal. The brand plays a role in helping the customer fulfill their goal, but is not the only means of doing so. Often, an eXperience map will start before someone comes in contact with the brand, and concludes after they leave.

No Fixed Length To Experience Maps

The length of a customer's eXperience is highly dependent on the scope of the goal the eXperience covers. Some eXperiences may be short. Some eXperiences may run a consumer's entire life.

There Is More Than One Experience

This is no single path or single eXperience from the customer to the brand. Each customer eXperience is unique, and brand interaction is part of that journey. The key is identifying and defining the specific personas with which the brand has a relationship and understanding their unique scenarios and their distinct eXperience maps.

Experiences Evolve And Change Over Time

As customers have different eXperiences with a brand, its competitors, and across industries, their expectations evolve and change. They will continue to encounter new eXperiences and learn better ways of doing things. As a result, their change in expectations changes the eXperiences they choose to repeat. eXperience maps need to be updated on a regular basis to reflect the changing expectations and eXperiences they have with the brand.

OPPORTUNITIES TO CREATE EXPERIENCES

Consumers have many scenarios every day, but not every scenario will be an opportunity for an eXperience. What types of scenarios should brands be focusing on in order to find the opportunities? There are three types of scenarios that are useful for brands to identify new opportunities: eliminatinging pain points, improving existing solutions, and inspiring innovations.

Eliminating Pain Points

As we discussed earlier, pain points are moments when consumers encounter problems as they try to complete a task in pursuit of accomplishing their goals. They're moments consumers hope to avoid in the future. If the pain point is associated with a particular brand, it becomes an opportunity for other brands to lure customers away with more desirable eXperiences. If a customer has a negative experience with one online merchant, it may be just as easy to buy a similar product the next time from a competitor.

Brands should identify pain points in their existing customer relationships to reduce customer attrition, and to identify the pain points of their competitors' customers as opportunities to develop new relationships. Brands should also look at pain points that are not being addressed by any brand as opportunities to innovate.

Improving Existing Solutions

Not all scenarios need to highlight a particular problem. Sometimes the method consumers choose to accomplish a goal is primed for disruption. The current way of doing things isn't broken, but it can be better. What if we substitute the people, objects, actions, or circumstance with something else? These scenarios often involve incorporating new technologies to replace existing technologies.

A great example of such an improvement is how smartphones are used to disrupt many industries. In the area of payments, cash and credit cards were not considered to be a pain point by consumers, but mobile payments were a way to introduce new technologies that offered a better and quicker way of paying. It is interesting to note that mobile payments have not taken off everywhere in the world. In China, WeChat Pay and AliPay have transformed how people pay for their goods and services. However in the United States, Apple Pay and Android/Google Pay have had a less transformative impact in the market. The success is highly dependent on how much better consumers perceive the new solution to be compared to the existing solutions.

Inspiring Innovations

In the process of understanding users and how they complete objectives to accomplish their goals, sometimes we come across solutions that consumers develop on their own. We call these user-inspired solutions. Often, we find that lead users will take existing products and services and use them in an unintended manner. Brands can work together with lead users to develop new offerings that leverage the same approach as their unique solutions.

When Sherman Poppen began tinkering in his garage on Christmas Day, 1965, he didn't expect to revolutionize winter sports. As he bound his children's skis together, his intent was to mimic the thrill of surfing on the snow covered slopes of his native Michigan. It would take more than a decade before various incarnations and additional inventors further refined the idea. By the time Jake Burton successfully lobbied ski resorts to allow the novel alternative on their lifts, he was already selling them as fast as his company could make them. Burton Snowboards offered a solution to a new scenario, capturing both the versatility of surfing and brisk exhilaration of skiing. [38]

SCENARIOS AND IDEAL EXPERIENCES

Understanding customer scenarios is such a powerful tool for identifying opportunities that it has long been used in various design fields. Scenarios are a core tool for approaches such as Activity-Centered Design, Design Thinking, Goal-Directed Design, Service Design, and User eXperience Design.

The approach has also been gaining popularity in business schools. Famed Harvard Business School professor and author of The Innovator's Dilemma Clay Christensen recently published a book titled Competing Against Luck: The Story of Innovation and Customer Choice, where he introduces the Theory of Jobs to be Done (JTBD), which leverages the core ideas of scenarios and their benefits. The theory focuses on helping brands understand customer contexts and what they are trying to achieve:

"Focus on deeply understanding your customers' struggle for progress and then creating the right solution and attendant set of experiences to ensure you solve your customers' jobs well, every time."

While there are differences in each of these approaches, they share the common thread of focusing on what consumers do, the situation in which they do it, and the goal they are trying to achieve. The application of scenarios in X Thinking is to identify, refine, and create Ideal eXperiences.

* * *

Summary

We opened this section with a famous quote about faster horses and how some believe this is evidence that the outside-in approach does not lead to Ideal eXperiences. They argue that if brands ask consumers what they want, the solutions will lack the imagination necessary to help them better achieve their goals — or to improve or create entirely new solutions.

Scenarios help solve this shortcoming by considering the activities and actions, additional support, and thoughts and feelings that contribute to an eXperience. To better illustrate these concepts, eXperience maps following customers along their journey, identifying potential opportunities to reduce pain points, improving existing offerings, and innovating through user-inspired solutions.

Section 3
PRIORITIZING THE SEVEN TYPES OF CONSUMERS

Understanding Ideal eXperiences requires starting from the consumer perspective. But with so many existing and prospective customers, where should we begin? With whom should a brand have a relationship?

Some companies hope to connect with everyone. They want to maximize their ROI by investing the minimum amount of resources to yield the maximum return possible. As a result, they hope that one marketing campaign will convince everyone to buy one product that meets all of their needs.

Unfortunately, this approach doesn't work; it is neither efficient nor effective. You hope you'll persuade everyone, but may end up convincing no one. Creating, managing, and maintaining relationships with customers requires a more nuanced approach, one with surgical precision. We need to be selective to make the best use of our time and resources, to be highly efficient and effective. We want consumers to know they are valued by creating Ideal eXperiences for them.

Just like interpersonal relationships, some consumers are a better match with a brand than others. Brands need to find the consumers who are the best match. So how does a brand identify and prioritize the consumers worth developing a relationship?

START WITH YOUR BUSINESS OBJECTIVE

In our daily lives, we have different types of interpersonal relationships that serve specific purposes. We spend most of our time during the week at work, interacting with colleagues and clients in our industry or individuals connected to our career. We have friends who are foodies with whom we try new restaurants. Some relationships are based on hobbies or sports, such as baking or tennis. Some relationships help us learn and grow, such as a professional mentor, financial planner, or someone who is teaching us how to play a musical instrument or another language.

Though many of these interactions and activities may include the same people every time, many of us have different groups of friends for different activities. The same is true with brands and consumers — brands have different types of relationships with different types of customers. Some are a better match than others for helping the brand achieve certain objectives.

The key is clearly defining the business objective and activity — increasing retention by improving existing products and services, creating new relationships through innovative offerings, maximizing revenue by extending brand reach into existing markets, expanding into an additional market by introducing a new brand, identifying the next generation of customers to prioritize brand development — then matching the brand with the proper target audience, the right consumers to help the brand achieve the objective.

FIND THE RIGHT CONSUMERS

Through our work with our clients at TANG, we have identified seven types of consumers who can help your brand achieve its objective: lead users, seed users, influencers, followers, majority users, upcoming users, and aspirational users.

Lead Users – Inspire New Products and Services

Lead users are those who encounter needs months or years before the general market. Their leading-edge needs exist prior to the development of a product or service offering that can satisfy them. They will often creatively adapt, modify, or transform other products in the market into custom solutions to meet their needs. Lead users offer crucial insights into future customer behaviors.

These users may not have an existing relationship with your brand, because their needs are not currently met by any existing product in the marketplace. Participation in the development of new or updated offerings empowers lead users and leverages their enthusiasm to the benefit of the brand. Think of them as an informal test market, constantly curious and quick to identify both oversights and opportunities.

Understanding these users, their needs, and their creative solutions can generate insights that lead to innovative and breakthrough products and services. These innovations can result in offerings that have a first-mover advantage, the competitive advantage of being the first to bring a new product or service to market.

Seed Users – A Startup's First Customers

Seed users are the first users of your offering. They're vocal enthusiasts who are particularly passionate and may often be professionals or experts in the industry. They're willing to try out new products, services, and technologies. Seed users are particularly important for startups. They are your early adopters and brand ambassadors rolled into one.

When new brands are trying to break into the marketplace, it is critical for them to identify their seed users. Seed users create the first opportunity for the brand to gather information about their customers and their opinions about the new offering. Seed users are also the first advocates for a new brand and can help generate testimonial marketing to persuade others to try the brand.

New offerings occasionally have some initial issues with quality and functionality. They may also be limited in availability due to difficulties with manufacturing and distribution.

As a result, the first availability of your product is targeted toward your seed users. They are excited to be the first to try new products and services, growing their relationship with your brand from strangers, to acquaintances, to friends. And as your brand grows, they will continue to deepen their relationship with your brand to the status of family, becoming the most loyal customers and spreading awareness of your brand through personal endorsements.

As the first users of your offering, seed users are often forgiving of buggy early versions of new offerings, and they often contribute ideas and suggestions to improve the product before the wider rollout. In return, they may expect preferential treatment in terms of early access, support, and attention.

Influencers – Generate Word of Mouth

As mentioned above, influencers are particularly important for brands when a large portion of their users are followers. Influencers are the people who followers look to for advice and opinions regarding new brands and brands they can trust. There are three types of influencers to pay attention to: experts, key opinion leaders, and key opinion consumers.

When making decisions, consumers often turn to those in their social circles who are perceived as experts in a selected field. These may or may not be professionals, but they are extremely passionate or knowledgable. They might not be primary users or even customers of your brand, but they may still recommend it to friends and family due to its reputation or their previous experiences.

For example, we all have a friend who is our go-to technology expert. While they may use a particular brand, such as Apple, for their personal phone, they are still familiar with many of the offerings from competing brands, such as Xiaomi or Huawei. Consumers often turn to this type of friend for all sorts of technology-based recommendations. If you ask them to recommend an affordable smartphone, they might recommend the Xiaomi, even though they don't use one personally. These experts enjoy staying up-to-date on the latest technologies and helping others with their technology needs.

Key Opinion Leaders (KOL) and Key Opinions Consumers (KOC) are high-profile users on social media networks, such as WeChat, TikTok, as Facebook, Twitter, and YouTube, where their combined perspectives reach millions of followers. Both are more commonly called influencers in the West. But in China, the term KOL is more specific while the definition of influencers is more broad. KOLs may be celebrities, professionals, or "gurus" in a particular field with enormous individual followings, while KOCs may be everyday social media users with a particular passion, but whose audience is far smaller. They post brand information, reviews, and endorsements and actively engage with desirable target audiences. However, they may not be primary users or customers of your brand.

Wanghongs are internet celebrities in China who have a large number of online followers. The American equivalent would be a YouTube star. Unlike experts, KOLs, or KOCs, they are not experts of any specific subject matter. Instead, they draw in their followers with their appearance, personality, sense of humor, and entertaining content. They are highly in tune with current popular culture, including the latest viral trends, buzzwords, slang, and memes. Compared to movie stars and music celebrities, wanghongs are more approachable and relatable compared to their more famous counterparts. Brands often leverage the celebrity status of wanghongs by using them as spokespeople. They can help brands connect with consumers by associating the brand and its products with pop culture, making it more socially relevant.

One example of this is the social network and short viral video platform, mobile app TikTok, also known as Douyin (抖音). Less than a year after launch, the platform reached a billion views, attracting wanghongs and their followers with more than 150 million daily active users and 300 million monthly active users. Brands have taken notice and registered official accounts and recruited wanghongs to be their brand ambassadors to help promote their products. [39] [40] [41]

When followers do not trust traditional advertising messages, brands can leverage influencers to help introduce their brand. Influencers can help followers develop relationships with the brand from strangers to friends in a more effective, efficient, authentic manner.

When there are no experts in a consumer's social network, customers from first and second tier cities tend to seek out KOLs and KOCs. Customers from third and fourth tier cities are more likely to be influenced by wanghongs. One major difference between experts compared to KOLs, KOCs, and wanghongs is that the latter can be paid to push a brand to their followers.

Followers – Influenced By Word of Mouth

Followers are customers who may have limited knowledge or opinions about the product or service category. They often seek the advice of fellow users who can introduce new brands and/or recommendations on the best offering to purchase, basing purchasing decisions on these recommendations.

These prospective customers may not have an existing relationship with your brand and are looking for offerings in your category. They could also be existing customers, but have not had a particularly great experience with your brand to push them to pursue a deeper relationship. They can be easily persuaded by influencers, contributing to brand growth — or pulled away from your brand.

If a large portion of your brand's users are followers, it is critical to understand the customer journey — how they discover brands, evaluate their options, and make their purchase decision as it pertains to their relationships with brands. In particular, who introduces these users to your brand and gets them to engage with your brand as they transition from strangers to acquaintances? As they consider their options, who can influence their decision to deepen the relationship with your brand as they transition from acquaintances to friends?

Majority Users – Improve Your Brand's Existing Offerings

Majority users are a group who represent the highest usage of the product or service offering. Their use-case scenarios make up the majority of use-cases. As existing users, they are already friends with your brand. They are most concerned with how useful, usable, and desirable your offering is.

Deepening the relationship with these users by meeting and exceeding their expectations in the use of products and services will create loyalty in the form of future repeat sales. Disappointing these users with negative experiences will push them away from your brand. Their loyalty leads to long-term relationships, which can become stranded over time.

All majority users don't necessarily have the same expectations, and this divergence may prove frustrating for brands. Some users will be completely satisfied with the status quo, resisting changes in products and services. Others who were satisfied may become less so as competing offerings adapt to changing tastes and use-cases. This group of users can provide insight toward improving the usability of existing products and services and making evolutionary design improvements through gradual changes.

Upcoming Users – The Future Customers of the Brand

Upcoming users are not currently customers, primary, or secondary users. They have no need for the brand's offerings. However, in the future, changes in life stages will also change their needs, prompting these upcoming users to seek out offerings from your brand and your competitors.

Though upcoming users do not currently have a relationship with your brand, starting early by becoming acquaintances and building their trust puts your brand in their consideration set when the time is right. For instance, younger consumers may be more practical or limited in their transportation choices, finding and favoring ride sharing, commuter rail, or bicycles more suitable for urban life. But as they age, their needs for an automobile may change over time as well — from the efficiency of a compact to the additional capacity of an SUV.

Upcoming users are especially important to brands when existing customers may eventually age to the point where your offerings are no longer relevant to their next stage of life. Developing a relationship with upcoming users ensures you will have customers to fill the void left by your current customers.

Aspirational Users – Who the Customers Want to Become

The final type of consumer, aspirational users, does not actually represent any existing group of real users. They represent a fictitious set of users whom some consumers aspire to be, or how they want to be perceived. Brands help consumers become the aspirational user.

While this type of user is fictitious, the consumers who hope to become this user are real. It also incorporates the social and emotional elements behind consumer behavior. Brands must understand this aspiration and determine how you can craft a brand and offer to help them realize these needs, wants, and desires.

PRIORITIZE THE RIGHT CONSUMERS

Now that we've identified the seven types of consumers, let's look at them from a practical perspective. This S-Curve represents the various roles users play at different stages of product and service development (Figure 4.4).

Brands should engage Lead Users in the Innovation of new offerings, incorporating their experience and insights. Upon Launch, the passion and enthusiasm of Seed Users eager to adopt new solutions move them into the mainstream. Rapid Growth is achieved through the interaction of Influencers and Followers, propelling the offerings forward. The Inflection Point marks the beginning of mass adoption, when Majority Users accept offerings as proven products and services.

However, even the best brands must continue to innovate. Though adoption by Upcoming Users may persist, as Diminishing Returns emerge, the cycle must begin again to avoid eventual Decline. Perhaps the next iteration will attract additional users, or they may remain just out of reach, as brands further refine their offerings and build better relationships with their customers by helping them find new ways to achieve their goals.

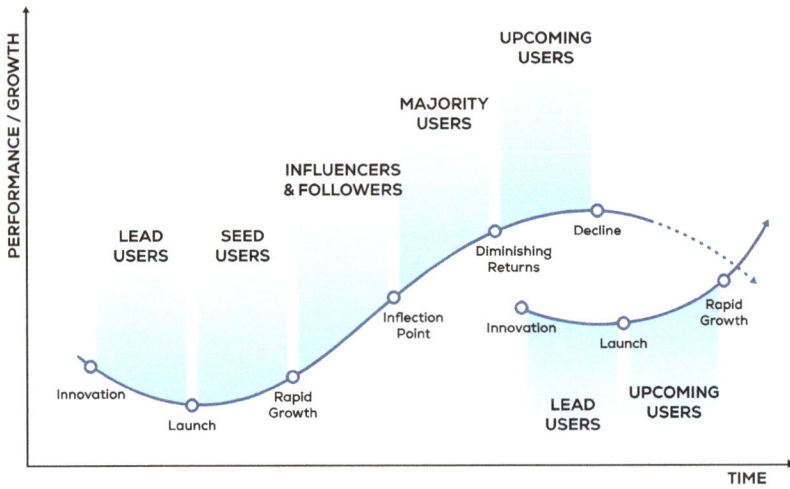

Figure 4.4, *The Seven Types of Consumers and Their Roles*

* * *

Summary

The seven types of consumers have a different value based on objectives, and brands should prioritize them depending on the desired direction and development of the brand — to understand how to create relationships with their target consumers. For example, brands that aim to extend their growth should target Upcoming Users, while those that seek to elevate their image should analyze their Aspirational Users. Brands that prefer to improve and iterate existing products should focus on Majority Users, and those hoping to increase awareness should concentrate efforts on Influencers and Followers.

However, if the brand is searching for an innovative offering requiring enthusiastic adoption, it's most beneficial for product development departments to focus on Lead Users and Seed Users. The key is matching the right type of consumer based on the needs and objectives of the brand, as well as the stage of development of the product or service.

Case Study
CHINA MERCHANTS BANK

Who Are They?

China Merchants Bank (CMB) has always been a bank of firsts. It was the first shareholding commercial bank in China to be wholly owned by corporate legal entities. Founded in 1987, the bank prioritized delivering exceptional customer service by applying the latest technologies. Pioneering achievements include introducing the first customer call center, the first domestic online banking platform, and the first wealth-management brand for high-end customers in China. CMB's dedication to providing customers with the best eXperience has earned industry accolades, including the Best Retail Bank, Best Wealth Management Bank, and the Most Popular Bank Brand.

Still recognized as one of the country's leading commercial banks, China Merchants Bank provides personal and commercial banking, financial leasing, fund management, life insurance, and overseas investment banking. CMB, headquartered in Shenzhen, operates more than 1,800 branches worldwide, including 130 cities in mainland China.

What Did They Need?

Facing an increasingly commoditized industry and the emerging threat of mobile internet financial services, China Merchants Bank partnered with TANG to evolve and differentiate their product and service offerings across their collective online and offline channels.

What Did We Do?

TANG helped China Merchants Bank identify innovative opportunities to deliver their core brand promise, which translates to "Change for You" (因您而变). By gaining a deeper understanding of their customers, the products and services they used, and the scenarios and contexts in which they used them, TANG developed a mobile-centric eXperience strategy for CMB that fostered a deep emotional connection with their clientele. The strategy was applied to their mobile app, website, and retail bank branch design — touchpoints that helped create a younger, fresher image for the brand.

Industry Context

In 2013, China's financial industry was at a crossroads. Banks were facing three major challenges: the commoditization of the financial industry, the emergence of the era of internet finance, and increasing customer expectations.

The traditional financial industry in China had achieved parity through the emulation of features between brands. Bank brands became homogenized with little differentiation, making it difficult for customers to identify unique desirable eXperiences amongst the brands. The commoditization also resulted in low customer loyalty across the industry.

Beyond of the financial industry, 2013 is also known in China as the First Year of the Era of Internet Finance (互联网金融元年). In addition to commoditization, the traditional financial industry was also facing the rising threat of mobile payments, digital banks, and the availability of internet financial services.

Yu'e Bao, an investment product offered by Alibaba's affiliate Ant Financial, disrupted the sector (Figure 4.5). Introduced in June 2013, Yu'e Bao is a money market fund that invests leftover cash from online spending. Initially, the product offered customers an annual rate of return of more than 6 percent, compared to a 0.5-percent interest rate in savings accounts. In just four short years after its launch, Yu'e Bao surpassed JPMorgan's US Government Money Market Fund to become the world's biggest fund. [42]

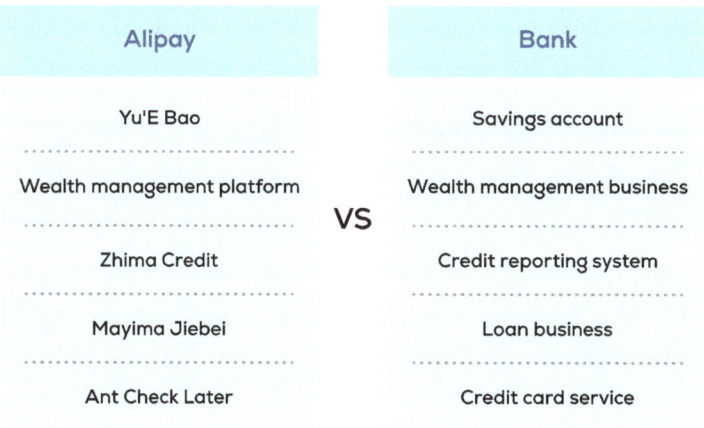

Figure 4.5, *How Alipay Compares to Traditional Banking*

Traditional financial institutions were put on notice, and recognized the need to change and adapt to retain their existing customer base.

As consumers grew accustomed to using their mobile phones extensively with other industries, their expectations likewise increased for the type of eXperiences the financial industry should deliver. Customers were becoming less forgiving of the perceived lower levels of service quality, reducing customer satisfaction throughout the financial sector.

Business Objectives

China Merchants Bank knew it could not rest on its success. As a leader in the industry, they could foresee banking was going to continue to shift toward online and mobile platforms. The question wasn't what this new future might be, but how to lead the banking industry into this new future? Through a series of strategic and tactical projects, TANG and China Merchants Bank created a comprehensive and compelling answer to:

- **Improve customer interactions with their financial institution.** Increase value to customers by improving their banking experience.

- **Generate new sales opportunities among current customers.** Offer an array of banking services that reinforce continued brand loyalty.

- **Acquire additional customers who are dissatisfied with competitors.** Meet the emerging demands of younger customers through brand differentiation.

The Solution

From "Mobile-First" To "Mobile-Centric"

To position China Merchants Bank to compete in the complex and evolving mobile banking space, TANG first sought to understand their diverse customer base: who they are, how they think, and how they live. They needed to understand under what scenarios customers use financial products and services as well as how they use them (Figure 4.6).

Because the overarching objective was to change the way customers bank, they identified affluent young customers as a lead user group for China Merchants Bank due to their familiarity with mobile devices. This subset of customers was accustomed to using their mobile phones for both personal and professional life, expecting a high level of efficiency from the products and services they used. They were already weary of cumbersome offerings typical of more traditional service providers, like hailing a taxi versus requesting a rideshare, shopping at a store versus placing an order online, or grabbing a quick meal at a restaurant versus food delivery.

Though this group of customers would often reach first for their mobile phones to access such services, TANG discovered these users did not necessarily prioritize mobile devices. Instead, smartphones are a central tool integrated into the lives of affluent young customers for their work, social, and financial needs. This subtle but important distinction suggested that the need to shift strategy from "mobile-first," where brands should prioritize the online mobile app before and ahead of other channels, to "mobile-centric," where the mobile app is at the center with the customer facilitating connections to additional online or offline touchpoints (Figure 4.7).

Just because customers carry their mobile phones all the time doesn't mean they prefer to do everything through the mobile app. Instead, the mobile app actually empowered customers to do more across additional channels. This wasn't just the case with the lead users. There was evidence of this trend in varying degrees among every customer group.

This led to a fundamental shift in strategy for China Merchants Bank. By understanding what, where, when, and how people used

X THINKING

STUDENT

CONSUMER ADVOCATES
- CAPITAL: Less
- KNOWLEDGE: Less
- CHARACTERISTICS: Consumeristic

- Capital funds are used for consumption
- No rolling consciousness and knowledge of wealth
- The remaining funds are basically idle in a current state

LITTLE ATTENTION
- CAPITAL: Less
- KNOWLEDGE: Less
- CHARACTERISTICS: Value of interest

- Growing up in an ordinary family
- The amount of funds is not high, planned consumption
- Expect to increase income through their own abilities, and wealth rolls
- Initial account: Yu 'ebao

PROFESSIONAL BACKGROUND
- CAPITAL: Less
- KNOWLEDGE: Medium/High
- CHARACTERISTICS: Consumeristic

- Have certain professional knowledge
- Try financial investments for the first time

WORK

- Enjoy life, keen to spend
- Part of the money is given to family members to control consumption and accumulate wealth
- Limited financial knowledge

- Money is not much, open source throttling
- Preferential strong attention, consumption moderation
- Penny earn
- Limited financial knowledge

- Rich knowledge of investment and financial management
- Trust your own judgment
- Dare to venture capital
- Consumption financial planning

MARRIED

HOSTING
- CAPITAL: Medium/High
- KNOWLEDGE: Less

- Don't know much about wealth
- Only responsible for own consumption
- Let the other half take care of the family's wealth

CONSERVATIVE
- CAPITAL: Medium/High
- KNOWLEDGE: Less

- Afraid of risk
- Manual accounting, preference to pursue concessions
- Build wealth in a safe environment

CONFIGURATION
- CAPITAL: Medium/High
- KNOWLEDGE: Less

- Learn about information through multiple channels
- Control risks independently and reasonably
- Pursue wealth and freedom at your own pace

COMMERCIAL INVESTMENT
- CAPITAL: Medium/High
- KNOWLEDGE: wide

- Investment biased towards commercial investment
- No strong interest in bank financing
- Rich social resources
- Work is still the main business, business is just investment

Figure 4.6, *China Merchants Bank's Diverse Customer Base*

CHAPTER 4: The Source of All Change | 215

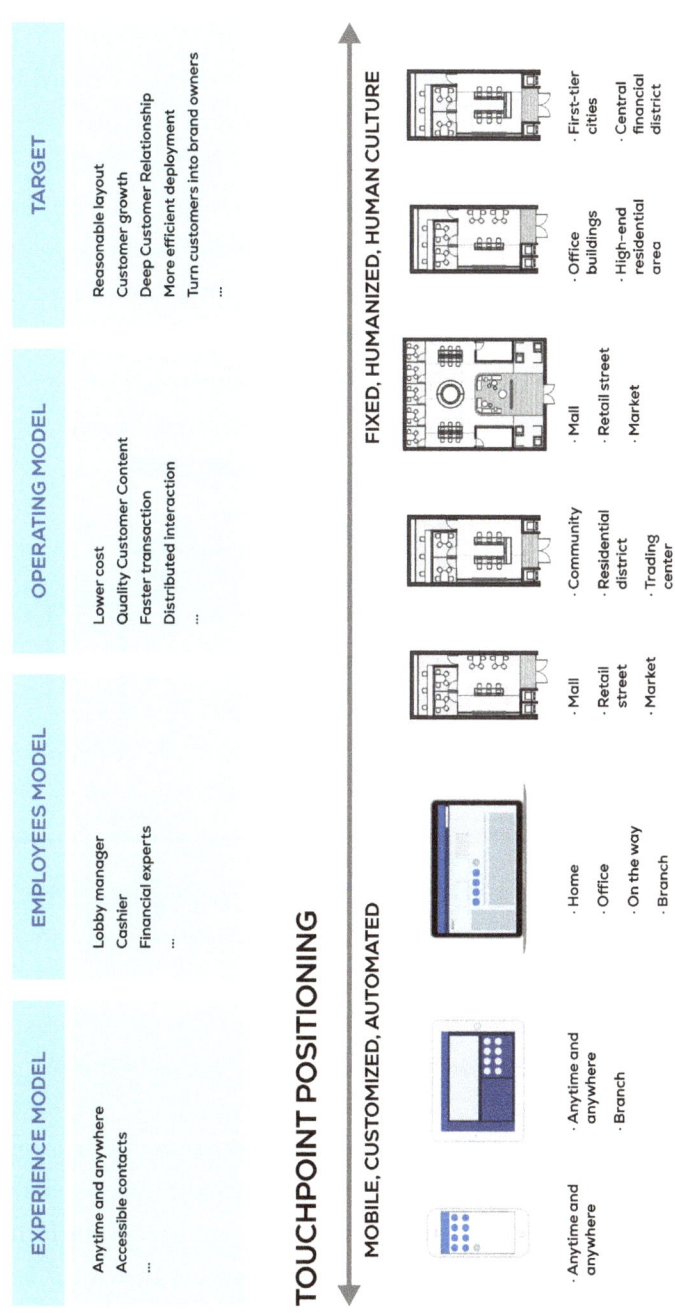

Figure 4.7, *Transition from Mobile-First to Mobile-Centric*

CMB product and service offerings, TANG was able to position product and service touchpoints in the appropriate channel based on specific customer scenarios (Figure 4.8). Online channels were best for delivering fast and frequent transactions such as checking account balances, making bill payments, money transfers, and scheduling appointments. But, offline channels were best suited for delivering more personalized interactions such as wealth management, when customers rely on the expertise and experience of a financial advisor when making significant investment decisions.

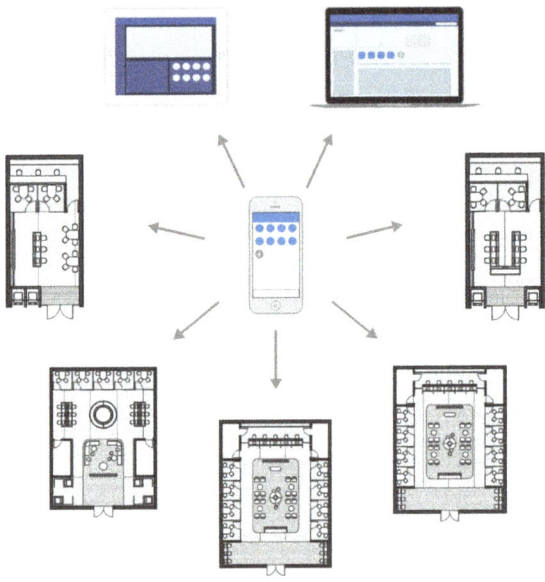

Figure 4.8, *Online and Offline Touchpoints are Determined by Scenarios*

In addition to delivering improved eXperiences to customers, repositioning the products and services based also supported a Chinese banking trend known as "transaction-type bank transformation." Banks were struggling to transition customers from their low-profit offerings (such as checking account balances and money transfers) to their high-profit transaction-based offerings (such as wealth management products and loans).

It changed the way people would bank in the future by redefining how products and services are provided through each channel based on the needs and scenarios of the customer. It equipped CMB with a perspective for positioning each touchpoint along the customer journey. Though this provides an approach for delivering better eXperiences and higher profit margins, a strategy is just a starting point.

From "Bank-Centric" Mobile Banking To "My" Mobile Banking

In a mobile-centric strategy, the mobile app plays a pivotal role in the brand eXperience. China Merchants Bank's mobile app has always been one of the country's leading mobile banking apps. It achieved its position and reputation by introducing emerging technologies before their competitors. Even though version 2.0 was performing well for the bank, China Merchants Bank was always looking to improve upon their industry-leading mobile banking app and extend their competitive advantage — and generate sales from current customers.

The early versions of the app were essentially an online version of the offline bank. Each of the features in the app was based on an organizational department structure. Though institutions are often structured to maximize the efficiency and effectiveness needed to deliver products and services to the customer, this "bank-centric" approach was neither an efficient nor effective way of organizing the functions of app for mobile customers.

Rather than structuring the app from a "bank-centric" approach, TANG and China Merchants Bank created a "My" mobile banking eXperience, developing a functional architecture that reorganized the features of the app. By creating an app that was easier and more convenient for consumers to use, CMB increased the frequency of use of the app, achieving a higher customer-retention rate.

For example, information and features that customers commonly use to gain an understanding about their financial situation, such as account balances, credit card statements, and living expenses (生活缴费), were all placed on one page — so that customers could easily make financial decisions based on how much money they currently had available and what expenses they needed to pay. Features such as overseas remittance or visa applications that customers prefer to handle in-person were given lower priority in placement within the app.

Within two months of the launch of version 3.0 in October 2014, the app had amassed 25 million installs, with 11.6 million active monthly users, and 100 million logins — more than a 300 percent increase in traffic within the app.

Following this success, China Merchants Bank worked with TANG to develop a roadmap for the planning and development of the subsequent 4.0 and 5.0 versions of the app focused on the "My" mobile banking strategy. With each new iteration, the app transformed from a basic smartphone tool to a financial service platform delivering more content, products, and ultimately value to customers.

From "One Size Fits None" To "Personalized"

One of the fundamental challenges China Merchants Bank faced was despite identifying distinct groups of customers, they didn't have a deep understanding of these groups, what they had in common, or more importantly, how they differed. So when CMB wanted to expand their customer base to include new, young, well-educated customers with white-collar jobs, they collaborated with TANG to understand how the bank could deliver value to them. If CMB could connect with these young professionals early in their careers, the brand could develop a deep relationship and grow with them as their lives and careers progressed.

What TANG uncovered was that this particular group of customers were not well served by the existing product and service options in CMB's portfolio offerings. If China Merchants Bank approached all their customers with the exact same products and services with a "one size fits all" strategy, providing everyone with acceptable service, then no one received exceptional service. It just ended up being "one size fits none." Instead, CMB needed to approach this group of customers, in fact all their customers, with a personalized approach tailored to each of them to create a closer relationship, with products and services designed to meet their specific needs.

One of the key findings among young professionals was that they cared deeply about any change in their financial situation, regardless of how much or little money they had in their account or how minor the change. The amount of money they had was important and meaningful to these customers. Though they may not require more frequent transactions, easy and immediate awareness of any changes to their account satisfied both a functional and emotional need for this group of customers.

This insight led to the development of a program just for them branded as M+, where M stands for merchant. The program provided special services that help young professionals better understand their financial situation, such as "Sheng" (省) and "Zhuan" (赚). Sheng helped customers track how much they saved by using the bank's services, such as free money transfers and preferential treatment from the bank's partners. Zhuan helped customers track how much they earned through the bank's financial investment products.

In addition to these services, a custom interface was developed specifically for these customers in the mobile app with features unavailable to other customers. They were only available for M+ account holders. The design of the page was simple, distinctive, and perhaps most importantly "cool", matching the brightly-colored bank card that came with the account.

The personalized M+ service helped China Merchants Bank build a more personal connection with young professionals, introducing another innovative opportunity to meet their needs with a service that would accompany them as they grow, and help them accumulate wealth along the way.

Result

When China Merchants Bank first partnered with TANG, they were already the industry leader. However, with commoditization and emerging threats from internet finance, CMB was able to evolve and differentiate their brand by delivering extraordinary eXperiences: updating their brand image, developing a mobile strategy to build a deeper emotional connection with customers, and shifting to a customer-centered model that further delivered on their core brand value of "Change for You".

But simply creating deeper relationships between customers and the brand was only the beginning. It transformed China Merchants Bank by breaking down the silos between departments to focus on the customer first, to understand the changing industry landscape. The end result extended CMB's advantage over its competitors, raising expectations, and going from the best to a brand that is even better — with a pulse on the present and an eye on the future.

"A brand is a living entity, and it is enriched or undermined cumulatively over time, the product of a thousand small gestures."

— *Michael Eisner*

CHAPTER 5

The Challenge of Execution

Understanding Brand Value Proposition

Delivering, Planning, and Managing eXperiences

Creating an eXperience Strategy

Case Study: WM Motor (Weltmeister)

INTRODUCTION

Before we continue, let's do a brief recap of what we've covered in the book so far. In Chapter 2, we examined how brands should build deep, long-lasting relationships with people. We introduced the relationship model and how relationships are not created overnight, but require time and energy to build and maintain. In Chapter 3, we discussed how eXperiences are the key to developing relationships. We dove in deep to understand how eXperiences work and how eXperiences generate value for businesses with the concept of return on eXperience, or ROX. And in Chapter 4, we talked about how brands can deliver eXperiences by understanding consumers. Because people are the source of all change, brands need to understand who they are to identify opportunities to help them achieve their goals in the appropriate context.

In this chapter, we put all these concepts together to help brands develop an eXperience strategy to deliver Ideal eXperiences to build deep relationships.

In Understanding Brand Value, we'll examine how eXperiences are currently delivered versus how they should be delivered. We'll discuss the consumer perspective, introduce the four Domains of eXperience and why we believe this is the best model to realizing brand value — as well as the shift from disconnected channels to our omni-touchpoint strategy for delivering these eXperiences.

Many touchpoints are needed in order to deliver Holistic eXperiences. To create these touchpoints, organizations divide the work up into manageable chunks of work where each department, group, or team is focused on a set of business activities. But the nature of large organizations inevitably creates some challenges which we'll also discuss. In Planning, Delivering, and Managing eXperiences, we'll propose that brands develop strategies to help overcome these challenges as they plan, deliver, and manage eXperiences.

A well-devised eXperience strategy establishes an objective, a means of accomplishing the objective, and a plan for development and execution. In Creating an X Strategy, we introduce three tools: eXperience Vision, eXperience Flows, and eXperience Masterplan. Together, they help brands envision the experience, align customer experience with brand touchpoints, and prioritize tactical projects for implementation.

Then we'll get behind the wheel with Weltmeister and discover why the road ahead for electric vehicles, and every industry, requires more than just innovative ideas. It involves engaging customers through entirely new strategies that bring them closer to brands than they've ever been before.

Section 1
UNDERSTANDING BRAND VALUE PROPOSITION

Take a minute and try to recall as many eXperiences as you can remember. How many of those eXperiences would you classify as superior?

If you're like us, you'll find such eXperiences are few and far between. In fact, according to a study conducted by Bain & Company, only 8 percent of customers categorize their eXperiences with brands as superior. However, in the same study, 80 percent of brands believe they are delivering these eXperiences to their customers.

Think about that — 8 percent of customers versus 80 percent of brands. That's a huge disconnect between what brands and people consider to be superior eXperiences. The problem lies in how brands deliver value through their eXperiences.

DEFINING BRAND VALUE PROPOSITION

Determining an organization's brand value proposition is a combination of understanding how the brand aligns the organization's capabilities and values with customer goals and needs. The organizational capabilities and values determine what the brand is able and willing to deliver. Customer goals and needs determine the potential demand for the brand.

It should be noted that brand value has more than one definition some may confuse with what we're describing here. Another definition of brand value is the financial worth of the brand, as in how much someone would pay to purchase the brand. The term brand value is also often used as a synonym for brand equity, or the commercial/strategic value of a brand, and all the assets associated with it, contributing to the value of the brand's product and service offerings. There's also a difference between brand value versus brand values, where brand values are the brand's fundamental beliefs from an internal perspective.

DELIVERING BRAND VALUE PROPOSITION: FROM CHANNELS TO OMNI-TOUCHPOINTS

Every business, and every brand, needs an approach to deliver value from the brand to the people. Start-ups, small- and medium-sized businesses, small and medium enterprises, and large enterprises all develop means of getting their offerings into the hands of their customers based on their resources and capabilities.

Channels: From the Perspective of Business

As mentioned earlier, channels are the medium or conduit through which brands deliver offerings and communications. Traditional channels include physical retail stores, television, and telephone. Digital channels include websites, email, social media, and mobile and tablet apps.

Some of these channels are considered unidirectional, where communications are pushed from the brand to the customer, such as TV, newspaper, and radio advertisements. There are also bidirectional channels that facilitate instant two-way interaction between people and brands, such as shopping at a retail store, talking to a brand representative on the phone, and exchanges through a brand's social media accounts.

Brands have developed different approaches to using channels to deliver value to their customers.

Single-Channel: An Informational Approach

In its simplest form, a single-channel strategy focuses on delivering products or services to the customer through a singular means, such as retail stores or online stores. It's the point of acquisition. Marketing helps consumers discover their products and communicates how they can provide solutions to specific needs. Utilizing only one channel, brands can use a simple and clear message to pull customers to the channel where they can acquire the product or service and eXperience the value of the brand.

Many small businesses and start-ups begin with a single-channel strategy: a small coffee shop that only has a brick-and-mortar location to sell its drinks, or a start-up that sells its new product only through an online store. Marketing needs to drive people to only one channel. With limited resources, it's easier and more cost-effective to take the single-channel strategy. Because a single channel primarily depends on marketing communications to drive consumers, it uses an informational approach to connecting customers with the brand.

It's also difficult to define any business as truly single-channel. Even if a tiny, one-location restaurant relies exclusively on word of mouth and organic growth without any advertising or social media presence, simply offering dine-in and carryout, delivery or a drive-thru is arguably more than one channel. In-person, online, and phone orders aren't technically a single channel either.

When we speak of a single-channel, we're really talking about a strategy that may be clear, focused, and direct, but where business growth potential is inherently limited by the channel's reach. In order for a brand to reach more customers, it needs to expand into additional channels.

Multi-Channel: A Transactional Approach

A multi-channel strategy enables brands to reach more potential customers by using two or more means of delivering products and services. Additional channels create more pathways to realize the brand's value proposition. People can choose the channel that best fits their particular consumption preferences. By creating more ways to consume in a fast and convenient manner, a multi-channel strategy is a transactional approach to connecting with customers.

For example, consider customers who buy a product from an online store. After bringing the product home, they decide that they aren't satisfied with the product and would like to return it. They work next to a brick-and-mortar retail store and would like to return it after work at the physical location, rather than ship it back to the online store. Unfortunately, the online and offline channels are isolated and not integrated. The customers are only allowed to ship it back to the online store, even though it is more convenient to return it to the retail store.

From the customer perspective, a multi-channel strategy often leads to multiple brand experiences, isolated by channel. When each channel has its own eXperience, they work against creating one cohesive brand meaning in the minds of customers. Worse, when one channel fails to meet the expectations set in another channel, it results in mistrust and deterioration of the customer's relationship with the brand.

Touchpoints: The Perspective of Consumers

Touchpoints represent specific instances of interactions between people and brands. A series of touchpoints combine to create customer eXperience. Each touchpoint defines the details of the specific interaction, including goals, interactions for achieving these goals, and the medium of the interactions.

When customers want to learn about a product, follow a brand on Facebook, Twitter, or Instagram, buy a product, or share a review of their eXperience, they do so by interacting with the brand. In China, WeChat is an even more pervasive point of contact and interaction with brands. These interactions are what define a touchpoint: touchpoints are defined from the perspective of consumers.

Though touchpoints and channels seem quite similar, their differences are quite significant, and their impact on how we think about and design for eXperiences is crucial. Channels exist from the perspective of the business; they are how the business understands where the customers come from and how they interact with the brand. Touchpoints are more specific and precise. A touchpoint can occur on any channel, but not every channel is appropriate for every touchpoint.

Omni-Touchpoint: An Experiential Systems Integration Approach

An omni-touchpoint strategy focuses on delivering eXperiences to consumers in a manner that enables them to select their own pathways to access and interact with the brand. It ensures brands will always offer what they are seeking at every touchpoint and reduces the number of pain points and friction between touchpoints.

By utilizing an omni-touchpoint strategy, brands are able to focus on: delivering Holistic eXperiences, tailoring eXperiences for specific consumers, and deepening relationships with eXperiences that evolve over time.

Delivering Holistic eXperiences through an omni-touchpoint strategy is the best approach for brands to build a more clear and less complicated eXperience. This approach particularly helps with creating frictionless eXperiences between touchpoints and reducing the confusion introduced by the multi-channel approach. Some interactions are inevitably complex, so brands must focus on ensuring they aren't more complicated than necessary.

Tailoring eXperiences for specific consumers is another application of an omni-touchpoint strategy for brands to build and maintain different types of relationships with different types of consumers. Each type of consumer has a different journey with the brand and desires a different type of eXperience and relationship with the brand. An omni-touchpoint strategy helps brands determine which touchpoints are required on which channel, and how to prioritize them for each type of consumer based on who they are, their goals, and how they want to accomplish them. The results are individual eXperiences that flow through appropriate and effective touchpoints, or even dedicated channels for each type of consumer, whether they are an influencer, majority user, upcoming user, etc.

Deepening relationships with eXperiences that evolve over time at each stage of the relationship between brands and consumers requires different types of interactions. An omni-touchpoint strategy can help brands manage these evolving eXperiences needed to deliver value based on the stage of their relationship.

For example, when people are looking to buy a new car, they probably seek information about the product offerings through the brand's website or social media accounts. As the relationship deepens to friends and family stages after they buy a car, they may access a personalized eXperience through the brand's mobile app and offline maintenance services. Delivering these personalized eXperiences requires brands to deeply know and understand their customers through the data and information generated from these interactions.

Some of these channels will require more time, resources, and investment to develop, deploy, and maintain. But they provide a high ROX where consumers perceive the brand value proposition of the brand. The key is properly aligning the brand's users and prioritizing the most effective touchpoints and channels to reach them.

HOLISTIC EXPERIENCE MODEL: DOMAINS OF EXPERIENCE

Now that we know how people experience brands — and how through these eXperiences they perceive the value of the brand — we can begin crafting eXperiences that engage them in a way that reinforces the brand value proposition. These eXperiences need to appeal to current and prospective consumers and work toward developing a mutually beneficial relationship. Though all brands deliver experiences, they are not all desirable. And though there are many types of attractive experiences brands can deliver, not all desirable experiences convey the value of the brand. Not all experiences are eXperiences.

We believe the best way to create long-term relationships between brands and consumers is for businesses to focus on delivering eXperiences. As introduced in Chapter 3, Holistic eXperiences help customers advance in achieving their goals, the transition between each interaction and touchpoint is frictionless, and upon reflection, their eXperience reinforces the brand value proposition.

The Holistic eXperience Model connects brands and consumers. There are four ways brands can express their value through touchpoints to deliver eXperiences, or what we call the Domains of eXperience: offerings, communications, environments, and behaviors (Figure 5.1).

These four domains are inspired by renowned brand practitioner Wally Olins' four Vectors of Brand Tangibility. We call them domains because each requires a different set of knowledge, skills, mediums, and tools to express a brand and its value in the particular set of touchpoints.

Offerings

These are the products and services brands offer to people and businesses. Offerings realize brand positioning through their ability to do something for customers to help them achieve their goals and fulfill their needs.

A drink that satisfies your thirst, a car service that transports you from one place to another, or a shirt that makes you look fashionable — these are all offerings that deliver value in the form of satisfying consumer needs.

Figure 5.1, *Holistic eXperience Model*

Communications

The messages and the mediums through which brands communicate to current and potential customers, and the messages and mediums used by customers to communicate to the brand — these are communications, whether they are mass communications or interpersonal.

Messages communicated by a brand help establish expectations of the eXperience they will have with a brand. The medium may be through words, images, sounds, videos, objects, or even gestures, to express the information and emotion of the message.

Communications are not just unidirectional, from the brand to consumers, such as print advertising, television commercials, and environmental signage. They can also be multidirectional, creating a dialogue between the brand and people in which messages are interactive. Communications set expectations through expression of the brand's value.

Environments

In the broadest sense, environments where brands deliver offerings and communications to the consumer. They are the locations where people can access the brand. This may include physical environments, such as a retail store, and digital environments, such as a website. Brands need to choose the right environment for the context in which people interact with the brand.

But environments go beyond just the location of the interaction; they need to be created in a way that embodies the brand. Physical environments use the layout, materials, lights, sounds, smells, temperature, and air quality to create a space for consumers to eXperience the value of the brand. Virtual reality and augmented reality are also environments, and brands need to consider the devices that provide such access to both physical and digital spaces.

Behaviors

A business consists of employees who interact directly with people and the world. Each employee has a role and associated behaviors in the brand's relationship with people. How do these employees, as representatives of the brand, treat people and the world? What are their actions and mannerisms when they engage customers? For example, when you walk into a retail store, how a store employee welcomes you and offers help when you are browsing are behaviors that represent the values of the brand.

With a new understanding of how people perceive the value of brands through eXperiences and the need to deliver Holistic eXperiences to realize the brand value proposition, brands will require a shift in their strategy, determining the best touchpoints to turn Holistic eXperiences into Ideal eXperiences.

* * *

Summary

Understanding the brand value proposition is essential to helping consumers differentiate why brand relationships are beneficial. Many consumers eXperiences are not directly attributed to how a product performs or how a service is delivered. Instead, the channels, or points of interaction determine the value. Even if all brand channels deliver great eXperiences, yet do so only in isolation from the other channels, brands will still be unable to deliver superior eXperiences to everyone.

The deciding factor is how well brands are able to interconnect touchpoints to work together. Only by understanding the Holistic eXperience Model and Domains of eXperience — offerings, communications, environments, and behaviors — are brands able to help consumers accomplish their goals, thus delivering Ideal eXperiences.

Section 2
DELIVERING, PLANNING, AND MANAGING EXPERIENCES

For brands to deliver Holistic eXperiences, every touchpoint needs to be aligned across the whole customer eXperience as an expression of the brand value proposition. That means everything a brand communicates through its offerings and employee behaviors delivered at every branded environment must be aligned to deliver an eXperience that consistently resonates with consumer expectations.

It's similar to how many manage their public image. There are things they believe that they should not say or do in public. They've carefully curated a Facebook presence, one where every photo and post communicates their lifestyle and thoughts. They decorate their desks at work with tchotchkes and souvenirs to express who they are, where they have been, and their passions. They also treat the people, animals, and world around them in a way that reflects their values. Every aspect of their lives — what they wear, how they act, how they talk, and the places they visit — say something about how they want the world to see them.

The challenge for brands is that rather than a single person managing their personal public image, brands rely on an entire organization of people to manage their brand eXperience through touchpoints spread across space and time. Each person in the organization has a different idea of what the Ideal eXperience should be and how the brand should express it. For this reason, organizations need a strategy to align and manage their brand eXperiences.

A BRAND STRATEGY SETS CUSTOMER EXPECTATIONS

Many businesses have a strategy to manage and maintain a consistent brand. In particular, it helps them communicate who they are, what they do, how they do it, why they do it, and why it matters. It defines the brand's look and feel (including the logo and visual language), tone of voice, and guidelines for implementing the brand in print and digital communications materials and environments. Frameworks are used to plan and manage the brand, including personas, brand positioning, brand promise, brand personality, brand hierarchy, and messaging. These assist businesses in developing and communicating a clear, compelling, and consistent brand story so that customers will recognize, understand, and remember the brand.

Brand strategy helps set expectations for the interactions consumers have with a brand. But communication is just one aspect of the brand eXperience. Businesses need to go beyond just setting expectations; they also need to be able to create and manage how consumers perceive their interactions with the brand at every touchpoint. Remember, eXperiences are a reflection of their perception of interactions with the brand compared to their expectations. What brands need is a strategy that can handle the nature of Holistic eXperiences and the meaning that customers derive from these eXperiences. X Thinking helps solve these problems, as well as additional problems through a different approach.

AN EXPERIENCE STRATEGY

An eXperience Strategy, on the other hand, is a mid-term to long-term strategic and tactical plan for the development of brand eXperiences in order to achieve business objectives. It helps brands envision the Ideal eXperience people would like the brand to deliver, identify the touchpoints that deliver such an eXperience, and prioritizes the business activities required to realize the vision, aligning the eXperience and the brand value proposition.

Because brand eXperiences are extremely complex, they are not something brands can build and deploy overnight. The process of delivering eXperiences requires a long chain of connected business activities: from identifying business goals, selecting and understanding the customer, conceptualizing the direction of the brand eXperience, prioritizing business activities to implement, to finally executing tactical projects to deliver eXperiences to consumers. It involves many people within the organization, from top-level executives guiding the strategic direction, mid-level managers implementing corporate strategy, the backstage employees working behind the scenes, down to the frontline employees interacting directly with customers, and even extending out to third-party partners and vendors outside the organization. It's a difficult task for all brands to execute a brand value proposition from the beginning to the end of the chain. Even when brands know exactly what customers want, it's difficult to enable the entire organization to work in unison to create offerings, environments, communications, and behaviors that deliver the Ideal eXperience.

An eXperience Strategy can help businesses apply an omni-touchpoint strategy to deliver Ideal eXperiences through: identification of the brand value proposition, consistent delivery of eXperiences, translation into touchpoints, prioritization of high-impact touchpoints (Figure 5.2).

Let's take a closer look at the four benefits of an eXperience Strategy and the business challenges it addresses.

POSITION

Determine Target Audience
(Persona)

Identify Value Delivered
(Brand Value Proposition)

Align Consumer Need with Brand Value Proposition
(Ideal eXperience Model)

PLAN

Plan Customer Relationship Development
(X Thinking Relationship Model)

Envision the Ideal eXperience and Outcome
(eXperience Vision Framework)

Prioritize High-Impact Touchpoints
(eXperience Masterplan)

DESIGN

Create Seamless and Consistent eXperience
(Holistic eXperience)

Create Meaningful eXperience
(eXperience Map)

Align Scenarios with Touchpoints
(eXperience Flows)

IMPLEMENT

Pilot and Iterate the eXperience

Standardize and Scale the eXperience

Operate and Optimize the eXperience

Figure 5.2, *eXperience Strategy*

Identification of the Brand Value Proposition

This step may sound obvious, but is often overlooked as the necessary starting point for any eXperience Strategy. Brands must identify why consumers value their products and services. If that answer is unclear or unknown, there are several approaches we've discussed to help brands reveal why customers choose their offerings over a competitor.

It may help them accomplish their goals. It may be a relationship with the brands that has developed over time. It might be a particular set of customers eager to embrace a new technology given a specific use scenario. It could be a combination of all of these factors, or another set of factors, but it's almost certainly not a single factor.

For example, Apple used to be a computer company that has evolved to become far more. From the first iPods, iPhones, and iPads, Apple slowly reinvented itself. Apple TV and Apple Watch started as companion devices, but the company's shift from content distributor to content creator and forays into fitness and health monitoring marked a notable shift in trajectory and influence. Apple Pay likewise revealed additional ambitions in financial services.

The Macintosh maker remains most recognized as an integrator of enterprise, education, and entertainment markets by creating seamless hardware and software solutions. However, all of these products and services share the same underlying brand value proposition that has endured this evolution. A brand value proposition should transcend every offering. It's singular and synonymous with the brand, evoking an implicit set of expectations among its customers. Apple makes complex tasks and technologies simple and accessible to everyone, regardless of the product or service.

But if businesses can't identify their own brand value proposition, it's unlikely consumers will, and it's impossible to develop an eXperience Strategy to reinforce it.

Consistent Delivery of eXperiences

One of the biggest challenges for brands is the management of the eXperience across all the brand touchpoints. The brand needs to deliver a consistent eXperience that reflects its brand value proposition, where interaction with every touchpoint should reinforce the brand positioning.

The delivery of consistency is challenging whenever work is divided among multiple groups, let alone across an organization. At any given moment, a company concurrently works on multiple projects that contribute to customer eXperiences with the brand. In order to handle the workload, organizations divide the work into manageable units and form organizational structures, such as divisions, departments, and teams, that focus on their specific unit of work. While these organizational structures maximize efficiency, they also form silos. Silo behavior is a mentality where divisions, departments, groups, and teams of people do not share information and knowledge with other parties within the organization.

Compartmentalization can help brands focus on specific tasks, prevent leaks of confidential information, or even to promote competition between departments. But there can also be unintended consequences for companies that have grown too large and too busy to effectively share information and knowledge across the whole organization and from the top to the bottom.

Such compartmentalization may become an impediment to the delivery of Holistic eXperiences. People need to share information and knowledge to maintain consistency across all the touchpoints of the brand. In addition, people need to work across the organizational structures that cause division to create the connections between touchpoints to support the interconnected nature of Holistic eXperiences, and by extension Ideal eXperiences.

What brands need is a shared vision across the entire organization where everyone works toward delivering the same desired eXperience. Brands also need a comprehensive plan that outlines the interconnected nature of all the touchpoints and how to ensure consistency among them.

Translation into Touchpoints

Many brands have a clearly defined brand value proposition, but occasionally organizations find their brand strategy difficult to execute. They may not know how to take these theoretical concepts and interpret them into practical projects that create tangible touchpoints delivering Holistic eXperiences. It's not a matter of how to make something; many brands know how to make just about anything. It's a problem of determining what to make.

Each of the Four Domains of eXperience are so different from one another. How a brand touchpoint is expressed in one domain is drastically different from all the other domains. It requires pulling people from multiple disciplines with different domains of knowledge in order to express a brand in all four domains.

For example, if an insurance company is positioned as always being "the one brand that knows best how to protect you," how is it expressed as an insurance product? Then how is this feeling of protection expressed as a physical environment? Does it use materials that make customers feel safe and secure? What sort of language does its communication use? Should it be strong, so customers feel the brand will protect them from harm, or should it be soft and caring like a protective mother? And how do employees treat the customers? Is there a difference between their behavior when people sign up for an insurance plan compared to when they are making a claim after an accident? These are just some of the ways a positioning can be translated into touchpoints.

What brands need is a way to translate abstract concepts into actionable strategy. This requires defining how a brand's value proposition and positioning can manifest in each of the Four Domains of eXperience. Brands also need a way to identify which touchpoints could serve as potential projects that can express the brand value proposition and positioning by delivering the appropriate eXperience. And lastly, brands need a way to communicate how these touchpoints fit into an eXperience map, as well as the company's overall direction and future plan.

Prioritization of High-Impact Touchpoints

A brand value proposition may manifest as an infinite number of potential touchpoints that can deliver eXperiences. The challenge is not necessarily determining what all those touchpoints are, but deciding which projects to say no to, which ones to say yes to, and prioritizing the projects brands decide to move forward with.

How should a brand evaluate which initiatives to pursue? What sort of criteria should brands use? Some touchpoints are considered to be essential to the Ideal eXperience, and others are just nice to have. Some touchpoints may already exist, but require changes and upgrades. Some touchpoints don't currently exist, but if they did, they would make a significant impact on customer experience with the brand. Some touchpoints that do not exist may require significant resources to develop, while others are quick and easy wins. Brands will need to evaluate for low-impact vs. high-impact, short-term vs. long-term, existing or non-existing, and essential vs. non-essential.

Brands need a way to plan for all the touchpoints that deliver the Holistic eXperience. It should provide brands with a comprehensive view of the entire eXperience and every existing touchpoint as well as future near-term and long-term touchpoints.

* * *

Summary

An eXperience Strategy aligns every touchpoint, from customer engagement to employee interactions. It's comprehensive, incorporating both expectations and perceptions. It's a combination of strategic initiatives and tactical plans involving interconnected activities that use personas and scenarios to understand customers and help them accomplish their goals.

There are four essential components to an eXperience Strategy. Identification of the brand value proposition ensures businesses are focused on the distinct advantages their products and services offer. Consistent delivery of eXperiences requires the alignment of groups that may be isolated through compartmentalization. Translation into touchpoints that connect the Domains of eXperience reinforce the brand. The prioritization of high-impact touchpoints provides the highest ROX by creating Holistic and Ideal eXperiences for customers.

Section 3
CREATING AN EXPERIENCE STRATEGY

Have you ever noticed how we describe our eXperiences? There is something quite intriguing in the language we use. When we talk about eXperiences, we might say:

"It was so much fun!"
"It was an 'interesting' eXperience."
"It was so frustrating!"
"It was a learning eXperience."
"It was boring."

eXperiences are often described using adjectives, which are abstract in nature. The challenge with abstract descriptions is that what one person finds to be fun, another person may find less inspiring. And it's this abstract nature that makes it inherently difficult for organizations to deliver eXperiences that consistently reinforce the brand value proposition.

An eXperience Strategy helps brands deliver the value through a process of interpretation. It begins with envisioning the desired eXperience in the form of an abstract description of how it should be perceived across the four Domains of eXperience and the lasting impression it creates. The eXperience is made tangible in the form of an eXperience map by aligning goals and needs with possible touchpoints that might be used to realize the brand value proposition. The touchpoints that make up the eXperience map are incorporated into clearly defined business activities the organization needs to execute to implement the eXperience. Simply put, an eXperience Strategy helps brands plan at the abstract level, determine the tangible means to bring the eXperience to life, and becomes tactical in determining what the brand needs to do.

We'd like to introduce to you three eXperience Strategy tools to help brands plan, deliver, and manage Ideal eXperiences: eXperience Vision, eXperience Flow, and eXperience Masterplan. These tools help brands describe, document, and communicate the eXperience in a manner that allows everyone across the organization to interpret, understand, and execute the desired eXperience.

EXPERIENCE VISION – ENVISION THE EXPERIENCE

Brands sometimes have trouble delivering a consistent eXperience across every touchpoint. Some touchpoints are on-brand, where the touchpoint is aligned with the brand value and positioning. Other touchpoints are off-brand, where the touchpoint feels out of place and inconsistent with the overall brand eXperience.

When Netflix co-founders Marc Randolph and Reed Hastings launched their now iconic company in 1997, it was dismissed by critics as a novelty. The process of selecting DVDs online that would arrive days later by mail completely contradicted the instant gratification of browsing for something to watch that evening at Blockbuster, the fledgling brand's most notable movie rental rival.

A monthly membership for as many movies as you could watch was an obvious bargain for some consumers. Most were less convinced, including then Blockbuster CEO John Antioco, who had the option to buy Netflix in 2000 for a mere $50 million, but according to Randolph and Hastings, he thought it was "a joke". [43]

Then Netflix took a different approach. They gave memberships away. Not to everyone, at least not a first. A campaign coordinated with nearly every major electronics retailer in the US put millions of postcards for one-month free memberships on the box of every DVD and Blu-Ray player sold. For those already planning to subscribe, it was essentially a discount on the player. For those buying players and looking for fresh content, it was a free gift they could use with their new purchase.

It was simple, but highly effective, integrating every touchpoint from the purchase of the player to selecting their first movie on the Netflix website. Best of all, it was a surprise that reached the right customers at the right time.

But Blockbuster's undoing wasn't Netflix's lack of late fees. It was the difference in selection. Blockbuster banked on the immediate availability of new releases, while Netflix focused on an exhaustive inventory of options. It was a stark disconnect for a company built for fans of all kinds of film, but had become one only for those interested in seeing what they may have missed in theaters last year. Selection was Blockbuster's brand, but Netflix was now delivering a better brand value proposition. Blockbuster stores, their primary touchpoint, were suddenly out of sync — and sales suffered.

Netflix still ships discs on a far more limited basis, but their industry dominating streaming service is available in nearly 200 countries and has more than 200 million subscribers. They're now a $40 billion company. Two decades later, there is just one Blockbuster location left in the world, in Bend, Oregon — a nostalgic destination dedicated to a bygone era of home entertainment. [44]

What brands need is an eXperience Vision to ensure that all touchpoints are on-brand and deliver an eXperience that reflects the brand value proposition. An eXperience Vision is the Ideal eXperience that the brand aspires to deliver to customers in the future. This point in the future can be as short as one year away or much further out, such as five to ten years into the future. A vision serves as a guiding star, where everyone in the organization can see a clearly defined direction for the types of eXperiences the brand should deliver and the criteria for evaluating the touchpoints created to deliver these eXperiences (Figure 5.3).

A successful eXperience Vision clearly defines three things:
· WHY consumers desire a relationship with the brand
· HOW value is expressed through brand touchpoints
· WHAT meaning is created from the eXperience

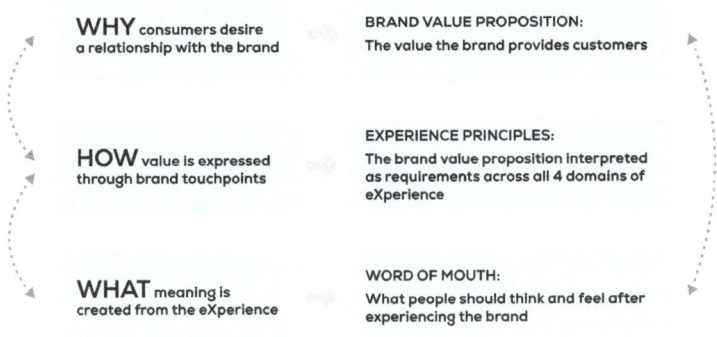

Figure 5.3, *eXperience Vision*

WHY Consumers Desire a Relationship with Brands

As we've discussed throughout this chapter, businesses must define their brand value proposition and how it helps customers accomplish their goals. It's the reason why they prefer to have a relationship with one brand over its competitors.

It may be a short phrase consisting of several adjectives that can be applied to everything the brand does across all the Domains of eXperience. It should communicate the value the brand provides customers and distinguishes the brand.

Here are some examples of a brand value proposition:
· Apple – Making Life Easier
· China Merchants Bank – Extremely Simple Finance, Extreme Experience (极简金融, 极致体验)
· Volvo – Safety
· Xiaomi – Affordable High Quality for Everyone
· Disney – Family Magic

HOW Value is Expressed Through Touchpoints

Brand value can only be perceived through the eXperiences people have with the brand. And these eXperiences occur through the interactions people have with the brand at each of the brand's touchpoints. For people to perceive the value of the brand, the brand value proposition must manifest in every touchpoint across all four domains of eXperience in a manner that people can see, hear, touch, smell, and taste.

Brand eXperience principles are an interpretation of the brand values into the form of requirements for the touchpoints. And because each of the domains manifests touchpoints through different forms, it requires a different interpretation for each of the four domains. These requirements are used as a starting point for creating new touchpoints, as well as criteria to evaluate existing touchpoints.

Let's take a look at Disney and its brand value proposition and the concept of "Family Magic" as an example (Figure 5.4).

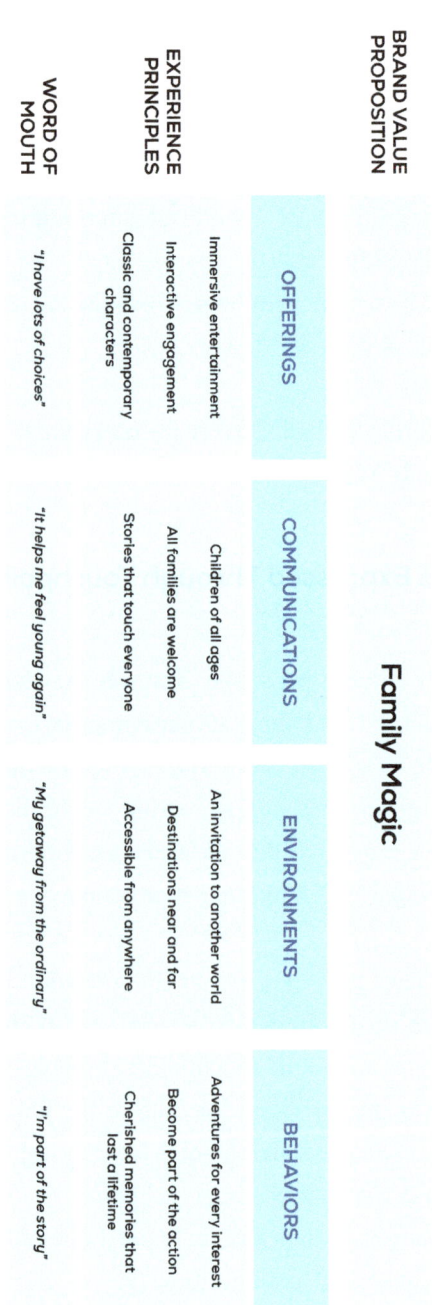

Figure 5.4, *Brand eXperience*

Offerings:
- Immersive entertainment.
- Classic and contemporary characters.
- Interactive engagement.

Communications:
- Children of all ages
- All families are welcome.
- Stories that touch everyone.

Environments:
- An invitation to another world.
- Destinations near and far.
- Accessible from anywhere.

Behaviors:
- Adventures for every interest.
- Become part of the action.
- Cherished memories that last a lifetime.

Whether it's a visit to one of their amusement park attractions or interaction in theaters or at home with the Pixar, Star Wars, or Marvel universes, Disney's "Family Magic" is founded on the suspension of disbelief in worlds where anything is possible.

WHAT Meaning is Created from the eXperience

For brands to evaluate the success of an eXperience at each touchpoint, a successful eXperience Vision must define the desired outcomes of people's eXperiences when they interact with a brand touchpoint. These outcomes are what people should be thinking and feeling, and are often best expressed from their perspective.

Revisiting the Disney example:
- Offerings: I have lots of choices
- Communications: It helps me feel young again
- Environments: My getaway from the ordinary
- Behaviors: I'm part of the story

Using the eXperience Vision: Align, Guide, and Inspire

An eXperience Vision is not just a dream for the distant future. It can be used to solve common problems when brands try to deliver eXperiences such as fragmented eXperiences, off-brand touchpoints, and lack of alignment within the organization. When used correctly, an eXperience Vision can align, guide, and inspire the organization to deliver Ideal eXperiences through Holistic eXperiences.

Experience Visions Align

Delivering eXperiences requires multiple people from across the organization working on multiple initiatives with different objectives and key performance indicators. This often takes the brand in conflicting directions.

When stakeholders from across the organization work together to create an eXperience Vision, it helps define a shared aspiration for the brand's future eXperience. The vision serves as a common direction for the entire organization to ensure all business activities reinforce the brand value proposition and appropriate positioning. It also serves as a tool for communicating the common direction for all employees within the organization who play a part in crafting people's eXperience with the brand.

Experience Visions Guide

As we discussed earlier, eXperiences can often be ambiguous due to their abstract nature. As a result, different people may interpret the description of an eXperience in different ways.

An eXperience Vision guides an organization by removing ambiguity around the nature of the desired brand eXperience from an individual perspective. It establishes clear expectations and requirements for touchpoints in each of the four domains as well as a clear end-state of what people think and feel after they interact with a touchpoint.

The eXperience Vision can be used to guide the brand's direction of innovation by focusing brainstorming and idea generation, helping to maintain the brand's differentiation from competitors. It's also a guide for strategic decision-making by creating clear criteria for what is on-brand and what is off-brand. This enables employees to say "no" to business initiatives inconsistent with the vision of the brand.

Experience Visions Inspire

Organizations often become so vast that it's easy to lose an understanding or appreciation of their contributions to the bigger picture. They may not see how their daily contributions create value for the brand's customers.

An eXperience Vision inspires employees by providing a sense of purpose by connecting what they work on day-to-day to the vision of the brand. The vision humanizes the brand's mission and purpose, energizing employees and making their work meaningful.

EXPERIENCE FLOWS – ALIGN TOUCHPOINTS WITH SCENARIOS

Banking eXperiences can often be cumbersome, particularly in China.

Going to the bank isn't quite as common an apprehension as going to the dentist, but it's an activity some still dread.

Let's suppose you're interested in purchasing an investment product. You decide to go to the closest bank branch, where you already have a bank account, to learn more about their products. When you arrive, you need to get a number, then wait until your number is called. While you wait, the bank staff offers you a form to fill out your basic information, such as your name, address, phone number, ID number, etc. When it's your turn to meet with the financial manager, he asks you a series of questions to get a better idea of your investment goals. He explains the products and makes a recommendation. As helpful as he has been, you need some time to consider the options carefully, so you choose to sleep on it and come back another day.

Though this eXperience isn't negative, it could be improved simply by moving around the sequence and location of the touchpoints. Before ever heading to the bank, you could use the bank's mobile app to learn about their wealth-management products. Within the app, you could also answer a simple investment preferences questionnaire to generate several product recommendations for you. Even though the information has been helpful, you still find it difficult to make a decision, and you choose to talk to a financial advisor in person. The app also has a list of recommended financial advisors, and you notice that there is one at your local bank branch office. You're able to schedule an appointment right away within the app.

When you arrive at the bank, there is no need to take a number and wait; the receptionist leads you straight to the financial advisor's office. The advisor says hello, and after confirming your identity, is able to review the investment preferences questionnaire you took in the mobile app as well as some of the products that were recommended to you. The advisor gets to know your needs, as well as your concerns, and develops an investment strategy to suit your personal investment preferences, explaining the plan and products in detail to make sure you understand the advantages of each recommendation.

You are confident with the plan you've developed together and impressed by the expertise. You decide to purchase the product, and because you're already a customer, there is no need to fill out the forms with the information they already have in their records. Extremely satisfied with the experience, you extend the relationship, choosing to work with the financial advisor online.

By moving some of the information from the bank to the mobile app and sequencing it earlier in the process, leveraging existing customer records the customer supplied in previous visits to avoid the need to fill out forms with information the bank already had on file, and extending the amount of time the customer was engaged in the decision-making process allowed the bank to create a superior eXperience that was more efficient and assuring for the customer. It just required rearranging the sequence and location of the touchpoints.

Delivering Ideal eXperiences requires a brand to become a master of space and time — always wherever and whenever the customer needs it to be. Though brands are capable of generating endless ideas on how they might be able to deliver value through the four Domains of eXperience, if people do not interact with the brand with the right touchpoint, at the right location, and at the right time, they never perceive value from the brand.

What brands need to do is determine exactly which touchpoints are best suited to deliver value to achieve their goals. An eXperience Flow visualizes how people flow through multiple brand touchpoints in pursuit of their goals. It consists of two key components: scenarios and touchpoints (Figure 5.5).

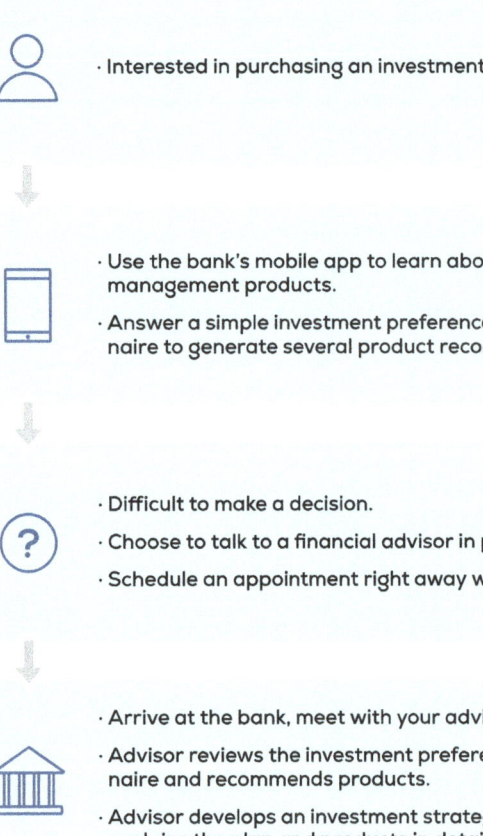

Figure 5.5, *eXperience Flow*

WHERE and WHEN People Interact with the Brand

In the previous chapter, we discussed the role scenarios play in innovation by identifying pain points, opportunities for improvement, and user-inspired solutions.

Here, we apply the insights we've gained about the consumers, their context, and their goals toward planning new scenarios to create opportunities for the brand to help them achieve their goals in a preferred manner and sequence. The focus here is on selecting the exact locations where and moments when the brand can deliver value.

Remember, touchpoints are the interface between the brand and people. They are how brands deliver value and eXperience. Brands need to determine the right type of touchpoint that will deliver value. Is the touchpoint an offerings, communications, environments, or behaviors? Which touchpoint will best help customers achieve their goals?

It's not enough just to define scenarios and touchpoints. Brands need to avoid creating new scenarios that create friction between customers and their goals. In the earlier financial investment example, all the touchpoints existed as well as a scenario. However the interaction with the customer was in the wrong order and at the wrong touchpoint. Brands need to align touchpoints in the proper order and sequence that makes the most sense from the perspective of the customer, thus increasing the brand value proposition.

Using the eXperience Flows: Clarify, Identify, and Connect

An eXperience Flow helps brands find the best sequence of events and touchpoints by making the eXperience tangible through a visualization of new scenarios with the brand. Though eXperience Flows seem simple, they are extremely powerful for helping brands solidify eXperiences, identify touchpoints, and connect touchpoints.

Experience Flows Clarify Experiences

An eXperience Vision is abstract in nature so that it can be used to inform all eXperiences involving any type of touchpoint. But this also makes it challenging to fully comprehend how an eXperience may unfold in detail for a person interacting with the brand.

eXperience Flows fill this void by interpreting the intangible eXperience Vision into tangible eXperience scenarios. An eXperience Flow can be created for every scenario, and multiple eXperience Flows can be created for every type of persona. Together, they create a complete picture of all the different scenarios and resulting eXperiences everyone might have with the brand.

Experience Flows Identify Touchpoints

When it comes to describing touchpoints, an eXperience Vision focuses on how touchpoints should express brand value, rather than which exact touchpoint should be used to express brand value. As a result, people within the organization have difficulty determining which potential touchpoints are required to deliver the defined eXperience.

By thoroughly visualizing all of the scenarios for every persona, a complete collection of eXperience Flows paints a picture of every touchpoint the brand needs to deploy to materialize the eXperience Vision. The more often a touchpoint appears in eXperience Flows for multiple personas, the more likely it should be prioritized. The fewer times a touchpoint is used and the fewer personas use it, the less it should be prioritized. There are other criteria for identifying the priority of touchpoints, such as the pain points they resolve, how substantial a WOW moment they create, or the significance of the persona with which they interact.

Experience Flows Connect Touchpoints

Because eXperience Flows focus on developing scenarios of individual interactions with brands, they're an extremely effective tool for helping brands ideate Holistic eXperiences. Rather than focusing primarily on one channel that serves every customer's needs, an eXperience Flow should focus on helping achieve goals within a specific context. This may require multiple touchpoints that span different types of channels.

An eXperience Flow helps visualize how customers transition between multiple touchpoints across different locations over time. This visualization will help brands identify which touchpoints need to be interconnected so the transition between these interactions is smooth and frictionless. In doing so, teams or departments responsible for different touchpoints can begin to work together to ensure that people's eXperiences are holistic.

EXPERIENCE MASTERPLAN – PRIORITIZE TOUCHPOINTS

A strategy is only as good as its ability to produce positive change for the organization, and an eXperience Strategy is no different. The eXperience Vision serves as the goal for X Thinking's approach to eXperience Strategy, but the eXperience Masterplan serves as the plan for achieving that goal.

An eXperience Masterplan is a dynamic, long-term planning document that outlines the brand touchpoints to guide current and future development. The document is an inventory of every current and future touchpoint, providing a complete picture of the entire ecosystem of touchpoints, allowing brands to determine actionable next steps (Figure 5.6 & Figure 5.7).

264 | X THINKING

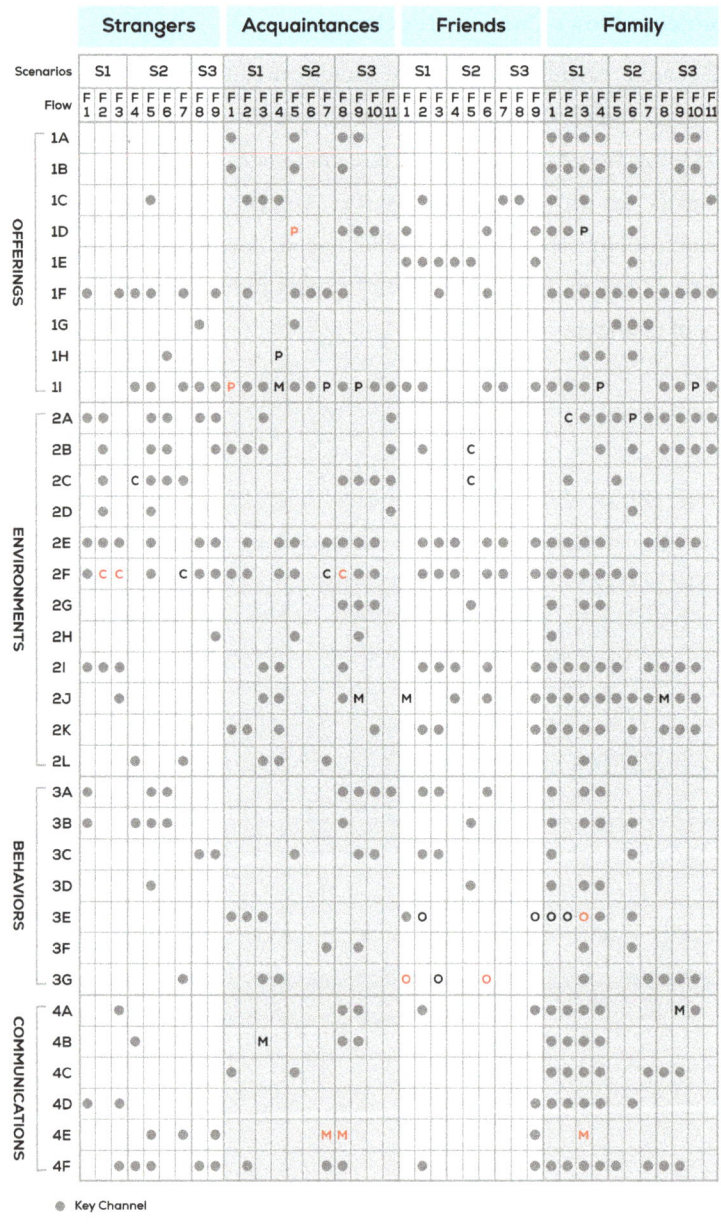

Figure 5.6, *eXperience Masterplan*

CHAPTER 5: The Challenge of Execution

	Scenarios	Family — New Product Promotion			
	Flow	New Product Recommendation	New Food Flash Sale	Brand Co-branding	New Product Collection
OFFERINGS	Hamburger	●	●	●	●
	Fried Chicken/Snacks	●	●	●	●
	Toy	●		●	
	Combo	●	●	P	
	Birthday Party				
	★ Member Points	●	●	●	●
	24-hour Meal Delivery				
	Other			●	●
	★ New products/Services	●	●	●	P
ENVIRONMENTS	★ CBD Stores		C	●	●
	Community Stores				●
	High-speed Rail/Airport stores		●		
	Drive Thru				
	★ McDonald's APP	●	●	●	●
	WeChat Mini Program	●	●	●	●
	Store Ordering Screen	●		●	●
	Third-party Takeaway Software	●			
	WeChat Service Account	●	●	●	●
	★ WeChat Public Account	●	●	●	●
	Social Media (Douyin/Xiaohongshu, etc.)	●	●	●	●
	New Environment			●	
BEHAVIORS	Order Clerk	●		●	●
	Coffee Salesperson	●		●	●
	Takeaway	●			
	Store Manager	●		●	●
	Happy Sister/Brand Member	O	O	O	●
	Other			●	
	★ New Staff			●	
COMMUNICATIONS	Store Advertisement	●	●	●	●
	Outdoor Advertisement	●	●	●	●
	TV Advertisement	●	●	●	●
	Brand Activities(Promotions/New products)	●	●	●	●
	Brand Activities (Cross-border/Title naming)			M	
	New Content/Communication	●	●	●	●

★ Important Scenarios

Figure 5.7, eXperience Masterplan (Detailed)

Using the eXperience Masterplan: Identify, Develop and Manage

An eXperience Masterplan is extremely versatile in providing multiple views of the brand eXperience touchpoint ecosystem. It can provide views at both the 30,000-feet level as well as ground-level implementation. It can also show the current state, as well as the future state, and every state in between. Because of its versatility, the eXperience Masterplan can help brands manage touchpoints, identify priorities, and develop implantation roadmaps.

Experience Masterplans Identify Priorities

The eXperience Flows help brands develop many possible touchpoints that can express the brand value to people in a way they can perceive it. But out of the potentially endless number of touchpoints that are conceptualized, brands need a way to identify and prioritize which touchpoints to pursue. An eXperience Masterplan can help in multiple ways.

For established enterprises, the eXperience Masterplan can help identify existing touchpoints brands have as well as the non-existing touchpoints that still need to be developed. Among these touchpoints, some may require only minor tweaks that can be improved in the short term. Changes that are more fundamental are more of a long-term initiative.

Brands can also identify which touchpoints are high-impact, that would yield a high ROX versus others that might be more low-impact. This may include eliminating significant pain points or generating major wow moments. These would also be evaluated based on whether the time, energy, and resources required to modify or create a touchpoint is worth the potential benefits.

Experience Masterplans Develop Implementation Roadmaps

Due to the scale and complexity of Holistic eXperiences, they require a long-term plan to develop and deploy. An eXperience Masterplan can help show brands how the eXperience touchpoint ecosystem system might evolve over time from the current state to the desired future state. By creating multiple versions of the masterplan at key phases of the implementation, a brand can forecast from the present toward the future states as well as backcast from the desired future state toward the present.

Experience Masterplans Manage Touchpoints

A Holistic eXperience comprises a large number of touchpoints throughout the relationship between a brand and a persona. Multiply the management of every relationship between the brand and different personas, and the number of touchpoints can quickly become unwieldy to oversee over time.

An eXperience Masterplan organizes these touchpoints, allowing the brand to see current and future touchpoints to be developed. By organizing them based on relationship stages, brands can focus on certain touchpoints aligned with the goals of the organization. By categorizing them based on eXperience domains, brands can more easily see multiple touchpoints that may exist in the same channel.

An eXperience Masterplan can also be adjusted to show only touchpoints relating to one persona to see their journey. Likewise, the masterplan can be adjusted to show only touchpoints that are relevant to one department within the organization to highlight who is responsible for deployment of each one.

FROM STRATEGY TO REALIZATION

For X Thinking, our eXperience Strategy is more than just defining the brand value or brand positioning of the organization. It takes into consideration how the strategy materializes in the form of touchpoints that deliver a Holistic eXperience. It also provides the tools brands need to develop a roadmap for implementation.

At the onset of many development sessions, significant resources are invested to develop a new strategy for the future of the organization. But these strategies often have trouble finding life after conception if they are too abstract and lack detailed plans for realization.

An eXperience Strategy is a living and breathing set of tools that not only help the strategic conception and tactical execution of the eXperience, and continue to evolve with the brand eXperience.

* * *

Summary

Every brand needs an eXperience Vision to help create consistency by ensuring all touchpoints are on-brand and differentiating the brand from the competition. It promotes collaboration from across the organization working in one direction. Ultimately, it ensures that the brand delivers an appropriate eXperience that results in people thinking and feeling about the brand in a desirable manner.

eXperience Flows help brands create more clarity around which touchpoints are needed, where they are, and when they deliver value. Specifically, they identify the particular order in which people interact with touchpoints so brands can deliver a Holistic eXperience. The clarity helps identify tangible projects for the organization and connects otherwise unrelated departments across the organization to work together to ensure frictionless transitions between touchpoints.

eXperience Masterplans are an extremely powerful tool in providing multiple views of the entire ecosystem of brand touchpoints. It helps avoid the trap of losing focus, the inability to prioritize immediate needs, or not looking at the long-term development of the brand eXperience. The prioritization of touchpoints leads to the creation of actionable tactical short-term projects and long-term initiatives. When used properly, it can help brands identify how to move the eXperience from where it is today to where the brand wants to be in the future.

Case Study:
WM MOTOR (WELTMEISTER)

Who Are They?

WM Motor, better known as Weltmeister, is a Chinese automaker that produces electric vehicles in Wenzhou, Zhejiang Province, with additional research and development facilities in Germany and the United States. Their first model, the compact crossover Weltmeister EX5, was announced in December 2017, unveiled to the public in May 2018 at the Beijing Auto Show, and entered mass production in September 2018. The EX5 is built around three core technologies – the Living Motion electric powertrain, the Living Pilot intelligent driving assistance system, and the Living Engine, which combines smart connectivity and interactivity in the cabin.

In its first year of manufacturing, Weltmeister delivered more than 16,000 EX5s, vehicles that earned a customer satisfaction score of 97 percent. In 2019, the EX5 also achieved a C-NCAP 5-star safety rating and became the first electric vehicle company in the world to offer a lifetime warranty on its battery packs.

Weltmeister gained extensive attention from the media, market, industry, and also the recognition of brands from other industries. In 2017, Weltmeister ranked 18th in China Unicorn Startup List, with a valuation of $5 billion, and was ranked first among NEV startups with the delivery of 4,085 EX5s in the first quarter of 2019, and in March, Weltmeister was honored the Golden Service Award at China Vehicle Aftersales Congress 2019.

What Did They Need?

Weltmeister needed to strengthen its relationship with prospective owners who would pay higher prices for electric cars — particularly younger drivers in China's so-called "pan-post-'90s generation" who are defined by distinctive expectations and lifestyles.

What Did We Do?

TANG helped Weltmeister understand the motivating factors that contribute to customer loyalty among pan-post-90s consumers (defined as those born in the late 80s/early 90s). By creating a comprehensive strategy for building relationships between customers and the Weltmeister brand, WM Motor developed a holistic, smart mobility ecosystem that recognizes new-energy vehicles (NEVs) as both a product and a service.

Industry Context

NEV is the collective designation in China for zero and low emission automotive technologies, including battery electric, fuel cell, and hybrid vehicles. In 2010, NEV was identified by the State Council as an emerging strategic industry, and vehicles powered by electricity were subsequently introduced into Chinese automotive market. With the combined stimulus of favorable policies and increasing mobility needs in the past decade, NEV production has rapidly expanded in scale. However, in 2019, NEV subsidies to both manufacturers and buyers were reduced by 50 percent, and companies dependent upon government offsets have struggled to maintain their market positions.

With increased quality, advanced intelligence, premium features, and lower emissions, NEVs have proven popular among younger car buyers around the world. Both traditional automakers and emerging startups are tapping into the NEV market, shifting attention to China's prosperous post-80s-and-90s consumers — the primary focus for China's automotive industry, accounting for 47 percent of present and prospective NEV owners.

Younger car buyers have distinct expectations, and highly homogenous NEV brands are attempting to define key differentiators. Younger consumers in China still make purchasing decisions based on utility, but also appearance, status, personalization, lifestyle, and environmental impact. NEV startups like Weltmeister, NIO, Byton, Xpeng, and Singulato are developing new products and services, recognizing both the challenges and opportunities market consolidation presents.

As favorable policy initiatives gradually fade, the NEV industry will face increased and intense competition, resulting in inevitable consolidation. NEV companies driven by the development of core technologies will soon realize a larger share of an expanding market with fewer competitors.

Business Objectives

As part of an emerging and competitive industry, Weltmeister needed to engage customers in new ways that ensure sustainability, even in the absence of state subsidies for NEVs. Younger consumers have expectations unique from previous generations, placing value on experience and service as much as product features. By creating authentic relationships that grow over time through an innovative retail strategy, Weltmeister and TANG focused on developing a new brand eXperience to:

- **Appeal to the distinct expectations of pan-post-90s car buyers.**
  Establish sincere relationships with customers navigating modern urban life.

- **Develop an immersive eXperience for comprehensive smart mobility solutions.**
  Service beyond the sale is essential for brands to break through the crowded NEV market.

- **Create a comprehensive ecosystem that informs every business decision.**
  Understand the interactions and relationships that define the brand at every level.

The Solution

NEV is a smart mobility solution, unlike a conventional product or service alone. Consumers value traditional gasoline vehicles for performance and quality; for NEVs, consumers prioritize ancillary services and environmental impact. NEVs offer a comprehensive suite of services, from charging stations and car rental to online feedback and real-time monitoring, creating more opportunities for value-added interactions and brand loyalty.

Customer focus is the starting point for smart mobility. As the NEV industry and customer expectations evolve, every automaker must rethink the conventional mindset of selling a product to offering a smart mobility solution driven by an ongoing relationship with the customer.

As a commodity, vehicles are typically sold through car dealerships which are managed independently of the automaker. They are the first touchpoint for customers, for maintenance and concerns, potentially leading to inconsistencies in service — eXperiences that may jeopardize the relationship with the brand.

Weltmeister and TANG adapted the conventional demographic analysis used in the automotive industry by redefining the pan-post-90s generation. By mapping the ambiguous boundaries and traits of this group into four personas, we were able to explore the value propositions for each.

Weltmeister studied the diverse mobility needs that drive decision-making among this demographic. Buyers who once made brand purchases based largely on societal trends and conspicuous social status are now as likely to choose a vehicle based on a balance of practicality and personal identity. The value propositions behind vehicle purchases were evolving.

Based on insights into this target audience, Weltmeister designed its products and services to appeal specifically to this demographic. The pan-post-90s are more objective and open to change. Rather than seeking fulfillment from product features, they are more likely to become emotionally invested in brands that share their values.

TANG advised Weltmeister to gradually deepen its connection with customers through the X Thinking Relationship Model — from communication at the stranger stage, to product experience at the acquaintance stage, then the shared experience of the friend stage, and eventually to the intense bond of the family stage. All while promoting the value of its ambitious smart mobility ecosystem.

Weltmeister leverages different approaches to enhance the connection with customers at different relationship stages. To reach consumers with limited exposure or familiarity with the brand, the company organized activities like the Weltmeister Hygge Lifestyle Exploration and the Weltmeister EX5 Test Drive to create immersive emotional eXperiences. As customers gradually learn about the brand, Weltmeister deepens the degree of services to cater to their needs (Figure 5.8).

Figure 5.8, *Weltmeister's Suite of Services*

The Weltmeister's Experience Spaces are flagship showrooms in major cities where customers learn the latest news about the brand, experience Weltmeister's leading-edge technologies, and share in the enthusiasm and passion of fellow Weltmeister followers. The Weltmeister User Stores are the sales and service centers Weltmeister Motor jointly builds with its smart mobility partners (SMP). The Weltmeister Service Stations offer charging, maintenance, and repair. The Weltmeister E-Spots connect customers to the company's entire service network.

Weltmeister divides pre-sale and after-sale services within its ecosystem. Before visiting a store, in-person, customers can schedule and customize their visit online. Once in the store, customers can use their Super ID to access the in-store guide from the touch desk and select custom services. During the visit, customers may also shop for digital accessories at the Manufacturer Lab as an extension of the in-store experience. Through these touchpoints, Weltmeister shares its brand stories, value of products and services, and vision with visitors.

After purchase, owners move from brand friend to family through owner exclusives. The Pioneer Service Plan includes a lifetime warranty, unlimited data service, and 24/7 roadside assistance — all creating a relationship of reliability, connectivity, and security that's synonymous with brand. As the level of service increases, so too does customer opinion of the Weltmeister.

Today, Weltmeister's brand image is differentiated through multiple touchpoints and relationship stages. Weltmeister Home provides mobility services for customers new to the brand; Weltmeister Class connects car owners to share life and smart mobility experiences, and WMate, a platform that organizes test drives and similar events to engage customers in Weltmeister culture. Weltmeister Motor, together with its followers, organize compelling meetups, like the competitive WMate Karting Championship and the Weltmeister University Talk Show, featuring key influencers in a captivating format. Appearances on streaming content providers like iQiyi and Bilibili also transformed Weltmeister followers into a thriving community.

Result

Weltmeister's complete process of online appointment, in-person visit, after-sales guarantee, and mobility services creates a Holistic eXperience. The company delivered on the promise made by CEO Freeman H. Shen that the company would launch a smart, affordable, and practical electric vehicle, even without state subsidies. WM Motor's consistent and seamless retail approach creates an ecosystem where both the brand and the customer benefit — an eXperience Strategy that aligns Weltmeister's operations internally and collaboration externally.

Through our collaboration with Weltmeister, our greatest takeaway was the role relationships play not just in customer interaction and individual brand satisfaction, but also influence. The persuasive power of customer loyalty spread among family, friends, acquaintances, and even strangers has inherent, but often unmeasured value for the brand and their customers. Weltmeister now recognizes the benefits of this ancillary eXperience and how it fulfills customer needs beyond product features and service beyond the initial sale.

"Every organization has to make the transition from a world defined primarily by repetition to one primarily defined by change."

— *Bill Drayton*

CHAPTER 6

The Evolution of Engagement

Understanding Connectivity

Driving Digital Transformation

Case Study: Starbucks

INTRODUCTION

Some companies and consumers are internet native, founded or born after the global information and communications network changed our everyday lives by incorporating digital connections into nearly every personal or professional interaction. But for brands that preceded this evolution, digital transformation has often been a daunting transition.

In Understanding Connectivity, we'll reflect on how consumers embraced the internet, and how China's adoption was both similar and distinct from the West. From the early days of dial-up to the latest iPhone, brands often mistake incremental change as intuitive, when it is far from it. Understanding the industries and eras that preceded smart devices and artificial intelligence is essential to predicting the future of consumer behavior and building relationships that are valuable and sustainable.

In Achieving Digital Transformation, we'll break down complex concepts and highlight how digitalization, dataization, and intelligence capture previously unknown insights and drive innovation. Convenience and efficiency are soft metrics, but data gathered from every transaction inform opportunities to improve and enhance every exchange. We'll also examine customer journeys, the scenarios that motivate decision making, and how brands can apply these to deliver a more modern consumer experience.

Then we'll take a look at Starbucks, and how their digital transformation from the American incarnation of a "third place" to a more immersive social destination where customers can participate in the roasting, preparation, and enjoyment of coffee in a way that was completely reinvented just for China.

Section 1
UNDERSTANDING CONNECTIVITY

Consumers spend hours on smart devices everyday. They're an integral part of life at work, home, and the places in-between. The digital era is constantly evolving. With the increased popularity and frequency of device and service upgrades, digital transformation has become an essential path for every brand in every industry.

DIGITAL EVOLUTION IN CHINA

When the digital era was still in its infancy, China was a keen observer and emulator. During the early days of the Internet, China in many ways lagged behind the rest of the world. Yet as the significance of the mobile Internet emerged, China emerged as a leader in digitalization with the robust development of mobile payment and O2O, the interplay of online and offline.

So far, China's digital era can be divided into three phases: internet connectivity, mobile connectivity, and smart connectivity (Figure 6.1).

The period from 1986 to 2010 ushered in the digital era. China Academic Network, or CANET, was launched in 1986 and the first email was sent the following year. CANET was connected to the Internet in

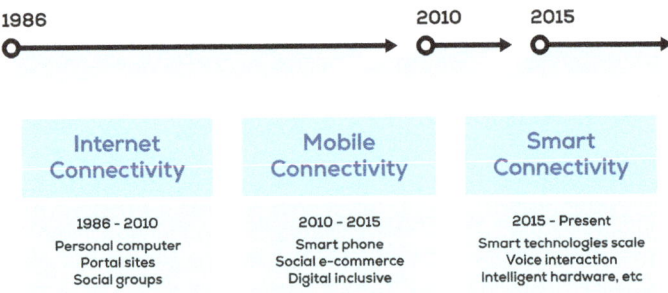

Figure 6.1, *China's Digital Era*

1994, and the Chinese public was connected in 1995. The performance of personal computers significantly improved, and portal websites and web communities became pervasive and prosperous. Consumers began to interact with one another and the world via the Internet. During the period from 2010 to 2015, the mobile Internet expanded rapidly. The wide adoption of smartphones hastened the improvement of inclusive, mobile applications that profoundly changed the social lives of consumers.

Since 2015, China has gradually started the large-scale application of smart technologies. Voice interactions, smart hardware, as well as smart furniture and home devices have improved lives beyond the Internet, and artificial intelligence has become a part of the progress of human civilization. As Internet connectivity, mobile connectivity, and smart connectivity continue to iterate, consumer experience has also undergone its own transformation.

Internet Connectivity

Internet connectivity and the widespread adoption of Internet technologies enriched consumer experience. The virtual world became a part of everyday life, with social networking, shopping, and entertainment all easily accessible via the internet, creating entirely new experiences. Internet technology broke through the information silos between companies, consumers were given more choices, and online activity gradually became the center of business.

Companies were no longer dominant by traditional metrics, because the Internet became the conduit of information between companies and consumers. As the economic environment improved, consumer options continued to expand, even when staying home. In the meantime, information sharing online accelerated personal testimonials. The popularity of blogging in China provided a relatively open and equitable online platform for anyone to record personal feelings, interactions, and opinions in blogs and photos shared with strangers. Now individuals could make their voices heard more easily and effectively. Brands didn't dominate the communications anymore. The focus started to shift to consumers.

Mobile Connectivity

Mobile connectivity further improved the access, convenience, and inclusiveness of the online experience. Smartphones, online shopping, instant messaging, mobile payment, online learning, location services, and mobile games became popular in China and transformed consumer life completely. Take mobile payment as an example. In March 2018, Alipay became the largest mobile payment platform in the world with more than 870 million users. Mobile payment has become an integral part of Chinese life because it can be used anywhere with greater convenience, doesn't require change, significantly boosts transaction efficiency, and eliminates the circulation of counterfeit currency. Compared with other countries worldwide, China is at the forefront of adopting and popularizing mobile payment. [45]

Adoption of these technologies in the education industry increased access to opportunity. In 2018, the number of active users of online education apps in China reached 220 million, with more than half of users living in third-tier and fourth-tier cities. The rapid popularization of mobile devices, to some extent, addressed concerns about the uneven distribution of resources that hadn't been solved by traditional education, thus creating long-term societal value. [46]

In less than a decade since mobile phones surpassed desktop computers to become the most common connected device for consumers, mobile internet users have become the driving force propelling the development of China's digital innovation across all industries.

Smart Connectivity

Smart connectivity and machine learning have created improved eXperiences. In 2017, Alipay introduced "Pay with Face Recognition" on KPRO, KFC's food ordering mobile app, with a recognition accuracy rate of 99.99 percent. As technologies like artificial intelligence (AI) and image processing mature, the commercial adoption of facial recognition will continue to increase. Payment with facial recognition can efficiently reduce customer wait times during peak hours and significantly boost cashier efficiency. The potential savings are so promising, Alipay is investing ¥3 billion RMB ($420 million USD) in the technology, with an anticipated 760 million Chinese consumers expected to use facial recognition payments by 2022. [47]

In the same year, Alibaba officially introduced its first smart hardware, Tmall Genie, a series of smart speakers with various models similar to Amazon's Echo. In the first year, Tmall sold more than 3 million. With its built-in AliGenie operating system, the Tmall Genie helps consumers control smart furniture, order food delivery, top up their mobile phone plans, and place orders via voice commands.

Though Internet connectivity, mobile connectivity, and smart connectivity are the three phases of the digital era, the degree of development in China has not been consistent geographically. First-tier and second-tier cities have a higher adoption rate of mobile connectivity and smart connectivity, yet some remote areas are still in the early phase of popularizing the Internet.

CHANGING THE WAYS BRANDS INTERACT

The continuous interaction between consumers and technology changes the business environment. For brands in the three development phases of the digital era, how they create value and obtain benefits is changing as well. The providers and purchasers of products and services were aggregated organically, as the business model of free online services became prevalent. The mobile internet further extended the interaction between consumers and brands. The mobile internet is portable, accessible, and convenient, encouraging consumers to stay connected constantly to share product and service experiences. Therefore, companies needed to provide an omni-channel, seamless, and consistent eXperience. As the "Internet of Things" evolves into the "Internet of Everything", consumers and technologies will become further integrated. Forward-thinking brands will likely become more media-less, or even channel-less.

Free Online Services: New Value Creation Enabled by the Internet

In the early days of the Internet era, search engines primarily served as portals for online visitor traffic — a business model designed to compete directly with the online service providers that preceded them. Such portals attracted visitors with free content. Much like Google and Yahoo, the business model was based on advertising revenue. The two most significant characteristics of this trend were the massive scale of the audience coupled with high frequency interaction. Consumers weren't simply passive participants similar to the broadcast media business model. They were actively engaged, giving advertisers the opportunity to monetize content in a new manner. Business was no longer a reciprocal exchange, but a more sophisticated form of value creation.

All companies that emerged successfully from this era used internet technology to create better experiences for more consumers. Value is created based on exchange of benefits, but mutual benefit reduces the gap between consumers and brands. In 1997, NetEase started as one of the four major portal websites in China, with a successful IPO in the US just three years later. NetEase then extended its reach to online games, email service, online education, e-commerce, and online music, all aimed at deepening the connection with consumers and catering to their increasingly diverse needs. By launching multiple service platforms, NetEase increased its brand value, and its business and service expansion reflected how the Internet gradually reached a larger and more demanding audience.

Data Connection: Consolidating Multi-Touchpoint Experience on the Mobile Internet

Smart devices were more consumer-centric. Therefore, companies needed to provide consistent services anytime and anywhere. Constant connectivity satisfied the basic needs of netizens in the digital era. Because products were highly homogeneous, the competitive edge and brand differentiation were gradually reflected through experience. Fragmented and inconsistent experiences would quickly weaken favorable impressions of a brand.

Providing interactive experience based on individual data was a critical foundation for companies to expand business scope and continuously create value in the mobile internet era. Consumers placed orders through all types of mobile applications, and enjoyed convenient services anytime and anywhere. Meanwhile, data generated in the process became the core basis for companies to better serve their core customer groups. Data gathering on customer behavior helped companies quickly create new connections with core groups. For example, JD Finance, launched in 2013, utilized the transaction data of users of JD.com as the reference for the loan evaluation and approval. As privacy considerations globally have become more present, brands have carefully navigated and adapted to changing customer expectations.

Human-Machine Interaction Enabled by Smart Technology

The value of AI has become more prominent after its commercialization. A large amount of scenario-based data provides the prerequisite for AI to prosper, which allowed Alipay's facial recognition payment system to thrive. Even when smartphones are removed from this process, smart technology can directly connect people to services, allowing technology, especially digital technology, to serve consumers.

Smart connectivity enables the interactions between people and people, people and things, things and things to be intelligently connected to make services smarter and empower brands to better anticipate their needs. To serve individual needs, companies need to formulate a vertical ecosystem which collects comprehensive, scenario-based data from end to end and utilizes it to create added value. Chinese tech giant Tencent proposed the "AI in All" strategy in 2017, combining AI with various industries. By realizing AI in eight major scenarios — covering content, games, healthcare, retail, finance, security, translation, and social networking — Tencent maximized the technical value of AI to better serve its users.

Company Strategy: Digital Transformation Driven by eXperience

Digital transformation is a strategic decision for companies to adapt themselves to global development and transformation. Focusing on Ideal eXperiences helps brands prioritize their digital transformation efforts. We expect this eXperience will become the next trend in the evolution of business across all industries.

Digital technology integrates the core resources of companies to enable a consistent digital eXperience from top to bottom. As introduced in Chapter 1, Freshippo's integrated retail grocery and delivery platform leveraged Alibaba's big data insights and algorithms to integrate the operations of warehouses and stores. Automated logistics systems helped to achieve a two-way flow of efficient sorting and unified distribution. In just one year, Freshippo opened 64 stores in 14 cities nationwide, and offered services to over 10 million users. Two years later, the average daily sales per store exceeded ¥800,000 RMB ($120,000 USD) with 60 percent of the sales coming from online orders. As of 2021, Freshippo's expansion has reached 21 cities with a total of 234 stores. [48]

But digital transformation and touchpoints don't need to become so efficient that they become invisible. Sometimes there's a downside to seamless integration that may inadvertently make a Holistic and Ideal eXperience so inconspicuous it's taken for granted — not necessarily hurting the brand, but also not increasing the brand value proposition.

In Chapter 5, we discussed Disney's concept of "Family Magic" and how it permeates every touchpoint. An example of a technology that integrates an entire eXperience is their "MagicBand". Originally free, but now available for a nominal price, guests at Disney hotels adjacent to their theme parks have the option of an RFID-enabled wristband that serves as their room key and park ticket, offering less to carry and less to lose during a day of rides, exhibitions, and adventure. But guests can also add credit card information to their MagicBand securely, making it a wireless payment device. They can also add FastPass and PhotoPass accounts to the wristband to make such premiums more convenient and secure.

Disney has since incorporated several of these features into a smartphone app, suggesting the MagicBand was in some ways a stopgap solution that preceded the hardware and software necessary to offer such options through existing mobile devices. But the more important lesson is that eXperience inspires transformation, not the underlying technology that enables it.

It's not just seamless integration, it's a tangible manifestation of Family Magic, making it easier for parents, children, grandparents, couples, or any guest to navigate the park and accomodations with ease.

The fundamental nature of digital transformation is to leverage digital technology to create value for desirable target audiences. In the digital era, sustainable brand development is about whether a company has the capability to use digital technology to provide an enhanced interactive experience that deepens its connection with customers.

* * *

Summary

China's digital evolution in many ways mirrored the migration from analog engagement to digital interaction in the US. The emergence of free online services subsidized by advertising revenue was based on the media business models that preceded it. But it soon diverged from the broadcast model and transformed into platforms built that encouraged consumers to become content creators.

The pervasive nature of the mobile Internet has resulted in a shift in expectations brands must answer. Smart devices coupled with the growing use of data aggregation present sincere concerns about customer privacy, as does advancement in artificial intelligence. Though these technologies can often prove intimidating, brands that embrace them respectfully and responsibly can gain insights to improve eXperiences in ways that were previously impossible.

Section 2
DRIVING DIGITAL TRANSFORMATION

Even the most beloved brands can't ignore the future forever. But change is often disruptive, and the culture of some companies, both within their workforce and their relationship with consumers can suffer unless the eXperience customers expect is preserved, and ideally improved, as brands embrace, incorporate, and align their strategies in the digital era.

Digital transformation is a systematic process that requires continuous planning, execution, and iteration. When consumers enjoy a smooth and seamless digital experience at the front office, companies need to continuously accumulate and utilize the operation and data capabilities from the middle and back offices.

This process is not without its perils. Customer privacy and the standards for acceptable information collection and sharing are neither standardized nor static. Seemingly benign efforts may result in suspicion, and negatively impact the brand. Efforts to provide more personalized interaction and offering could backfire. As brands wade deeper into these waters, the balance between improving the brand value proposition and potentially unsettling consumers must be carefully considered. But the benefits that such insights afford, applied respectfully and responsibility, have the promise of bringing brands and their customers closer together.

Digitization, dataization, and intelligence are the three phases of digital transformation. The three are not separated but integrated, and take place in sequence to continuously evolve (Figure 6.2).

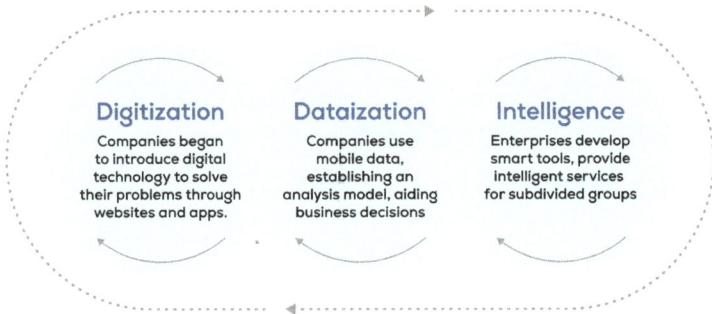

Figure 6.2, *Three Phases of Digital Transformation*

Digitization: Efficient Experience Brought by Functionality

The digitization phase is the most fundamental phase of the entire digital transformation process. In this phase, the way people interact with brands is shifted from physical to digital. Companies utilize digital tools to efficiently and conveniently provide access products and services to reach customers at a scale traditional retail simply cannot. Different types of companies with different starting points in the digitization phase often face different challenges and opportunities.

Taking the digital experience of end customers as the starting point, companies develop their own digital service capabilities. The interaction between consumers and a company is quick and clear. Prior to 2000, functionality was among the most important attributes for consumer satisfaction and interaction. Dangdang.com, one of the earliest online commerce platforms in China, was established in 1999, introducing the ability to view production information and place orders online, a new level of interaction enabled by digital technologies. This is how companies can use end customer functionality experience to identify an entry point to connect with target audiences.

Companies that are digitally native have first-move advantages in obtaining visits and frequent interactions, helping them achieve success faster than companies that are still behind the curve. For example, Chinese companies NetEase, established in 1997, and Sohu and Sina, established in 1998, all joined the NASDAQ in 2000. By providing premium content to online audiences delivered via first-generation search engines, their rapid expansion inspired a wave of internet adoption and innovation in China.

Compared to internet companies, traditional companies often have weaker digital capabilities and are less capable to reach, understand, and retain core groups. They evolved from the industry era, relying on offline stores and channels. How to leverage digital technologies to develop their own digital service capabilities is still the greatest challenge facing traditional companies.

The key to digital transformation lies in transforming the fundamental mindset. For example, when it comes to data utilization, big data is often about consolidating consumer behaviors into one persona that fits all, which is only one approach at the operation level. What brands really need is to evolve from the one-persona-fits-all positioning to the multiple-persona-fits-all strategy, and eventually a one-touchpoint-fits-one solution. Vanke, a Fortune Global 500 real estate developer based in China with US operations in New York and San Francisco, kicked off its company-level digital transformation in January 2016 with the "Fertile Soil Project". From the brand positioning perspective, Vanke evolved from a traditional real estate developer to an urban lifestyle service provider; from the brand strategy perspective, based on changing housing needs in the digital age, Vanke reconstructed its service eco-system by reshaping the business capabilities of the four major modules: development, marketing, service, and product. By experimenting with prefabricated construction, online-to-offline omni-channel precision marketing, multi-format lifestyle services, and flexible production, Vanke can provide customized service for each touchpoint. The transition from offline to online also represented a reinvention of Vanke's general business logic and management philosophy, instead of stopping at simply superficial changes like application design and website interaction. Nowadays, internet natives born in the 90s and 2000s are gradually becoming the primary consumer demographic.

Because digital transformation is still in its infancy, it's often challenging for companies to provide a more targeted service experience relying exclusively on the fragmented and insufficient data accumulated during the digitization phase. Therefore, brands need to advance to the second phase of digital transformation, dataization.

Dataization: Holistic eXperience Enabled by Channel Integration

This phase is the most important phase for companies to collect and accumulate data assets during the digital transformation process. The dataization phase serves as the link between digitalization and intelligence. In the digital era, data generation is never-ending. Accumulating data from multiple scenarios help brands develop customer personas and maximize the value of data from the customer perspective.

In this phase, consumer interactions become actionable data. In addition to Taobao, Tmall, Sesame Credit, and Alipay, Alibaba Group also developed or acquired businesses like Freshippo, DingTalk (an enterprise communication and collaboration platform), Ele.me (an online food delivery service platform), Idle Fish (an online marketplace for second-hand goods), and Youku (a video hosting service platform). Alibaba aims to consolidate data from online shopping, fresh grocery retailing, office working, dining and entertainment to further understand its core customer groups from multiple perspectives, thus enhancing its capability to know and serve its current and prospective customers.

Companies that collect and aggregate data from various sources can further extend the scope and enhance the capability of their service, but must be sensitive to customer privacy concerns. Sesame Credit analyzes customer online transaction and behavior data from five dimensions — including credit record, behavioral preference, ability to perform contracts, identity and personalities, and interpersonal relations — to create credit reports through a process similar to a college application weighing a balance of factors, not just a series of scores. Based on the credit report, customers can obtain credit extensions or installment payments much faster. Credit and credibility share the same word origin, and both represent a measure of trust. Sesame Credit is a prototype of the combination of Internet insights and the commercialized credit value. Its collaboration with residential rental platforms and financial institutions further converts social credit relationships into a new consumption model.

People-oriented data utilization maximizes the importance of data analysis on prediction. Data is the fundamental competitive edge in the digital era. The more individual data a company can accumulate, the more it can understand its core groups from multiple dimensions, and the more accurate the digital persona will be. This will further optimize this service experience. Fragmented data collected from individuals can be analyzed and applied to become an important data asset for companies. For example, the 3-1-0 online loan application service introduced by Ant Financial, an affiliate of Alibaba, is a highly-customized service based on data from multiple scenarios. The name is a nod to the process, a customer's loan application can be completed in three minutes and processed in one second, with zero manual intervention.

Distinct from general data obtained in digitalization, data collected from individuals in the dataization phase is more specific and targeted. As companies better understand their customers' needs and decision making, brands can offer more personalized products and services. When companies can obtain all scenario data for every individual and leverage cloud computing and restructuring capabilities to offer customized services, the era of targeted business truly arrives. With that, the digital transformation process enters its final phase of development.

Intelligence: Personalized eXperience Enabled by the Internet of Everything

The third phase of digital transformation, when customized services and smart devices are pervasive, digital technology will benefit customers in a more engaged and intelligent way. As AI continues to evolve, technology and people will become further integrated.

The best way to commercialize AI is to establish an ecosystem based on the ideal application scenarios. In the early days of AI, when major players launched their own AI products, neither Microsoft nor Google achieved early success. Yet Echo, Amazon's smart speaker, sold more than 80 million units in one year. The reason why Microsoft and Google didn't gain traction was because their approach was based on PCs and mobile phones with the interactions happening at customer's fingertips. However, Amazon combined voice interaction and AI into its smart speakers to help AI seamlessly integrate into their daily lives.

Intelligence means companies should be prepared to provide personalized intelligent services. As noted in Chapter 4, understanding the scenarios in which customers use specific products and services allows for precise insight into the changing needs of consumers is the foundation for offering services with added value. Data collected from individuals is the basis of targeted service, and brands that switch from offering digital platform services to seamless assistance leveraging smart data will serve core groups better.

In this phase, individuals and the environment are integrated and empowered by emerging technology. Xiaomi's smart home system leverages AI to elevate product experience by building an environment centered around customer needs. Its mobile apps are interfaces for functionality, including face recognition, voice control, and automated adjustments. Xiaomi, just like an increasing number of home automation brands, believes that creating products that understand our needs better than we do will become a growing trend. The company will continue to leverage AI and cloud computing capabilities to predict and satisfy these needs, as well as establish additional smart connections.

In the intelligence phase, brands and consumers form a convergence of value connected by digital devices, a reciprocal relationship which helps companies provide services in a smart way. Consumers can seamlessly experience all the benefits of digital intelligence. Consumers will instead be attracted to a brand by digital devices and remain for the brand-people relationships they create and facilitate.

In the intelligence phase, brands will become more personalized. Digital intelligence will help consumers find the right products faster. Brand competition in the digital era will be about more than products and services, but also about the Holistic eXperience and emotional connection with customers. People will understand a brand's personality via every interaction, then choose the brands that suit them best. Different from marketing, brand personalities in the digital era will focus more on deep value proposition, not superficial emotion (Figure 6.3).

BRAND | PEOPLE

Digitization

- Efficient problem solving (Use digital tools to handle tasks)
- Single point digital tools (Single channel)
- Digital task capability (Websites and apps)
- Decentralized industry data
- Universal collective data

Dataization

- More efficient, deep understanding & shaping of self (Become a digital entity)
- Digital portal/platform (Omni-channel)
- Data network construction
- Data acquisition capability
- Data operation capability
- Digital integration capability
- Integration of digital space
- Individual data capitalization
- Full scene data accumulation of target population

Intelligence

- Personality, wisdom, feedback (Gain digital wisdom)
- Smart Assistant/Smart Home (Omni-present)
- Personal-based intelligence service ability
- Demand forecast of target population
- Provide customized services
- Intelligent data

EXPERIENCE Point of Access
ABILITY Data integration and operation
ASSETS Population and Data

Figure 6.3, *Three Phases of Digital Transformation (Detailed)*

* * *

Summary

To serve the ever-changing needs of consumers in the digital era, companies must implement a comprehensive digital transformation divided into three phases. The digitization phase improves efficiency; the dataization phase deepens interaction; the intelligent phase personifies service experience. The value offered by companies is constantly increasing as individuals deepen their perception of value, but brands must be mindful of customer concerns about privacy as they engage in these efforts.

Digital Transformation is a process, one where the greatest risk is focusing too intently on the digital and insufficiently on the transformation. As George Westerman, chief scientist of digital economy at the MIT Sloan School of Management, noted: "Successful digital transformation is like a caterpillar turning into a butterfly. It's still the same organism, but it now has superpowers. Unfortunately, when it comes to digital transformation, many senior execs aren't thinking about butterflies. They're just thinking about fast caterpillars. And it's hard to keep up with your competitors if you're crawling ahead while they can fly."

Case Study:
STARBUCKS

Who Are They?

American consumers are well-acquainted with Starbucks, whether or not they are customers. Founded in 1971, decades of quiet success and paced growth in the Pacific Northwest laid the groundwork for an organic expansion throughout the country in the 1990s and early 2000s, eventually branching out beyond their signature retail presence to grocery store shelves and international markets. Brisk mail-order sales and retail partnerships informed the decision to transition to brick and mortar locations, but there was no obvious roadmap for growth past the saturation threshold achieved in the US market.

But much like tea, coffee until recently has been more of a commodity in China, and the concept of a so-called "third place" did not have a clear parallel in Chinese culture. Premium pricing always poses challenges for an undifferentiated product, and with an emphasis on retail stores as a destination versus those designed for quick-turn clientele, Starbucks entered a new market with a brand strategy crafted and refined for the US, but not the distinct and evolving expectations of Chinese consumers.

What Did They Need?

Starbucks entered a mobile-centric market without a mobile-centric strategy, one that would reach Chinese consumers through familiar platforms and interactions. Locally-grown internet brands like Luckin Coffee and Coffee Box, as well as those with American origins like McDonald's McCafé and K-Coffee from KFC, dominated the market by offering convenient online ordering and pickup for patrons only seeking a product, not a place to consume it.

China's pervasive e-commerce adoption and the rate of mobile internet users both rank first in the world, with phones emerging as the primary means of ordering food and grocery delivery, as well as accessing transportation solutions such as ride sharing. Mobile-centric, retail models like grocery chain Freshippo and convenience stores like Bianlifeng, have also played a dominant and formative role in setting new expectations for consumers. In short, Starbucks needed a digital transformation to succeed in cities and among consumers more fast-paced and mobile than their American counterparts.

What Did We Do?

TANG helped Starbucks identify and mitigate multiple factors adversely affecting their consumer adoption in China through a combination of research and strategy. Consumer personas were used to identify pain points and develop potential solutions. Brand strengths were analyzed and adapted to provide product distinction and differentiate the brand among better known and more established competitors. A focus on the seamless eXperience between online interaction and in-store transactions allowed Starbucks to evolve their third place concept to meet the distinct needs of the Chinese market while remaining true to their global brand.

Business Objectives

To meet the expectations of Chinese consumers accustomed to mobile ordering and payment, as well as highly efficient take-out service, Starbucks required "Digital Transformation of The Third Place". Appealing to audiences already familiar with local and international brands with established presence in China offering lower average price points, Starbucks and TANG needed to distinguish itself as a premium purveyor of coffee to:

- **Create a differentiated, difficult-to-replicate brand culture center.** Promote user brand recognition and connection to the brand.
- **Integrate and reinvent the digital and physical space experience.** Enhance the user experience when visiting Roastery.
- **Build brand-communication to raise conversion rate among the consumers.** Ensure the experience and promote the conversion of target customers.

The Solution

At the end of 2018, Starbucks developed a strategic partnership with Alibaba, and its membership system was fully connected, including delivery, points and gift system. Alibaba's third-party food platform Ele.me, similar to DoorDash, helped launch a take-out service named "Starbucks Delivers", to provide delivery services in its stores nationwide.

In 2019, Starbucks entered into a strategic partnership with TANG to jointly upgrade the digital experience of Starbucks' first Roastery in China. Beijing and Shanghai launched pilot initiatives for "Starbucks Now" the same year, and by late 2020, these pilot locations accounted for 26 percent of sales in China, with remaining stores nationwide going online the same year.

This was a dramatic reversal from the mobile app initially launched by the Roastery which faced two major challenges:

- **Difficulty in communicating coffee culture and branding.**
  With the large number of Chinese visitors and a complicated visitor flow design, coffee culture and brand stories were difficult to communicate to consumers.
- **Low sales conversion rate.**
  Roastery consumers tended to stroll around, take pictures and then leave, with low transaction rates and limited customer conversion.

Personal interviews and persona insights were employed to better understand and answer these challenges.

Starbucks in-store customers are predominantly digital natives long accustomed to the intersection of online and offline experiences. The digital experience has become an inseparable part of the product, service, and space. From these interviews, four categories of customers emerged (Figure 6.4).

Different types of users have different expectations and journeys in the store, but they have a common experience demand: a seamless online and offline experience.

After Identifying the core group of consumers who expect a more seamless online and offline brand experience, and considering the consumption patterns and development potential of the four groups, TANG and Starbucks targeted two of the groups to improve their overall Roastery experience.

Observers tend to be passive explorers. Though they are desirable for their enthusiasm and high-value consumption, despite their knowledge of coffee, interaction is often limited. If the space and experience don't satisfy their needs, the brand will fail to build a deeper relationship with them. A more robust online experience offers a more comprehensive tour of the Roastery and avenue for acquiring coffee knowledge.

CONNECTOR
Social Butterfly

"For me, the Roastery is like a latenight place to gather, to enjoy a drink and the company of baristas."

DESCRIPTION:
They love to connect with different people, and their social life provides a sense of belonging.

EXPLORER
Inquisitive Participant

"Since I came here, I'd like to find out the right coffee beans with the help of barista, so that it is not a waste of time."

DESCRIPTION:
They love to explore on their own, immersive journeys provide them a sense of active engagement.

VISITOR
Avid Photographer

"The process of roasting coffee is fascinating, it's so new and interesting."

DESCRIPTION:
They love the experience of acquiring new knowledge, providing a sense of achievement they tend to document with photos shared to social media platforms.

OBSERVER
Silent Recorder

"Even though I'm curious, I don't usually ask, and am more likely to look it up myself."

DESCRIPTION:
They love new experiences, taking notes, and getting to know more about coffee.

Figure 6.4, *Four Categories of Starbucks In-Store Customers*

By contrast, Visitors may become easily lost without clear wayfinding, and thus less likely to place an order. Though they are large in number, if the Roastery is only an attraction, without sufficient "hooks", it is extremely easy to remain simply a visitor, or even leave the venue without spending any money. A rich online experience likewise provides compelling and persuasive content, stimulating interest in coffee culture and customer conversion.

This digitalization of eXperience created an interactive space and stimulated coffee consumption, creating new opportunities for retail stores. The prevalence of check-in culture led to spontaneous exploration and social media sharing of the interactive Roastery eXperience. Though the first store economic effect accounted for a surge of early patrons, the integrated online-to-offline experience conveyed core brand value, helping customers experience coffee culture, many for the first time.

A premium brand eXperience was also furthered by standardized products and in-store coffee tours — from the spectacle of the roasting process to baristas led workshops for brewing better tasting coffee. Even offline orders featured online tracking.

Consistent and efficient brand communication from online and offline touch points, including a digital tour book of eXperience center to enhance interaction and interests and the Starbucks story from bean to cup, personalize the journey by design — adding an element of exclusivity to the experience, complimented in store with heartfelt interactions with passionate staff.

A consumer's journey in a brand experience center can be sorted into four steps: before entering, visiting, consuming, and leaving the Starbucks Roastery. By redesigning the entire journey customers went from a series of pain points to a series of wow moments.

Before entering the Starbucks Roastery jumbled information from different channels, making it difficult for customers to find key messages efficiently. The solution was a visual information structure and reminder mechanism. Customers could now make appointments and receive event promotion from Starbucks Roastery mobile app, providing clear expectations for the visit. The anxiety of waiting in line was reduced with the introduction of an online interactive experience — a "gamification" of the experience, with clear goals and tasks, stimulating a sense of achievement and generating interest through positive feedback.

The lack of direction when visiting the experience center was addressed by providing consumers with clear guides and instructions for each functional area, allowing customers to learn more about coffee and brand. Online ordering and offline pick up were disconnected, but a mobile app provided online ordering and tracking, ensuring customers were aware of the preparation process and time remaining, indicating the location of the bar and the steps for picking up online orders.

An increase in onsite coffee events helped customers gain more coffee knowledge and establish greater brand resonance with Starbucks, adding value to justify the premium price for their products. After leaving the Starbucks Roastery, customers could stay connected through personalized interaction that recognized achievements for one's coffee knowledge and rewarding customers for sharing their experience on social media platforms.

Result

By creating a functional, balanced, and efficient brand experience, Starbucks transformed their previous concept of a third space to one custom-tailored for Chinese consumers. Partnerships with dominant mobile payment platforms allowed Starbucks to quickly ramp up efforts to attract highly desirable consumers. Five months after Starbucks Now launched, the service was expanded to more than 4000 retail stores. Datatization, the combination of qualitative and quantitative measures, revealed and resolved pain points at every level of consumer interaction, building a complete customer portrait for future innovation efforts. Integration of digital space and simultaneous collection of consumption data and consumer insight will also inform these decisions.

Starbucks evolved from coffee selling to relationship building, enhancing a deeper connection between customers and the brand, one that will insulate the company against competitors. The reimagination of their retail stores into experience centers will continue to convert curious prospective consumers into loyal and reliable ones eager to share their interactions with the brand, now positioned as a leader in coffee culture.

"You can't transform something you don't understand. If you don't know and understand what the current state of the customer experience is, how can you possibly design the desired future state?"

— *Annette Franz*

CHAPTER 7

The Integration of X Thinking

Understanding People, Value, and Sustainability

Initiating Organizational Change: Chief eXperience Officer (CXO) and the X Thinking Maturity Model

Incorporating Insights from the Future

INTRODUCTION

When we introduced X Thinking at the end of the first chapter, it was aspirational, a new way for businesses and brands to improve the relationships they have with consumers. But as we learned more about eXperiences, this abstract concept became a process of discovery, one from which a vision of the future slowly started to emerge.

China is a country of ancient wisdom, and global influence. Beyond the obvious economic impact, its consumers are among the most astute, savvy, and sophisticated in the world. Any conversation about the role brands will play and the relationships they will have with their customers in the years to come that doesn't include observations and lessons from China is simply incomplete.

In Understanding People, Value, and Sustainability, we'll consider the evolution from consumers to co-builders, transactions to services, and the development of the ongoing relationships with brands upon which long-term loyalty is based — and how these concepts are independent and interdependent for the future of every business.

Then we'll break down the vertical silos of organizational hierarchy in Initiating Organizational Change: Chief eXperience Officer (CXO) and the X Thinking Maturity Model. Elevating eXperience to an executive level role is essential, but only after businesses reach the right stage in their efforts to make eXperience an inseparable part of their corporate culture.

Finally, we'll look beyond the horizon with Incorporating Insights from the Future, a series of lessons from the past and present leading to a portrait of consumer behavior, objectives, and values which brands must serve in the years ahead to survive and succeed.

Section 1
UNDERSTANDING PEOPLE, VALUE, AND SUSTAINABILITY

In this final chapter, it's fitting to end where we began with people, value, and sustainability — the three principles that comprise X Thinking (Figure 7.1).

People are no longer just consumers, but become co-builders of the brand. Value isn't limited to product transactions, but transitions to brand services. Sustainability is not simply supply and demand, but generates an entire symbiotic system. Each is part of a cohesive philosophy focused on bringing consumers and brands together.

Figure 7.1, *Three Principles of Business Innovation*

People: From Consumers to Co-builders

In addition to buying and using, people are redefining their understanding of value. All people were, are, and will be consumers. People who buy, use goods, or receive services are by definition consumers. But are buying, using, and receiving really enough? Of course not, instead, they are minimum, fundamental experiences.

As we discussed in Chapter 4, discerning consumers are increasingly seeking more — eXperiences that resonate with who they are, how they think, and how they live. The relationship consumers have with brands and the entire process of interaction are the basis of co-building, which comes in two main forms: creating eXperiences and sharing eXperiences.

Creating an eXperience isn't necessarily tactile in the traditional sense. Digital connectivity also allows consumers to participate in the process in a more intimate and in-depth way. Instead of viewing it as work, consumers actually enjoy contributing to the development of products and services.

Though not as well known in the US as Apple, Samsung, and Huawei, Xiaomi quietly became the third largest smartphone manufacturer in the world in 2020. But unlike its competitors, Xiaomi actively engages customers in the development of its custom variant of the Android operating system. Their MIUI (Mobile Internet User Interface) is feature rich, with each iteration the result of customers contributing directly to updated and expanded capabilities. The novel approach has even inspired fan clubs among passionate users, connected by their shared relationship with the brand. From Nike's online "Nike by You" initiative that lets customers create their own one-of-a-kind sneakers to American Idol, or any one of several similar singing competitions around the world where viewer votes determine the finalists and the champions, creating eXperiences together with consumers is becoming the new standard for brands across all industries.

Sharing eXperiences used to exclusively mean word-of-mouth, and in a sense it still does. Only the medium has changed. Conversations with friends, family, and colleagues may be face-to-face, but phone, texts, and email are all personal testimonials. The ways in which consumers and brands now share eXperiences has also evolved parallel to the technologies that connect them.

Brands that used to exclusively broadcast commercials or engage in more traditional advertising have started to embrace an interactive relationship with their customers, from text messaging campaigns to custom coupons. Social media has undeniably become a platform for shaping opinions about brands, in both formal and informal ways. It's a place where brands and consumers connect almost as equals. Then there is the often spontaneous proliferation of customers, end users, and audiences who create their own enclaves to discuss their eXperiences with specific products and services — online and offline, positive and negative.

Though testimonials continue to be highly influential, sharing eXperiences in all of these forms are also part of the co-building process.

Value: From Product Transactions to Brand Services

Harvard Business School Professor Theodore Levitt once quipped, "People don't want to buy a quarter-inch drill, they want a quarter-inch hole."

The observation is deceptively simple, possessing hidden insight. Consumers typically don't need a quarter-inch drill, or a quarter-inch hole. Perhaps they need to hang a picture to make a room feel more inviting? Their objective is to improve their experience.

As initially discussed in Chapter 1, the economic evolution from agricultural, industrial, to service has been more clearly delineated. eXperience combines these elements, meeting complex consumer expectations amid increased competitive pressures to offer innovative solutions to contemporary demands.

Changes in the grocery industry actually illustrate each of these distinct economies. Take Whole Foods as an example. The agricultural economy is reflected by the produce, bakery, butcher, fishmonger, even the florist. Everything is fresh. But in the aisles, the cans, jars, and boxes of shelf-stable foods are the industrial economy. There's more than harvest and transportation. It's more akin to a manufactured product. The service economy is represented by prepared meals, personal shopping services, even home delivery since their purchase by Amazon.

So what is the experience economy? It's easy to think of it in terms of the open concept of the store's layout and premium aesthetic. But it's also the in-store cooking classes, the diversity of inventory, and home gardening selection. Experience is the intersection of the previous economies, increasing sales, frequency, loyalty, all of the metrics any grocery store uses to measure success.

Value isn't defined by features, which are essentially the equivalent of a product. It's ultimately defined by benefits, which are a service. Taking a cooking class to learn how to prepare a new dish, then immediately purchasing the ingredients needed to make it at home is convenient, immersive, and participatory. It's an integrated eXperience. Interactions no longer focus on simple transactions, it's every contact between the brand and consumers. When consumers perceive and appreciate the value provided by the brand, transactions occur naturally. The more crucial question of innovation has changed from, "How to sell products to whom?" to, "How to create a valuable eXperience for whom?"

Sustainability: From Supply and Demand to a Symbiotic System

How do you make a brand last forever? It requires overcoming inconsistent development cycles, abandoning outdated, perennial product introductions to build a more diversified and integrated symbiotic system. The predictable press events for the latest laptop, phone, or mobile device to the annual Consumer Electronics Show in Las Vegas, new products don't necessarily increase the value customers require to replace devices that already serve their needs well.

A symbiotic system is mutually beneficial, connecting brands and consumers over time. It increases in value as brands accumulate understanding and insight into their customers. The ongoing relationship also makes it easier for consumers to gain and share experiences. Acquiring new customers for any brand is often more costly than maintaining them. By adapting to the changing needs of customers, the value of the relationship increases for both brands and customers over time instead of diminishing.

The relationship between brands and consumers requires a longer term and more holistic perspective. Consumers often focus on incremental growth, a series of short-term interactions with gaps between phases of development or product upgrades. For longer-term sustainability, brands and consumers both need persistent points of contact, to interact with one another, and move forward together. As introduced in Chapter 2, the X Relationship Model isn't just a series of stages. It's essentially a guide to building sustainable relationships.

A symbiotic system also involves the relationship between consumers and consumers. As mentioned above, the sharing of eXperiences among consumers creates both interest and trust. The relationship between consumers is among the most persuasive. Consider how social media exchanges among friends, family, colleagues, or even strangers change your opinion of a brand. How does discussion among an interest group, online forum, or similar customer community affect your long-term loyalty?

The relationship between brands and brands introduces the opportunity for mutually beneficial eXperiences for shared consumers. Such brand collaborations range from unexpected to almost obvious. The collection of outdoor apparel illustrated by The North Face and

Gucci brought two brands together that could hardly be farther apart, a convergence of function and fashion. Both sell clothing, but were never really competitors. Now, they're collaborators. Taco Bell and Doritos weren't competitors either, but the Doritos Locos Taco brought both brands together more than 50 years after founder Glen Bell sold his first taco and Disneyland served the seasoned, fried tortilla chips that would soon become the iconic snack. Though it helped that the two brands are distant corporate cousins, the cross-promotion created cross-pollination among their customers.

A more recent example of such a symbiotic system is Alibaba's "88 VIP" program, which launched on August 8, 2018. The number eight isn't just considered a lucky number in China, it's the luckiest number, and the more the better. In fact, the pronunciation of eight or "ba" sounds very similar to the word for "prosperity". In many regional dialects, it's phonetically similar to the words for "fortune".

Alibaba connected various individual online membership systems — from shopping destination Taobao and travel hub Fliggy to food delivery service Ele.me and movie ticket platform Taopiaopiao. This brand aggregation and shared experience included a five-percent discount for Alibaba brands, including Tmall's Supermarket, Luxury Pavilion, and Global — as well as Glamour Sales and Ali Health. The venture was so well-received by customers, Alibaba expanded the concept, launching the "Alibaba 88 Member Festival" exactly one year later on August 8, 2019. (That's the eighth month and the eighth day, in case you missed it earlier.) The cross-promotional convergence is more than just a loyalty program based on perks and privileges. It connects commerce and community by issuing points for online activities like social media posts and product reviews. It doesn't simply reward purchases, it encourages participation. Even American brands like Levi's and Old Navy have taken note and joined what has become nothing short of a retail ecosystem built entirely on brand relationships.

Sustainable development is the convergence of strategy and values. The symbiotic system, based on sustainable ideas and driven by eXperience, deeply integrates brands and consumers, consumers and consumers, and brands and brands. All three are fundamentally driven by eXperience, constantly iterating, creating sustainability.

* * *

Summary

X Thinking is a philosophy that connects brands and consumers through eXperience. People are the foundation of this relationship, where co-building allows consumers to participate through previously unprecedented access and interaction. Value is an ever-changing measure of the significance products and services play in the lives of customers. Sustainability is the ongoing connection they have with a brand, an ongoing symbiotic exchange from which both become closer over time.

Brands that understand the principles of People, Value, and Sustainability improve their relationships with customers, expand their offerings, and create long term loyalty.

Section 2
INITIATING ORGANIZATIONAL CHANGE: CHIEF EXPERIENCE OFFICER (CXO) AND THE X THINKING MATURITY MODEL

As discussed in Chapter 5, one of the difficulties of delivering Holistic eXperiences is management of the eXperience across all the brand touchpoints. Companies need to ensure interactions at every touchpoint accurately reflect the brand.

One of the contributing factors to this challenge is how organizations are structured. Most companies use a hierarchical organizational structure; the CEO sits alone at the top with a clear chain of command. Those who report to the CEO are in charge of highly centralized divisions within the organization, such as function (finance, operations, research and development, sales, and marketing), offerings (products and services), markets (consumer, business, and government), or geography (North America, Europe, and Asia-Pacific, Africa, South America). Within each division, the organization splits into even more narrow and specialized duties. The problem is that each one of these divisions, as well as each group within a division, has a different set of mandates, objectives, and key performance indicators they must meet — all of which often lead to silo behavior.

Though an eXperience Strategy attempts to help companies overcome these obstacles, it sometimes isn't enough.

CHIEF EXPERIENCE OFFICER (CXO) – CONNECTING EXPERIENCE INITIATIVES ACROSS THE ORGANIZATION

Once brands begin to incorporate the philosophy of X Thinking and companies reconsider their organizational structure, they often realize it is not enough to have a standardized process for developing and delivering eXperiences. What they need is someone who focuses on the strategic connection between each of the touchpoints across the entire organization. What they need is a CXO.

Traditionally, an organization's executives are focused on vertical aspects of the business. Each of these aspects are highly specialized, yet they each control different parts of the brand eXperience. Organizations still need someone to take the lead to oversee the strategic direction of the Holistic eXperience. The CXO functions horizontally across the organization, connecting all the eXperience initiatives. Their job is to create and manage eXperience Strategy so that current and future touchpoints are aligned and interconnected.

However, for many organizations early to adopt the idea of a CXO, the role was inconsistent, frequently aligned with marketing and operations, mostly in tourism, mobility, hospitality industries, who were responsible for recording, analyzing and sharing their perspective working as a product manager to constantly optimize customers' product eXperience. Even in the technology sector, CXO roles were often created because companies knew they probably needed one, even if they weren't quite sure how the role should serve their organization, and ultimately benefit their customers.

The CXO may not begin as a fixed role, but an organizational capability reflecting how much importance the management team attaches to experience. The functions of the CXO may be undertaken by several senior executives led by the CEO, or by another senior executive. In service-oriented industries, the CXOs become increasingly important. For brands focusing on marketing, the functions of a CXO are often an extension of the responsibilities of a Chief Marketing Officer (CMO). For brands focusing on operations, the role of a CXO is often undertaken by the Chief Operating Officer (COO).

But more recently, CXOs are senior management, at the same level as the CEO and CFO, very different from their earlier incarnations. The mission of the CXO is to define and manage the eXperience Strategy, enhance the external brand awareness among core user groups, make each department aligned with brand eXperience, and focus on accelerating the launch and realization of the eXperience Masterplan. In recent years, the CXOs also oversee value growth, for example experience premium, word-of-mouth management, and innovative growth.

However, none of these changes happen overnight, and even organizations that have adopted many of these concepts may still struggle to adapt. Brands that want to develop relationships with their customers and deliver a Holistic eXperience through an omni-touchpoint strategy will find that it involves more than learning and applying the methods and tools we have introduced in this book. It's also not enough to change how people think within an organization. It requires transforming how the whole organization works to empower the employees to plan, deliver, and manage the Holistic eXperience.

X THINKING MATURITY MODEL – EVALUATE YOUR BRAND'S ACCEPTANCE AND CAPABILITY TO DELIVER HOLISTIC EXPERIENCES

Every organization has a different level of acceptance and capabilities to deliver Holistic eXperiences. Informed by earlier models, then combined with our own experience, we have developed the X Thinking Maturity Model to help brands understand and evaluate their own organization's maturity level and the five stages of transformation (Figure 7.2).

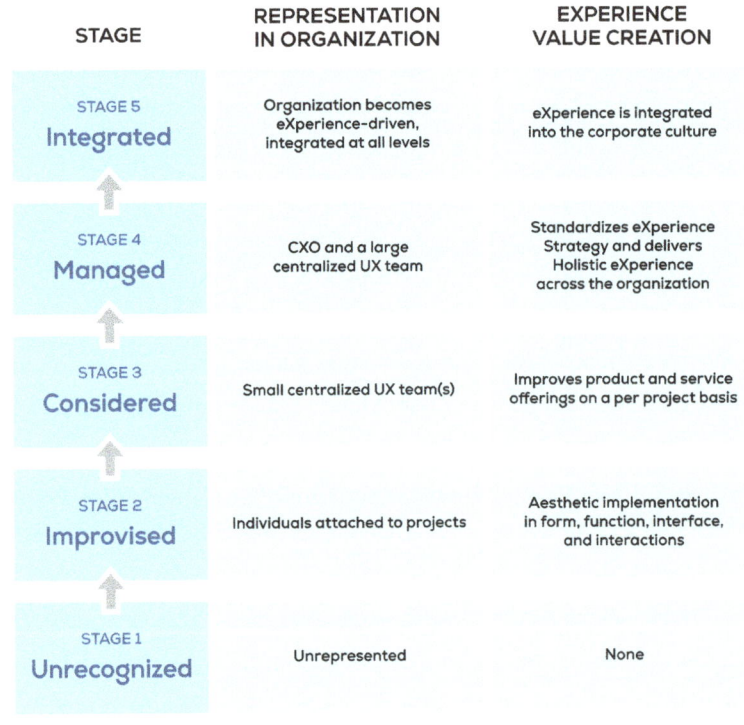

Figure 7.2, *X Thinking Maturity Model*

Stage 1: Unrecognized

In the first stage, the brand may not be aware of the importance of eXperience. Businesses in this stage are often technology-driven, primarily focused on the development and application of new technologies. Though product and service offerings based on these new technologies can be useful and deliver new eXperiences, they may not be usable or desirable.

It is not uncommon for seed and early stage start-ups to be technology-driven. Because they are often cash-constrained and focused on developing a minimum viable product, they might not consider the product eXperience, let alone the eXperience of the brand's other touchpoints.

Stage 2: Improvised

When a brand begins to acknowledge the value of eXperience, limited resources are dedicated to the eXperience. The eXperience may be improvised on the surface and aesthetic level by product, industrial, graphic, and interior designers who determine the function, physical form, user interface, and communications of the brand's touchpoints. It is implemented only on a project-by-project basis and is highly dependent on those involved. However, the overall brand eXperience lacks leadership and coordination.

At this stage, organizations may think they are committing resources to the eXperience through the investment and efforts. But these organizations are still driven by technology or business; the eXperience is considered as an afterthought and not as a strategic differentiation.

Stage 3: Considered

This is when organizations begin to actively consider eXperience as a crucial part of the brand. The organization begins investing capital and human resources toward establishing a small user experience (UX) team or multiple small UX teams dedicated to improving the eXperience of certain brand touchpoints, focusing primarily on product and service offerings.

This team of UX researchers and designers serves as a centralized resource for the organization, and their expertise can be leveraged by multiple product teams. They focus on fixing usability problems with only some of the brand offerings on a project-by-project basis, but do not look at eXperience holistically.

Stage 4: Managed

By this stage, the organization acknowledges, as we discussed in Chapter 3, that the value of eXperiences are of critical importance and is aware of their contribution to the brand — perhaps adding the role of CXO to provide executive level support. It has a large centralized UX team, with active involvement from the executive level, focused on standardizing the brand eXperience across most of the touchpoints in the organization.

Unlike the previous stage, the organization focuses on establishing and implementing a systematic process for developing and delivering eXperiences across the whole organization. At this stage, brands are still primarily looking at the eXperience of individual touchpoints rather than how they work together as a Holistic eXperience.

Stage 5: Integrated

As the organization continues on its path of maturity, it elevates eXperience to a core element of organizational strategy. Despite the role of a CXO, the organization is less dependent on a centralized group to manage the eXperience of the brand and begins integrating X Thinking intuitively into every part of the organization.

At this stage, the organization is no longer focused on just fixing problems with the eXperience, but is leveraging eXperience as a strategic advantage through eXperience innovation. It begins focusing on Holistic eXperiences that unify the brand's offerings, communications, environments, and behaviors across the entire customer journey.

By the time organizations reach this final stage, X Thinking philosophy has been adopted as part of the culture. Every employee feels both ownership and empowerment to maintain it, because the journey never ends.

At TANG, the X Thinking philosophy has been implemented across the whole company. Consider the concept of UX. Now expand that idea to include Operations and Human Resources, or what we call Staff eXperience (SX). SX is responsible for creating a meaningful eXperience for everyone working at TANG. Our Business Development and Client Services are called Partner eXperience (PX). PX is responsible for developing and maintaining the relationships between our business partners and ensuring that they have an extraordinary eXperience working with TANG. Our Public Relations and Marketing departments are known as Brand eXperience (BX) — they do more than just promote TANG, they deliver the TANG eXperience.

These are more than a new naming convention. They are an alignment of focus and function that reflect a new approach to achieving priorities. We believe that organizations shouldn't exclusively deliver

Holistic eXperiences to customers and users of the brand. They must also deliver them to the employees and partners of the business.

However, naming conventions can sometimes create confusion, one of the perils of being ahead of the curve. When Jason founded TANG, his title wasn't CEO. He was technically the CXO, incorporating the duties of CEO as well as serving at the company's chief champion of eXperience, facilitating the collaboration of employees as partners throughout the entire organization. The role of eXperience was so ingrained in the company's culture, it was the most accurate job title.

He later changed his title to CEO — only as a practical matter, not a philosophical shift. When prospective clients and colleagues engaged with TANG, Jason was the face of the company. But they also wanted to meet the CEO. The lack of one eventually required one. Ideally, CEOs should champion the concept of eXperience just as much as the CXO. It wasn't a realignment of purpose, instead one that simply served customer expectations as the understanding and integration of X Thinking expands across industries, both in China and throughout the world.

* * *

Summary

As an organization matures based on the X Thinking Maturity Model, it requires a new organizational structure to support the cross-organizational collaboration needed to deliver Holistic eXperiences. It also requires leadership and oversight of the brand eXperience at an executive level.

We believe that as companies continue to evolve, the organizational structure and CXOs will play a critical role helping empower X Thinkers to deliver Holistic eXperiences.

Section 3
INCORPORATING INSIGHTS FROM THE FUTURE

X Thinking from its inception has focused on eXperience as a guiding business philosophy, built around perspectives and beliefs necessary to achieve it. Though it was created to improve a brand's understanding of consumer expectations, motivations, and behavior in China, the ultimate measure of success was to create new opportunities and competitive advantages. Yet the lessons soon proved more universal in scope.

China is quickly becoming a test market for the world due to its scale, history, and trajectory. It's not a demographically representative locale widely recognized as a predictor of emerging trends by traditional metrics. It's actually much more.

The generational alignments, technological advances, and retail reinvention in China offer an unprecedented and unparalleled glimpse into the years ahead — one where eXperience is the defining standard for all customer interactions.

These lessons can be distilled down to five insights that apply to nearly every industry and country, the foundation of relationships with consumers that transcend borders, revealing a portrait of the consumer of the future.

Aggregation requires Collaboration

From traditional department stores to digital marketplaces, the ability to reach more potential customers than a tiny boutique or exclusive online store isn't just desirable, it's increasingly essential. Almost all brands rely on aggregators. But aggregation and collaboration are not synonymous, especially when the purchases involve more than one brand, and whose roles aren't always clear to consumers.

Few promotions illustrate the power of brand aggregation better than retail holidays. They may seem like a uniquely American phenomenon, but are hardly so. Whether it's the post Thanksgiving sales of Black Friday and Cyber Monday, or those proximate to Christmas, Hanukkah, and Kwanzaa at the end of December, cultural celebrations and the deep discounts that follow have become intertwined in the minds of many consumers. But these were all tied to seasonal celebrations, or perennial events like Back to School sales.

Amazon was among the first to create an original sales day untethered to another calendar event. First held on July 15, 2015 to mark the twentieth anniversary of the online retailer, and the tenth anniversary of their subscription-based Amazon Prime service, it has grown exponentially into a global retail event.

In China, November 11 is Singles Day (单身节). Created in 1993 by college students as an ironic alternative to Valentine's Day, Alibaba embraced the idea of treating yourself and adapted it into a retail holiday which now generates staggering sales numbers. In 2019, the company's Singles Day sales topped $1 billion within the first minute, with total sales of nearly $40 billion. By comparison US sales on Black Friday and Cyber Monday for all companies the same year totaled less than $20 billion combined.

But Alibaba's entire approach is also bigger than Amazon's. As we discussed earlier, the Alibaba 88 Festival isn't an Amazon style shopping frenzy of random discounts and inventory overstocks. It's a brand bazaar that connects online and offline, entertainment and engagement. Brands reach new customers directly, not simply as an extension, through in-store promotions, hotel and travel deals, even exclusive concerts for influential members whose social media activity creates essential buzz through testimonials.

Amazon announced the 200 million member milestone in April 2021, driven in large part by the enormous popularity in home delivery spurred by the pandemic. Alibaba's 88 VIP isn't a subscription, it's a rewards program built on loyalty, not dependency. That distinction is subtle, but helps explain why Alibaba is now on target to exceed a billion customers by 2024.

Amazon has been described as an everything store, all but unrecognizable as the bookseller it was a mere quarter century ago. But it's really a logistics company, one that specializes in predictive inventory and efficient distribution, increasingly through its own delivery fleet. Amazon Web Services supports a vast clientele of business and government hosting that is transparent to most users. Alibaba is a brand aggregator. It still creates its own brands and acquires others like Amazon, but the relationship is still between brands and customers, not the behemoth behind it.

Perhaps the most meaningful distinction for both brands and consumers is that Amazon's approach is still largely transactional while Alibaba's is based on the overall eXperience. Customers may offer reviews on Amazon, but they aren't really brand ambassadors. Their personal opinions of purchased products don't extend to their social media accounts, nor are they rewarded for the influence their reach offers brands.

Historically, brands have relied on aggregators, from the first Sears & Roebuck catalog to the modern department store. Aggregators increase volume while reducing costs. But there is a trade off, a lack of control over the customer experience. Startups may rely on the reach of aggregators, but only to a point. Eventually even Apple moved almost exclusively to online sales to reduce overhead and reinvent their retail experience through the launch of their own branded stores. It's often the stage of a company that determines their dependence on or independence from aggregators.

Another aggregation risk for brands is becoming a commodity. Supply chains, particularly in the grocery industry during 2020, further fueled an existing trend. For many shoppers, some products are the same regardless of the brand. One banana is as good as another, perhaps with a premium for local or organic. But items from cereal to shampoo have a following.

Private labels are nearly identical to their name brand rivals, priced slightly lower, and are often manufactured by the same companies whose massive advertising campaigns still don't persuade some consumers to pay the difference. But when scarcity strikes, for instance with toilet paper, Madison Avenue magic doesn't matter if the shelves are empty. Immediacy and uncertainty suddenly became deciding factors, and whatever was available was often good enough. Brands like Costco, Kroger, Aldi, and Target are in the middle, names which customers trust that offer private label brands and have created a fierce following of their own. They have in many ways become part of a larger customer retention strategy. However, when some of those private labels were in short supply as production capacity contracted and distribution struggled, many consumers were forced to consider similar alternatives. Whether they reliably return to their former private label preferences, brand names, or their substitutes is always a risk after such disruptions. It's an extension of the longstanding risk brands face when they are mistaken for commodities — like Klennex, Jello, and Band-Aids becoming synonymous for facial tissue, gelatin, and adhesive bandages. Aggregation is always a balancing act, and private labels further blur the line.

That blurred line also exists in the restaurant industry. When dine-in options dissipated due to the pandemic, third-party services like DoorDash, GrubHub, and Uber Eats stepped in to close the gap. But when deliveries are late or wrong, that relationship with the restaurant's brand is jeopardized by extension, even if prior dining experiences were spectacular. Consumers understandably struggle to dissect experiences when aggregators are involved. But this too is not entirely new. If customers have an outstanding meal at a dine-in restaurant, but the service is only so-so, which will define their experience with the brand? If an item purchased online through Amazon fails to meet expectations, but the return and exchange experience is excellent, the customer's opinion of Amazon may improve, even if that of the brand that made the item is diminished. Meanwhile, Alibaba facilitates the success of the brands it serves, not just its own.

Collaboration isn't working in parallel to achieve independent business objectives. It's working together to realize common goals that benefit shared customers. Aggregation requires mutual responsibility, to ensure the entire customer experience is seamless. When brands collaborate effectively, though they remain distinct, the lines between them that often frustrate consumers should disappear.

Convenience drives Innovation

The adoption of mobile payments in China has been very different from the US for several reasons, some of which we've already discussed. But beyond the convenience and efficiency of smartphone apps, there are additional factors. Generational differences affect adoption rates for all technologies, but pain points also drive them. For instance, the largest denomination of paper currency in China is the ¥100 RMB note, equivalent to roughly $15 USD. Can you imagine how inconvenient it would be to carry cash in the US if the highest value currency anyone could carry was less than a $20 bill?

For many Chinese consumers, they leapfrogged past checks and credit cards entirely, because neither offered a compelling advantage over cash. They were, just as they are in many parts of the world, more expensive for retailers and less trusted by consumers. Cultural reluctance to "buy now, pay later" remains a significant factor. The same pattern is evident elsewhere. Nearly two-thirds of Kenyans use mobile payments, and almost a quarter of Columbians do as well — both ahead of lagging US adoption.

Mobile payment in China wasn't just a collection of features built into a smartphone app. It made everyday payments faster and easier for everyone. Counting out cash and making change at cafes, like Starbucks, and grocery stores, like FreshHippo, became almost obsolete at some locations. That advantage extended to the smallest shops and street vendors, who also accept mobile payments through AliPay and WeChat. Unlike the US, the two leading platforms notably grew out of their pervasive presence on mobile devices, not the traditional financial services industry. Competing and incompatible services in the US haven't encouraged adoption by stores, which in turn hasn't created similar incentives shared by customers and retailers in China.

Apple and Samsung as smartphone manufacturers have since stepped into the American market to advance the transition to cashless transactions, but with proprietary platforms and hardware requirements as a prerequisite. China's implementation is built around QR codes instead of near-field communication. Adoption of any technology is dependent on various factors. China's approach was universal and lower cost, which is why it became the expectation instead of the exception — appealing to consumers in countries where interim steps have proven unnecessary.

This also alludes to the larger concept of a mobile-centric development strategy for brands. Even in the US, more than half of all internet activity doesn't come from desktops or laptops, with tablets and smartphones outpacing their personal computing predecessors by widening margins. Brands that are digitally native meet consumers who are as well on the same level. Companies prioritizing traditional touchpoints to support legacy consumers risk losing prospective customers.

There is a balance to preserving established and emerging relationships between brands and consumers, but also an inevitable transition to innovative technologies customers trust, find more convenient, and are eager to adopt.

Customization is Crucial

The option to tailor experiences to individual customers has historically been limited until somewhat recently. Cost has always been the most obvious factor, with mass production making everyday items more affordable for centuries. From the printing press to the Model T, preference was secondary to availability and affordability.

But as physical products have expanded to digital ones, and physical stores have likewise expanded to digital ones as well, the cost of customization on traditional manufacturing has fallen dramatically, combining the economies of scale with the desire by customers to express their personal style.

We've discussed the auto industry a lot in X Thinking because it illustrates concepts in a context with which both consumers and brands are already familiar. It also happens to provide ideal examples of how the expectations of customers and their relationship with brands are changing rapidly.

When Ford revealed its reimagination of the Lincoln Zephyr in 2021, the storied model's sophisticated styling and innovative dashboard design were stunning. But what was even more surprising was the venue. The latest luxury release from Lincoln didn't debut in Detroit. It was unveiled in Shanghai.

Lincoln first entered the Chinese market in 2014. Familiarity with the brand was limited, but that created an opportunity to create an entirely new experience for prospective owners. Dealerships became an immersive brand destination, one that combined high-end hospitality with a personalized purchasing process entirely unlike an American dealership. The ecosystem approach was described as The Lincoln Way.

Unlike the US market, where Lincoln has focused on SUVs, Chinese consumers still want sedans, ones with premium features and appointments that reflect their personality. Customers compare options and design details through an interactive screen, allowing them the ability to see their new car take shape. The brand launched three showrooms that year in Shanghai, Beijing and Hangzhou. All three became the top performing dealerships in the world within the first month.

Choosing the color, trim, and options on automobiles was once exclusive only to luxury brands. The cost of creating one of a kind cars decades ago was dismissed as too expensive or impractical for the masses. But now, it's more standard, an expectation that determines which brands customers will even consider, and an experience where brands must compete.

For modern consumers, brands themselves have become vehicles of self-expression. Co-building brands is a collective process, with customization offering an appeal as individual as consumers themselves. From custom sneakers to feedback on the latest build of a mobile OS, we've seen brands embrace Chinese consumers in new ways. Buying "off-the-shelf" often falls short of delivering on the identity consumers want to embody.

Another emerging example of this trend is the rise of the gaming industry from a niche product to a multimedia industry disrupting the entire entertainment industry. Though Asia has dominated the video game market for decades, the cultural shift is a global trend. Since the introduction of multiplayer games in the late 1990s and early 2000s, the gaming industry discovered the value of their products was the interactivity.

When Activision Blizzard released their latest Call of Duty edition in 2019, it was the most successful digital launch in the company's history, generating $600 million in the first three days alone. That was nearly twice the worldwide opening weekend box office revenue for the final installment of the Star Wars saga. E-Sports events are quickly rivalling the audience size of major league sports in the US — and advertisers and sponsors have noticed. So have brands, with smartphone apps in particular incorporating points and promotions into game-like features that engage customers and encourage interaction.

However, brands don't need to create a destination showroom or gaming console sensation to tap into customization and gamification. Both come down to details and building a deeper connection to the brand. If your restaurant's app doesn't allow for customization of orders or an incentive program, why not? If your apparel line offers certain sizes and styles, does the limited selection cost more in potential sales than expanding them? If your product is manufactured on demand anyway, why not invite customers to participate in a process that is interactive, entertaining, perhaps even somewhat competitive?

Consumers are still individuals, and their expectation of involvement in developing new brand offerings will continue to increase. Commerce has become consumer centered, and the ability to customize has become a crucial consideration in creating unique products and services incorporating consumer participation.

Authenticity creates Loyalty

The first contact Chinese consumers have with brands isn't always a television commercial, radio spot, or online ad — at least not in the obvious sense. For many, it's through a Key Opinion Leader.

As we discussed earlier, KOLs are kind of like internet celebrities, but with the added influence of traditional celebrities. In the US, and throughout much of the world, online celebrities tend to get their start as offline celebrities first, from actors and athletes to musicians and whole families so famous, sometimes it's difficult to remember exactly why. (How exactly did the Kardashians become famous?) Like brands whose physical stores led to digital ones, typical celebrities were already well-established, and their social media following was simply an extension of an existing brand. Some KOLs were already known to fans. However, other KOLs had no preexisting fame, but emerged as an entirely new class of celebrity endorsement. In China, like similar influencers elsewhere, their status is changing.

When McDonald's introduces a new menu item in the US, the strategy is predictable. They rely on in-store promotions combined with television and large scale outdoor advertising like buses and billboards, with social media simply as another platform for the same messaging. When McDonald's in China introduced a new Jumbo Cone, they instead relied largely on the reach of Zhou Zekai, a highly popular video-game player, who shared the fast-food chain's super-sized ice cream offering on social media. With a push from Zekai, McDonald's sold 5.5 million cones in just 10 days.

But KOLs are also imperfect. Consumers are becoming more savvy when it comes to social media influencers. YouTube stars in the US have faced scandals and scrutiny, as have Chinese social media celebrities. Much like movie stars, the audience suspends a certain amount of disbelief in exchange for entertainment. But they also recognize these endorsements are compensated. Such constraints on credibility have given rise to a new class of internet influencers: Key Opinion Consumers.

Also noted previously, KOCs don't have the same cache or name recognition as KOLs. With followers in the hundreds or thousands instead of millions, what they may lack in reach they make up for in authenticity. When a KOC reviews a product or service, it's rarely compensated. More often, it's an offering they personally use or have decided to evaluate for themselves. The reviews aren't heavily produced, another hallmark that can quickly turn astute consumers off. The reactions are real, the posts are recorded live and unrehearsed, the language is conversational not carefully crafted.

Authenticity is the intangible and sometimes elusive standard brands everywhere struggle to achieve. But it's all but baked into social media, especially when it comes to individual users. In the case of KOCs, it's their expertise that connects with audiences the most. Even if their number of followers pales in comparison to celebrities, social media or otherwise, their power to persuade is far greater.

User-generated content is not a new concept. Google has included it as part of their relevancy algorithm for nearly two decades, occasionally prioritizing Wordpress sites ahead of brand sites back when Facebook, Twitter, and Instagram were still novelties.

However, TikTok's meteoric rise in China, before becoming a global phenomenon, is proof that timing and authenticity play a fundamental role in the appeal of the platform. Vine's six-second viral video service seemed revolutionary, but soon withered despite its acquisition by Twitter. And even Quibi struggled to gain a toehold with ten-minute cinema backed by Hollywood luminaries. Even the reboot of Vine in 2020 as Byte seems unlikely to topple TikTok, whose head start and adoption globally make its ouster a longshot at best.

But why is the service so pervasive and popular, even if those of a certain age still prefer to dismiss it as another internet fad? It's because the platform was seemingly built to identify and amplify trends. From personal takes on popular songs to signature dance moves, the service reflects trends and creates them in a quick and casual way, then aggregates them. TikTok is both a mirror and a window of popular culture that invites users to participate.

Brands have taken notice, but not always with success. Those that have kept it casual, like the NBA's light-hearted and comical approach compared to their larger social media presence. Chipotle takes it even further, curating customer experiences instead of shoehorning content from their existing channels into one that inherently exists to empower end users instead of distilling traditional marketing down to a few seconds. That's Tiktok's deceptively simple appeal, one that keeps content fresh, creates loyalty through authenticity, and has customers hungry for more.

The role of KOLs and KOCs is evolving. The former raises awareness, the latter is more persuasive, illustrating a key difference between the stranger and acquaintance stages of a brand relationship. Both foretell the future of consumers as a competitive part of every brand's efforts to reach and relate to prospective customers. But opinion shaping is never static or exclusive. New platforms will continue to create new influencers that deliver authenticity, thus creating greater loyalty.

Integration becomes Essential

Traditional boundaries between industries are beginning to blur, and not just due to converging technologies. But in China, even competitors have often found a synergy when it comes to consumer behavior and expectations that have become increasingly common.

Imagine if Apple, Amazon, Facebook, and Google were to dominate a market of more than 1.4 billion people, and their reach from innovation and commerce to social networks and internet search was so integrated that nearly every consumer interaction and transaction was ultimately made possible through one of them, if not all of them?

That's essentially the scope achieved by Baidu, Alibaba, and Tencent — whose reach is so pervasive, they're simply and collectively known in China as BAT.

Though the influence of the three is significant, it's not collaborative. In some industries, they are actually direct competitors. As Xiaomi's reach expands into additional industries, some have started to refer to the combined influence as BATX, recognizing similarities in the rise of the hardware manufacturer's market dominance.

Baidu's influence is broad, but all of its offerings come down to its leading development and deployment of artificial intelligence. Their search engine boasts more than 70 percent of the Chinese market, while Google queries account for a mere 3 percent. Apollo, their global open-source operating system for autonomous vehicles, has partnerships with Volkswagen, Toyota, BMW, and Daimler. Meanwhile, their conversational and facial recognition AI-enabled DuerOS has already been installed on nearly half a billion devices.

Alibaba, which we've discussed extensively, is more familiar to many, but still misunderstood. Founder Jack Ma continues to reject the comparison that his vast commerce and payment platform are just China's version of Amazon. In 2017, at the World Economic Forum in Davos, Switzerland, Ma offered his own distinction, "The difference between Amazon and us is Amazon is more like an empire — everything they control themselves, buy and sell. Our philosophy is that we want to be an ecosystem. Our philosophy is to empower others to sell, empower others to service, making sure the other people are more powerful than us."

To that end, Alibaba launched Cainiao Smart Logistics Network Limited as a joint venture to improve the entire supply chain, reducing deliveries from days to hours in some instances. It's a collective that offers next-day shipping to any region in China through resource sharing with smaller delivery businesses — not an end-to-end solution like Amazon Prime that cuts local carriers out of the equation.

Tencent is even more challenging to compare. When we've discussed the scope of the company's pervasive WeChat platform for mobile payments (a space likewise occupied by AliPay), that's somewhat superficial. The WeChat app is where Chinese consumers connect with friends and family, find their news, schedule a ride, even order takeout. The average consumer in China spends twice as much time on their mobile phones as their American counterparts. More than half of that time is spent within Tencent's suite of services. There's really no equivalent anywhere. And with that enormous, inordinate influence, unexpected opportunities emerge.

When Chinese liquor brand Xi Jiu wanted to create a campaign to promote its distilled spirits ahead of Chinese New Year celebrations in 2017, there were no traditional ad buys, no commercials, billboards, or slick magazine spreads. Instead, they partnered directly and exclusively with Tencent through a series of live-streamed cooking shows featuring renowned chefs preparing regional dishes, which were then paired with Xi Jiu products.

No promotional prices or seasonal discounts, not even soft sell, despite the coming holiday. It was more sincere as a result, an awareness campaign that reached more than a million viewers who watched, not on their televisions, but on their mobile devices. That's because Tencent was able to promote it to their users through their news and sports service, their social network, and their gaming platform — a reach that is unrivaled.

But the cleverness of the approach is still less remarkable than the process that led to its production. A typical media campaign nearly anywhere else in the world would have involved internal creative teams and external agencies, and been planned, revised, and implemented over several months, perhaps even a year. Xi Jiu and Tencent went from concept to broadcast in just five days. [49]

When we consider how Chinese brands build relationships with their customers, it is impossible to understate how integration like BAT fundamentally changes everything. So-called big data and fewer barriers allow brands to understand consumers, and reach them, with an ease and efficiency that also is impossible to compare to more familiar advertising paradigms. The speed of decision-making is the direct benefit and result of more informed decision makers.

Because Chinese brands already know their customers beyond the interactions of their own offerings, a more complete picture comes into focus. Ideas that might otherwise be dismissed are discussed, but not delayed. Timelines that are traditionally restrictive are suddenly less so. Initiatives that would otherwise prove too impractical become new possibilities.

Integration of a more comprehensive understanding of customer preferences and priorities, beyond the narrowly focused profiles most brands now possess, is more than an essential next step necessary to deliver meaningful experiences faster and more effectively. It's a prerequisite to defining the interactions consumers will expect and demand in decades to come.

CONSUMER OF THE FUTURE

Insight into consumer expectations and behavior is typically less about foresight than hindsight. After all, trends are really just a series and snapshots that when plotted point to a probable direction. But predictions are only as reliable as the observations upon which they are based. Disruptive technologies, sweeping social changes, and cultural shifts in a world with fewer boundaries for ideas make truly forecasting the future of any industry a best guess.

Fortunately, consumers tend to tell us who they are and where they are headed with less ambiguity. They create their own options when desirable ones don't exist, and invite their family and friends with them on these journeys. Brands are invited as well, but don't always follow. They're used to creating their own journeys for customers, who don't always follow either, or forge their own paths instead.

The future for brands and consumers is one of shared eXperiences, built on sincere relationships that benefit and create value for both.

Instant access is a dominant theme for the future of consumer expectations in China and throughout the world. The concept of online versus offline will evaporate at every level. The proliferation of constantly connected hardware and windows of limited availability will be intentional, not infrastructure limitations.

Already the idea of missing a television show is unknown to consumers of a certain age. There will still be live events — like sports, films, and television episodes with a premium for watching them in real time. But they will remain available indefinitely, or expire only as a means of concentrating demand. This perceived premium will become pervasive, with live-streaming conferring added status on the content, and those who watch it. Being the first in your cohort to have the latest digital device will still be a trend, but being the first to see new content, or to create it, will increasingly be a pattern that gives rise to influencers at formal and informal levels. Expertise will become a measure of experience at a social and professional level.

Consumer lifestyles will become more a la carte. Everything will be subject to customization, and an extension of personal brands. Shopping excursions, entertaining friends, social destinations, even courtship rituals and child-rearing will become designed experiences. Cultural elements will seem less rigid and clearly defined, resulting in a more curated, cohesive, and individual form of lived expression. Everyone will become an audience for everyone else.

The lines between work and home are already difficult to separate for industrialized and developing societies. The distinction between time spent between these two defining sets of tasks may disappear entirely in decades to come, replaced by a more flexible understanding and allocation of time and space. The intersection of professional and personal relationships will be less delineated. Daily routines will be more seamless and less structured, a collection of moments that ebb and flow.

Transparency will become a fundamental consideration for interactions, but far from a single standard. Determined by settings and scenarios, consumers will allow and anticipate greater degrees of disclosure — from a more intimate and prolific personal online presence to presumptions that brands should be more open and engaged as well.

Privacy and security will become nearly synonymous, though how they are defined will vary based on contextual, cultural, and generational alignments. Current expectations for socially and environmentally responsible behavior will inevitably extend to include privacy, and brands that violate this implicit and explicit trust with consumers risk the sincere relationships they've achieved with otherwise satisfied customers.

Separate lives lived online and offline will become less distinct as both converge into a balanced whole that is unified, but not uniform. Time connected to the digitally native world will become a default state, but time when consumers deliberately disconnect from the responsibilities and distractions of online interactions will be sacred, reserved for reflection and reconnection with the tangible and tactile elements of a less complex life.

The measurement of value has never been universal, though it will still have key components. Content as we know it will transform from mass-produced streams of information into an individually determined collection of interests and attributes manifested by interactions that are more than observational. Consumers will no longer be satisfied with assigned roles that are passive instead of participatory. Experiences will become eXperiences.

* * *

Summary

These five insights aren't bound by geography any more than the consumer of the future is bound by time. They are universal in their application, expanding in their relevance, and intentionally adaptive to account for an ever changing world.

The future is inherently unknowable, yet the elements that will define the relationship between brands and consumers are already visible. We've seen glimpses of it in China, and echoes of it elsewhere, from the proliferation of platforms for interaction in the US and Europe, the empowerment of individual expression throughout Asia, and the investment in enabling digital infrastructure in Africa and South America.

All of these advancements and predictions are predicated and contingent upon the precepts of People, Value, and Sustainability. Consumers and brands are intertwined and interdependent, a relationship that will define them in ways that are only now coming into view. When and how they meet will determine the journey they take together. X Thinking is the intersection where this future has already begun.

Acknowledgements

The origin of this book started over a decade ago when Jason proposed the concept and coined the term eXperience Thinking (体验思维), or what we now call X Thinking, in 2011. At the 10th anniversary of UXPA China in 2013, Jason introduced X Thinking to the public, the culmination of his ten years as president of the organization he led since its founding in 2003.

However, the roots of X Thinking run deeper, to the giants that preceded us. The idea that experiences create business value isn't new. In fact, our experiences are built on the experiences that came before us — so many influences that they are too numerous to list.

The journey to create this book was inspiring, with many people to thank along the way.

* * *

Thank you to Joseph Pine, whose endless curiosity makes the Experience Economy even more relevant today. His pioneering observations with James Gilmore echo our own, and affirm the universal principles of X Thinking.

* * *

Thank you to all the clients who partnered with TANG through the years. The challenges you provided were a proving ground for X Thinking. Thank you for your confidence and faith in us and X Thinking. It is only through our collaboration that X Thinking could be iterated and refined to create a new form of business value.

Thanks to Du Guoying, whom we admire for his industry influence and commitment to our culture. Xiao Guan Tea is reshaping China.

Thanks to Hu Tao, whose honesty and commitment create a lasting impact. China Merchants Bank has transformed China's financial experience, while Zhima Credit has defined China's personal credit services.

Thanks to Shen Hui, whose abundance of knowledge and enthusiasm are deeply contagious. WM Motors has become a recognized leader in the Chinese auto industry.

Thanks to Yu Fang, who helped revolutionize customer experience strategy. Amway's digital transformation in China has changed the way the company continues to grow throughout the world.

* * *

Thanks to all the TANGers, past and present, for bringing X Thinking to life in the work we create with our clients. Your curiosity and passion, the reflection of your work and thinking, have helped us with the formulation of X Thinking as our business philosophy.

Thanks to Tim Kobe, our long-time friend and strategic partner, whose 12 years of work with Steve Jobs have enriched our careers as well. We are proud and honored to work with industry leaders to create beautiful, consumer-driven experiences that put people first.

Thanks to TANG's co-CEO, co-founder and managing partner

Denny Huang for embarking and continuing on this journey with us. Your dedication to TANG and X Thinking is unparalleled.

Thanks to Xia Fangyu for co-founding TANG together with Jason. TANG would not be where it is today without all the hard work and sacrifices we made in the early days of the company.

* * *

We'd like to particularly thank the people that made this book possible, who worked on it, and were involved in its creation.

Thanks to Daniel Szuc for your guidance and serving as our sounding board. Our discourse with you has made X Thinking stronger.

Special thanks to Cai Qingqing, Wang Yuewei, Alan Fan, Dyas Wu, Bruce Li, and James Xu for your knowledge and insights into the case studies in the book.

Thanks to Tang Hsien-Hui for joining us on this X Thinking journey of researching, advancing and disseminating eXperience Strategy, eXperience Design, and eXperience Management. We're creating something special and meaningful together.

Thanks to Oasis Feng, Chen Weiqiao, Lily Zhou, Cai Yue, Xu Shanshan, Varson Wu, Liu Dongming, and Liang Kai for your contributions to the original Chinese version that served as the source for this English adaptation.

Thanks to Estella Yan, Mona Zi, Jenny Li, Zhuo Ziqing, Anna Shang and Blanco Shen at X Thinking Institute and Emily Zhao and Derisi Qimude at TANG for your support for the English adaptation.

Thanks to Gregor Gilliom and his team at Versatile Words, Andrea Clute and Bailey Martin, for editing those early drafts of the book.

Thanks to Peter Chan for your guidance on the design of the book.

Special thanks to J.R. McMillan of Notable Narrative for editing and adapting the final manuscript. Your insights helped bridge the concepts of X Thinking across cultures and bring them to the English-reading world.

* * *

Thank you to our families — Jason's wife Vivian Xu and three children, and Mike's wife Ellena Cheng — you are our driving force to keep us moving forward and creating value for this industry and for society, and to our parents and siblings for laying the foundation for our success today.

Endnotes

1 "Chinese Economy to Overtake US 'by 2028' Due to Covid." BBC News, BBC, 26 Dec. 2020, www.bbc.com/news/world-asia-china-55454146.

2 "China's High-Speed Rail Tracks to Hit 38,000 Km by 2025." Xinhua, Xinhua, 2 Jan. 2018, www.xinhuanet.com/english/2018-01/02/c_136867339.htm.

3 Jones, Ben. "Past, Present and Future: The Evolution of China's Incredible High-Speed Rail Network." CNN, Cable News Network, 20 May 2021, edition.cnn.com/travel/article/china-high-speed-rail-cmd/index.html.

4 "China to Add More than 11,000km of New High-Speed Lines by 2025." Asia Times, 15 Sept. 2018, www.asiatimes.com/2018/09/china-to-add-more-than-11000km-of-new-high-speed-lines-by-2025/.

5 Air Traffic By The Numbers, Federal Aviation Administration, 21 Sept. 2020, www.faa.gov/air_traffic/by_the_numbers/.

6 "China's Global Luxury Market Share Nearly Doubles in 2020: Report." Xinhua, Xinhua, 18 Dec. 2020, www.xinhuanet.com/english/2020-12/18/c_139601137.htm.

7 "The Road to Recovery for Chinese Outbound Tourism." Economist Intelligence Unit, 24 May 2021, www.eiu.com/n/the-road-to-recovery-for-chinese-outbound-tourism/.

8 "Alipay Introduces a Mobile Wallet App." Alizila, 18 Jan. 2013, www.alizila.com/alipay-introduces-a-mobile-wallet-app/.

9 Cramer-Flood, Ethan. "In Global Historic First, Ecommerce in China Will Account for More than 50% of Retail Sales." Insider Intelligence, Insider Intelligence, 10 Feb. 2021, www.emarketer.com/content/global-historic-first-ecommerce-china-will-account-more-than-50-of-retail-sales.

10 "2020年12月份社会消费品零售总额增长4.6% (Total retail sales of consumer goods increase by 4.6% in December 2020)." National Bureau of Statistics of China. 18 Jan. 2021. http://www.stats.gov.cn/tjsj/zxfb/202101/t20210118_1812428.html.

11 Ma, Jack. "2017 Chairman Letter to Shareholders." Alibaba Group, 17 Oct. 2017, www.alibabagroup.com/en/news/article?news=p171017.

12 Liu, Paul, et al. "The Accelerating Disruption of China's Economy." Fortune, Fortune, 26 June 2017, www.fortune.com/2017/06/26/china-alibaba-jack-ma-retail-ecommerce-e-commerce-new/.

13 Kwok, Ben. "Alibaba Hema Online Supermarket Records $116k Daily Sales." Asia Times, 18 Feb. 2020, asiatimes.com/2018/09/alibaba-hema-online-supermarket-records-116k-daily-sales/.

14 "Alibaba Tech Underpins World's Most-Interactive Starbucks." Alizila, 5 Dec. 2017, www.alizila.com/alibaba-tech-underpins-launch-worlds-interactive-starbucks/.

15 "Economic Watch: Service Industry Steering China's Firm Growth." Xinhua, 30 July 2018, www.xinhuanet.com/english/2018-07/30/c_137357795.htm.

16 "China Aims to Boost Services Share in GDP to 60 Percent by 2025." Reuters, Thomson Reuters, 21 June 2017, www.reuters.com/article/us-china-economy-services/china-aims-to-boost-services-share-in-gdp-to-60-percent-by-2025-idUSKBN19C1IB.

17 "China Urban Households Disposable Income per Capita 1978-2020 Data." China Urban Households Disposable Income per Capita | 1978-2020 Data, tradingeconomics.com/china/disposable-personal-income. Accessed 10 July 2021.

18 Luehrs, Adam. "The Cost of Living Comparison for the U.S. & China." Pocketsense, 2 Apr. 2021, pocketsense.com/cost-living-comparison-china-7757369.html.

19 "China's Per Capita Disposable Income Up 9.0 Percent in 2017." People's Daily Online, 24 Feb. 2018, en.people.cn/n3/2018/0224/c90000-9429702.html.

20 "China's Resident Income Rises 7.3 Pct in 2017." Xinhua, 18 Jan. 2018, www.xinhuanet.com/english/2018-01/18/c_136905784.htm.

21 "2020 年居民收入和消费支出情况 (Residents' income and consumption expenditures in 2020). National Bureau of Statistics of China. 18 Jan. 2021. http://www.stats.gov.cn/tjsj/zxfb/202101/t20210118_1812425.html.

22 Baan, Wouter, et al. "Double-Clicking on the Chinese Consumer." McKinsey & Company, McKinsey & Company, 22 Nov. 2017, www.mckinsey.com/featured-insights/china/double-clicking-on-the-chinese-consumer/.

23 Blue Technology "Chinese Young People Prefer Tea Drinks to Coffee." Sohu.com, 15 Apr. 2021, www.sohu.com/a/460805094_188923.

24 Heath, Alex. "Mark Zuckerberg Reveals That Facebook Paid More than We Thought for Oculus VR." Business Insider, Business Insider, 17 Jan. 2017, www.businessinsider.com/facebook-actually-paid-3-billion-for-oculus-vr-2017-1.

25 "Gartner Hype Cycle Research Methodology." Gartner, www.gartner.com/en/research/methodologies/gartner-hype-cycle. Accessed 10 July 2021.

26 Porter, Michael E. "Competitive strategy: techniques for analyzing industries and competitors." Free Press. 1980. Pg 370.

27 "'Immunity' Becomes the Highlight of Master Kong's Annual Report: Earn 35 Percent More in 2019 and Hold 17.4 Billion in Cash." Xinhua, Xinhua, 24 Mar. 2020, www.xinhuanet.com/tech/2020-03/24/c_1125759361.htm.

28 "The Road to Recovery for Chinese Outbound Tourism." Economist Intelligence Unit, 24 May 2021, www.eiu.com/n/the-road-to-recovery-for-chinese-outbound-tourism/.

29 iChinaStock. "Chinese E-Commerce Giants' Hype on Logistics." Business Insider, Business Insider, 20 Sept. 2011, www.businessinsider.com/chinese-e-commerce-giants-hype-on-logistics-2011-9.

30 "Recommendations From Friends Remain Most Credible Form of Advertising Among Consumers; Branded Websites Are the Second-Highest-Rated Form." Nielsen, 28 Sept. 2015, www.nielsen.com/eu/en/press-room/2015/recommendations-from-friends-remain-most-credible-form-of-advertising.html.

31 Teehan, Geoff. "The UX Fund: Investing $50,000 in 10 Companies, 10 Years Later." Medium, Habits of Introspection, 17 Nov. 2016, medium.com/habit-of-introspection/the-ux-fund-investing-50-000-in-10-companies-10-years-later-6fc65bd35e7a.

32 Kaplan, Jennifer. "The Inventor of Customer Satisfaction Surveys Is Sick of Them, Too." Bloomberg.com, Bloomberg, 4 May 2016, www.bloomberg.com/news/articles/2016-05-04/tasty-taco-helpful-hygienist-are-all-those-surveys-of-any-use.

33 Benn, James A. "Tea in China: A religious and cultural history." Hong Kong University Press, 2015. Pg 21.

34 "零售破 10 亿, 快速发展的小罐茶让人看不懂? 创始人杜国楹系统解读 (With retail sales exceeding 1 billion, the fast-developing small cans of tea make people incomprehensible? Interpretation of the founder Du Guoying's system)." 普洱茶网 (China Pu'er Tea Network), https://m.puercn.com/show-49-127679.html. Accessed 10 July 2021.

35 苏茶网络 (Su Tea Network) "4.7 亿中国人爱喝什么茶? 看完近 10 年排行榜我们发现这些真相 (What kind of tea do 470 million Chinese people like to drink? After reading the ranking list for the past 10 years, we found these truths)." Sohu.com, 1 Aug. 2019, https://www.sohu.com/a/330949327_99920953/?pvid=000115_3w_a.

36 Edelman, Joe. "Human Values." Medium, Human Systems / The School for Social Design, 12 July 2019, medium.com/what-to-build/human-values-a-quick-primer-b01ef9617925.

37 "Henry Ford, Innovation, and That 'Faster Horse' Quote." Harvard Business Review, 23 July 2014, hbr.org/2011/08/henry-ford-never-said-the-fast.

38 "Inventor Sherman Poppen, Snurfing His Way into History." National Museum of American History, 9 Sept. 2009, americanhistory.si.edu/blog/2009/09/inventor-sherman-poppen-snurfing-his-way-into-history.html.

39 Graziani, Thomas. "How Douyin Became China's Top Short-Video App in 500 Days." WalktheChat, 21 Oct. 2018, walkthechat.com/douyin-became-chinas-top-short-video-app-500-days/.

40 "抖音上成功的品牌营销 (Successful Brand Marketing of Doujin)." Hai Tao, 13 Apr. 2018, www.haitaoit.com/news-detail-4300.html.

41 "TikTok Announces That Daily Activity Exceeds 150 Million and Monthly Activity Exceeds 300 Million Users Aged 24-30 Account for 40 Percent." 网易 (NetEase), 12 June 2018, tech.163.com/18/0612/15/DK43FHHE00097U7R.html.

42 "Meet the Earth's Largest Money-Market Fund." The Wall Street Journal, Dow Jones & Company, 14 Sept. 2017, www.wsj.com/articles/how-an-alibaba-spinoff-created-the-worlds-largest-money-market-fund-1505295000.

43 Zetlin, Minda. "Blockbuster Could Have Bought Netflix for $50 Million, but the CEO Thought It Was a Joke." Inc.com, Inc., 20 Sept. 2019, www.inc.com/minda-zetlin/netflix-blockbuster-meeting-marc-randolph-reed-hastings-john-antioco.html.

44 Jarvey, Natalie. "Netflix Tops 200 Million Subscribers Amid Pandemic." The Hollywood Reporter, The Hollywood Reporter, 19 Jan. 2021, www.hollywoodreporter.com/business/digital/netflix-tops-200-million-subscribers-amid-pandemic-4118251/.

45 Cheng, Evelyn. "How Ant Financial Grew Larger than Goldman Sachs." CNBC, CNBC, 8 June 2018, www.cnbc.com/2018/06/08/how-ant-financial-grew-larger-than-goldman-sachs.html.

46 "2020年中国在线教育行业市场现状及竞争格局分析互联网巨头加速布局推动行业洗牌 (Analysis of China's online education industry market status and competitive landscape in 2020 Internet giants accelerate their layout to promote industry reshuffle)." 前瞻产业研究院 (Qianzhan Industry Research Institute). 26 Jan. 2021. https://bg.qianzhan.com/trends/detail/506/210126-a793db8c.html.

47 "刷脸付产品介绍 (Product Introduction)." 支付宝 (AliPay), 11 Dec. 2020, opendocs.alipay.com/pre-open/20180402104715814204/intro.

48 Tatum, Megan. "Alibaba Has Invented the Supermarket of the Future." WIRED UK, 21 June 2021, www.wired.co.uk/article/supermarket-future-alibaba.

49 "What Western Marketers Can Learn from China." Harvard Business Review, 16 Apr. 2019, hbr.org/2019/05/what-western-marketers-can-learn-from-china.

About the Authors

Jason Huang

Jason is Founder and CEO of TANG & Partners, a Shanghai-based experience design consultancy. Jason, a pioneer in China's eXperience industry, coined the term "X Thinking."

Jason entered the eXperience industry in 2003 and has explored the business value of eXperience since that time, promoting the industry's development. He co-founded China's first user experience (UX) professional association, UXPA China, in 2004. Jason has delivered more than 100 presentations at conferences, forums, enterprises and universities around the world, and is a guest professor at [Shanghai's] Tongji University. He has published multiple articles in Harvard Business Review China, and serves as a limited partner of InnoSpace Venture, helping entrepreneurs pursuing their innovation dreams.

Jason has helped more than 400 companies in FMCG, retail, fashion, catering, automotive, real estate, finance, medical and other categories to rebuild their brand eXperiences and achieve value growth, including China Merchants Bank, Zhima Credit, WM Motor, Vanke, The Palace Museum, People's Daily, Suning, Xiao Guan Tea, Amway, GE Healthcare, IHG, Richemont, Daimler AG etc..

He was awarded the Ram Charan Management Practice Award and named one of China's Top 10 in Outstanding in Design. He has a master's degree in Human-Computer Interaction, University of Bath, UK, and a bachelor's degree in Computer Science, Southeast University, China.

Michael T Lai, PhD

Michael is Senior Vice President of Knowledge Management & Senior Partner of TANG & Partners, Dean of X Thinking Institute, and Associate Professor of Tongji University, College of Design and Innovation.

As Dean of X Thinking Institute, Mike leads a highly skilled team of researchers, content creators, and educators in equipping business leaders with the knowledge and tools to create business value through the delivery of extraordinary experiences. In addition, Mike oversees the knowledge development and application for TANG & Partners to enhance the value and delivery of TANG's offerings to clients.

Prior to his work with X Thinking Institute, Mike spent 15 years helping clients position, envision, design, and deliver brand experiences. His experience covers a wide number of industries in the United States and Greater China, including creating insurance retail stores in the financial industry, innovating new ways of interacting with smart homes in the consumer electronics industry, redefining the car purchasing and ownership experience at dealerships in automotive industry, and positioning university brand experiences for prospective students in the education industry. His clients have included companies such as Nationwide Insurance, JPMorgan Chase, Legg Mason, Baojun, Amway, Changhong, Alliance Data, Big Lots, and more.

Mike currently teaches in the College of Design and Innovation, Tongji University (China). He has previously held posts at The Hong

Kong Polytechnic University (Hong Kong) and the Columbus College of Art & Design (United States).

Mike holds a PhD in Design from Tsinghua University (China), a Master of Design (MDes) in Interaction Design from The Hong Kong Polytechnic University (Hong Kong), and a BFA in Advertising & Graphic Design from the Columbus College of Art & Design (United States).

Lightning Source UK Ltd.
Milton Keynes UK
UKHW050241130522
402823UK00003B/12/J